DRAGON TACTICS

龙

BIS Publishers
Borneostraat 80-A
1094 CP Amsterdam
The Netherlands
T +31 (0)20 515 02 30
bis@bispublishers.com
www.bispublishers.com

ISBN 978 906 369 638 2

Design and illustrations:
Tine van Wel, tinevanwel.nl

Dragon Tactics

How
Chinese
Entrepreneurs
Thrive in
Uncertainty

Aldo Spaanjaars
Sandrine Zerbib

BISPUBLISHERS

TABLE OF CONTENTS

NOTES FROM THE AUTHORS

Between the time we decided to write this book, two years ago, and today, as we are putting the finishing touches on our manuscript, we are seeing a steady accumulation of what some might call alarming news about increasingly bold policies and actions by the Chinese authorities, some aimed at controlling the most dynamic companies in its private sector, especially in the tech industry.

Such initiatives are undermining not only the already fragile trust the rest of the world has in China but also, within the country, the confidence entrepreneurs may have in a stable future to develop their businesses.

We are also witnessing a worrisome rise of nationalism in China that slowly is becoming the new norm to which many conform, stifling alternative voices as well as potentially making it increasingly difficult for foreign brands and companies to succeed in China.

Yet, despite such circumstances, we believe more than ever in the relevance of the *Dragon Tactics* we describe in this book. We provide clear insights in what has made Chinese entrepreneurs successful in a rapidly evolving and often uncertain environment. Changing realities, political uncertainties, hyper competition, rapid digitalisation — none of these circumstances is new to them and they have learned to prosper within such uncertain surroundings.

The book is therefore less about China, but much more about what can be learned from companies that are able to thrive in uncertainty.

This book is not just aimed at entrepreneurs and company executives who do or are interested to do business in or with China, but mainly at business leaders worldwide who want to learn how to survive in fast-changing market circumstances.

With business uncertainties on the rise globally, driven by climate change, the increasing calls for firms to become more socially responsible and involved, the role of China on the world stage growing and changing, and its companies transforming and expanding, the world may only now start to experience what successful Chinese entrepreneurs have known since their very beginnings. In this fast-developing new reality, the lessons in this book are of vital importance to entrepreneurs and business leaders around the world.

To be clear, this book is not a political book. It does not intend to analyse the geopolitical tensions between China, the US, and other parts of the world, even less to take sides. Also, while we believe much can be learned from Chinese entrepreneurs, we are not giving in to blind fascination and enthusiasm about all things China. Instead, throughout this book we demonstrate our critical ability, including when it comes to Dragon Tactics.

With this book, we share some insights from our many years in the Middle Kingdom. We encourage you not to throw out the baby with the bathwater, to keep your eyes open and exercise a healthy curiosity for new ideas and new practices that may help you become or remain successful in tomorrow's world, rather than judge this world prematurely, without the necessary knowledge and insights.

The road to Dragon Tactics...
In June 2019, we came to the conclusion that this book needed to be written.

What instigated our decision was the announcement by the Carrefour Group, the French multinational retailing behemoth, that they were selling their China subsidiary because they were no longer able to compete in the Chinese market. Incredible! This after nearly two decades operating in the Middle Kingdom, a large part of that period very successfully and profitably. What had just happened?

We had some ideas about what led to their demise, and this book now provides many of the answers. Carrefour was indeed outcompeted. They failed to fully understand or take seriously enough the capabilities of local players. They moved too slow in a fast-changing, difficult-to-predict market. They did *not* thrive in uncertainty.

But many of their local competitors did and still do. Our book provides clear insights into how local enterprises have mastered operating in uncertain circumstances. In our view, there is much to learn from their experiences and capabilities.

...started with our own first steps in China, many years ago.
We both came to China relatively early in China's incredible journey from an economic backwater to the global powerhouse it is today.

Sandrine arrived in Shanghai at the beginning of 1994, on what was supposed to be a short-term mission. Requested by Robert-Louis Dreyfus, the new shareholder and CEO of Adidas, she came to explore commercial opportunities for the German sportswear giant. Sandrine ended up staying and starting Adidas China out of her living room.

Aldo first moved to Hong Kong in early 1992 when he found his first job, in marketing, at Dutch conglomerate Hagemeyer. He then relocated to the mainland in 1995 to be one of the co-founders of the Beijing office of J. Walter Thompson, an American advertising agency. Both of us did not know a lot about China when we arrived. For Sandrine in particular, it was a true cultural shock and a tough journey at the beginning: what could Adidas do in China when faced with immature (if non-existent) commercial infrastructures, very low purchasing power, and significant legal obstacles in place before China was granted access to the WTO?

And yet, Sandrine insisted on staying beyond her short assignment and volunteered to create the Adidas China subsidiary and business. Despite all the difficulties she encountered, she felt China had a unique energy that would make the place the epicentre of the 21st century.

She was proven right. Yet, as China was developing at lightning speed, she was still very sceptical about the first generation of entrepreneurs emerging back then. Her impression was one of chaos, lack of planning, wasted resources. And in the early days, that was all true.

The same belief as Sandrine's — that China was holding incredible opportunity — was behind Aldo's move to give up life in Hong Kong for an uncertain future in Beijing. Having travelled back and forth into mainland China from Hong Kong for a few years, he experienced a more subdued culture shock.

Whereas Sandrine was, at first, working with local entrepreneurs to create a supply chain and a distribution channel, Aldo initially worked with multinationals aiming to conquer the Chinese market, some of them achieving success, some of them a lot less. He vividly remembers discussions along the lines of 'if only a small fraction of China's 1.3 billion population would buy our product, we would be very successful', while the reality of enticing this 'small group' was a lot harder, especially, with not many companies willing to make tough strategic choices to appeal to this new Chinese audience.

Aldo's best example of this short-sightedness came when consulting for a well-known cereal company that was struggling to entice Chinese audiences to eat sugared cereal for breakfast. He was warned explicitly by the China management team, prior to a meeting with the APAC leadership, *not* to suggest during that session that the company should start creating local breakfast products, such as deep-fried breadsticks, for risk of being removed from the meeting. The company was a cereal company and it *was* going to convert the market!

Sandrine and Aldo met at Adidas China in 2004. Sandrine had meanwhile grown Adidas China from scratch into the second biggest subsidiary and had successfully convinced the Beijing Olympic committee to award Adidas the lead sportswear sponsorship at the XIV Olympiad to be held in Beijing in 2008.

Needing a marketer to strengthen the Adidas brand ahead of the Olympics, she turned to Aldo, meanwhile working for Siemens, who had just delivered an award-winning advertising campaign that was successful both globally and in China, quite a unicum at that time.

A lot has changed since then. Not just China itself, or our own careers, but especially our belief and understanding of how to become and stay successful in China.

Since 2004, we both have served in different leadership roles and have worked for, and with, a variety of different businesses, companies both global and local. And in Sandrine's case, advancing her own entrepreneurial endeavour. In all these positions we have had numerous touchpoints with Chinese entrepreneurs, ranging from Chinese franchisees and manufacturing partners of the brands we operated, to scouting possible partners for global brands we have represented, to actually working directly with or for these entrepreneurs.

With our initial and, in hindsight, limited knowledge, we first judged local businesses, like so many others before and after us, as not quite at a professional level. And yet, from those early days, and particularly over the last ten to twelve years, Chinese entrepreneurs have turned many of these shortcomings into strengths and have developed a whole new way of doing business, which is one of the key success factors of China today.

One thing of note is that throughout our career in China, we have both operated mostly in consumer markets. In the book, we therefore use many consumer-related examples because that is what we know best. However, it should be clear that there are many businesses in China, successful or not, operating outside the consumer space for which our thinking does and will apply. The management practices used successfully by Chinese entrepreneurs and business leaders that we describe in this book, are not category specific.

Dragon Tactics, explained.

Last, but certainly not least, we would like to explain the title of our book: 'Dragon Tactics'. On the surface these two words seem a simple amalgam that combines an iconic Chinese cultural symbol with a word to express how to get things done.

While this is perfectly true, there is more to the title than meets the eye. In our view, any other name would not have been appropriate for our book.

As you will read soon, many Chinese entrepreneurs, certainly the ones we have met and worked with over the years, revere wolves. Not necessarily the molar wolves — the aggressive lamb mauling, drooling kind despised in both Western and Chinese culture — but the more cerebral types that are smart, courageous, stubborn, and patient; the kind that cherishes independence and freedom and in a fight are fully cognizant of the limits of battle, highly organized, and disciplined; wolves that know how to make plans and set goals and then spy, encircle, ambush, attack, and intercept; the kind that can resist thirst and hunger, is family-oriented, possessing a collective spirit, unyielding, and indomitable.

In many ways wolf characteristics symbolize much of what drives Chinese entrepreneurs. Wolf Culture, which we will explain in-depth in this book, has become for many of them the most appropriate metaphor to describe the business culture they have built.

So, we could have considered calling our book Wolf Tactics, and yet we did not. While a lot of Wolf Culture is admirable and can lead to incredible success, you will read that not all that a Wolf does is amicable. Moreover, not every entrepreneur or business leader in China is necessarily a Wolf. But they are all Dragons!

While dragons feature in both Chinese and Western legends, they are perceived very differently. In the West a dragon often has a negative image as a fire-breathing beast that can only be slain by brave heroic men. In Chinese legend on the other hand, the dragon is perceived much more favourably. The Chinese dragon is a highly revered mythical creature.

In ancient Chinese times, the dragon was a sacred being, worthy of worship. The dragon was elegant, with a docile character. A benevolent symbol of fertility associated with water and the heavens. A god who controlled the rain and sunshine.

As feudal society developed, and with it hierarchy, the role of the dragon evolved with it. When Chinese rulers obtained the mandate of heaven and became Emperors, the position of the dragon followed in their footsteps. The Emperor, no longer just a man, but a god-like Son of Heaven embraced the dragon as the exclusive symbol of his aristocracy. Gradually the emperor became a dragon. A golden dragon.

Today, the dragon is still a highly respected symbol, representing wealth, wisdom, success, power, and luck. The Chinese proudly declare that they are the descendants of dragons. Western media often use the dragon as a symbol of China.

In our book, we describe the role which a Chinese founder, entrepreneur, or leader fulfils inside his or her organisation. Often that is as an absolute, yet benevolent leader looking after his people. An Emperor. And thus in our view a Dragon (龙, pinyin: Lóng).

The word Tactics (策略, pinyin: Cèlüè) is also carefully chosen. As we describe in this book, Chinese entrepreneurs are masters of speed, flexibility, and improvisation. With their history and culture pervaded with the succession of the four seasons and its resulting expectation of permanent change, the only constant is their need to adapt.

Operating in a hyper competitive, fast-changing world, they plan with a long-term vision in mind. Yet, with how the world around them changes, they don't chisel their plans in stone tablets. We once heard very aptly described that the only time you see a Chinese company create a five-year plan is when they are preparing for an IPO or sell themselves to a Western firm.

The market is simply moving too fast to plan far ahead. In fact, in an environment where things change as rapidly and fundamentally as in their increasingly modern and digitalized world, entrepreneurs in China need to keep their engine running, even while they upgrade it.

As we will explain, strategic planning as we know it in Western thinking therefore does not exist in the Chinese entrepreneur's mind. In a flexible world, inflexibility equates to stupidity. Vision, on the other hand, is scope, is long-term and anticipates the future based on the potential of the situation here and now.

While working toward a long-term goal, the short term therefore can be as flexible as the here-and-now requires. After you have a clear vision, you can start to act. Tactics are what will get you on your way and will keep you directed, no matter how winding the road will be.

This is also how we see the role of this book. Dragon Tactics is your scope. It shows you where you can go. How you apply the lessons, here and now, in your reality, is for you to decide.

PROLOGUE

In June 2019, the Carrefour Group of France, the multi-national retailing behemoth, announced it had sold 80% of their China business to Suning, a large local retailing conglomerate. The reason, they admitted, was that they were no longer able to compete because they had been too slow to adjust to the realities of the fast-paced Chinese market.

Carrefour was an early China entrant, did many things right from the outset, and traded profitably for nearly two decades. Numerous foreign businesses never even get off the ground in China (often erroneously) blaming 'unfavourable business conditions', but in reality, not adapting a global business model fast enough to a market and consumer that is very different from their home market.

Seeing Carrefour, a once successful corporation, falter in an environment where many local competitors flourish, while admitting to their own shortcomings was refreshing, but also alarming.

How can it be that a globally successful European company can lose its way so quickly in a market they had initially conquered? What is happening in the China market that even a player that had managed to navigate its way in challenging conditions and had figured out a business model that actually worked in this so very different marketplace was throwing in the towel?
Why was what worked so well initially, obsolete so quickly? How did local competitors out-compete Carrefour so fast?

Since China opened up to the world in the late 1980s, its economy has gone through various stages of development. Central to most of these phases was not just a reliance on foreign capital and technology but notably management expertise. Foreign executive skills and practices were a key inspiration early in the industrial and consumer economies.

Leaders of the first successful Chinese corporations looked abroad or learned from the many overseas Chinese active in mainland China to run their business. They also hired local tal-ents that had honed their skills at multinational firms.

But we have come a long way since...

Today's business success in China — and, as we see it, increasingly outside its borders — is based on a new set of management beliefs that go beyond commonly accepted international practices. The current principles are deeply rooted in China's thousands of years of history, the cultural environment in which Chinese entrepreneurs and business leaders matured and amplified by the hyper competitive environment in which they operate.

That, combined with a rapidly digitizing society and its inherent increase in scale, speed, and complexity, means successful Chinese companies now rely on a very different skillset: survival skills, platform organisations, horse races, long term goals intertwined with complete short-term flexibility, opportunity over efficiency, amoeba style organisations, extensive data reliance, an entrepreneur's mentality to staffing, and a 'try, fail, try again, fail again and try again until something works' methodology among them.

Western management theory can easily deride all that as leading to chaos, lacking sufficient business sense, or worse, lacking a 'business case', and proclaim that such will never work.

Yet, as the Carrefour example dramatically proves, much of it does.
For many people and business leaders around the world, China remains an enigma. A faraway place with an unfamiliar culture.

But as the world becomes more intertwined and digital and the presence of China and its entrepreneurs likely to grow in global business in the coming decades, there is much to learn from Chinese management practices for business leaders around the globe. And for Chinese business leaders to better understand what possible challenges lay ahead when venturing abroad.

China may not yet have produced widely accepted new management approaches like these of Peter Drucker or what Japanese companies achieved with continuous improvement and just-in-time systems. But as we will demonstrate in this book, Chinese entrepreneurs have mastered management skills needed in today's increasingly unstable and rapidly digitizing societies: flexibility, adaptability, speed, agility, tenacity, and rate of learning.

These abilities already give them a critical edge. Studies (such as those by Qiao Liu and Alan Siu of the University of Hong Kong) suggest that China's private unlisted companies earn higher returns — 14%, on average, versus the 4% earned by state-owned companies.[1]

A guide to Dragon Tactics.
In this book we detail what makes modern Chinese companies and leaders successful, which of such management beliefs and techniques work and why, and how they can be applied in a more Western-focused business arena: a manual for businesses around the world on how to adapt to a rapidly changing and digitizing world with its increasing levels of uncertainty.

In PART 1 – THE NEED FOR UNDERSTANDING DRAGON TACTICS, we will explore what it takes to become successful in the rapidly changing Chinese market, from the point of view of global businesses.

In the first chapter, *Why in China, Do Some Fail and Others Succeed?* we take you through a brief history of the failure and success of multinational companies in the Chinese market. In the early days of operating in the Middle Kingdom, or even for entrants that arrived at a later stage, the road to success, albeit not easy, was relatively clear. We will show that businesses that were willing or able to adapt to local market conditions and by default compromise global strategy, positioning, and efficiencies to create and deliver a 'China for China' approach had a real chance of success. Many businesses, for myriad reasons failed to do so. And thus, they failed quickly against emerging Chinese competition, Amazon being a surprising and high-profile victim.

Success stories of companies like Adidas, KFC, or Starbucks will show that building a profitable business is possible. Companies able to leverage their global strengths, while adapting product offering, go-to-market strategies, and how they operate in this competitive and fast-changing environment with limited global interference, had a real chance of achieving success.

The importance of this willingness and ability to adapt has only increased.

Over the last ten years and accelerating yet, the Chinese market has seen a significant change in market dynamics. A dramatic digitalisation and the rise of increasingly very capable local competition have made an already fast-moving business arena even more challenging.

Rapidly changing market environments require loosely structured and flexible management systems which can process new information quickly and that are led by empowered managers who can act independently and swiftly.[2] Chinese companies have only ever known such operating circumstances and have developed the skills to survive and prosper.

In Chapter 2 *Dragon Tactics*, we will demonstrate this based on the realities of Carrefour. As noted, they were initially successful and profitable, but the market changed too fast for the French retailer to keep up. Underestimating local competition added to their demise. Based on how Carrefour was outcompeted, we will form the basis for 'Dragon Tactics': the five management skills Chinese business leaders have developed and mastered to survive in their unstable, fast-moving, and increasingly digital business world — a world we see as the blueprint for the future of commerce around the globe.

In PART 2 – MASTERING DRAGON TACTICS, we explore five Dragon Tactics in depth.

In five chapters, one for each tactic, we will describe the historical context that has formed each skill. We will highlight the key characteristics of each ability and draw lessons for a global audience. Not all skills will be transferable one-on-one in a Western business environment, but we will explain why and what can still be learned from them. Not all skills are perhaps uniquely Chinese, but where they are not, Chinese entrepreneurs are often more able to implement them. We explain why and what can be learned from that.

Chinese companies have developed extensive survival skills and are masters of adapting to rapidly changing market environments. They build organisations that are laser focused on consumer needs, are adopting digital capabilities fast, and that enable decision-making and execution at incredible speed.

We will explore:
1. WOLF CULTURE – How survival skills influence business culture and behaviour.
2. ADAPT OR DIE – How fast-changing circumstances require constant nimbleness and innovation.
3. THE EMPEROR DECIDES, BUT AGILITY RULES – How fast decision-making and agile organisations are possible, even under central control.
4. PEOPLE COME AND GO – How the right people stay and contribute.
5. IT ALL STARTS WITH DATA – How data is enabling an even sharper consumer focus.

In PART 3 – EMPLOYING DRAGON TACTICS, we will summarize our thinking and place it in a context of recent geopolitical reality and developments.

Over the course of writing our book, we have sadly witnessed a deteriorating global relationship between China and large parts of the world. With dissimilar values and visions at a political level, disputes may not be so easy to solve or to bridge.

In the first section, *Demons and Dragons,* we will however make a clear case that despite such differences we believe a closer cooperation is still inevitable. Complete decoupling in our view is not desirable nor is it a realistic alternative. We will plead our case that both sides can benefit from investing in a better understanding. There is much to learn from each other for both sides to be better equipped for our rapidly changing world.

In Section 2 we then list what we see are the 16 core components of Dragon Tactics and what their historical, cultural, and contemporary contexts are. This summary serves as a quick reference guide to recap the essence of the capabilities we discuss throughout the book. The list includes references to where in the text examples or more details on the topic can be found.

We conclude our writing with words of advice both for leaders of multinational companies around the world as well as for companies from China.

In Sections 3, *Not all Dragon Tactics are sustainable, especially outside China*, and 4, *Facing reality*, we look at elements of Dragon Tactics that will have their limitations particularly outside a Chinese business environment. Not all Dragon Tactics are exportable or sustainable, and we will explain why and what the possible consequences may be if left unchanged.

Section 5, *Following the Dragon's path*, concludes our book. In it, we provide a clear way forward with what companies need to and can do to equip themselves with the capabilities we describe in this book.

The world around us is changing. It is up to you to change with it.

PART 1

THE NEED FOR UNDERSTANDING DRAGON TACTICS

各有成败

WHY IN CHINA,
DO SOME FAIL
AND OTHERS
SUCCEED?

1. WHY IN CHINA,
DO SOME FAIL AND OTHERS SUCCEED?

1.1 FAILURE TO ADAPT, THE BASIS FOR FAILURE

Carrefour was not the only enterprise admitting defeat in China in 2019. Arguably an even higher profile casualty was Amazon.

April 2019: Amazon announces it will stop operating its China domestic marketplace.

Amazon's leadership role within the e-commerce industry is indisputable. Without any doubt, its global success can be attributed to the vision of its founder, its relentless drive as an innovator, and the speed at which the company has been evolving since its infancy.

And yet while highly innovative and successful in many parts of the world, Amazon was forced to admit they were not good enough to achieve success in China. Twice!

To the surprise of many, in March 2015, Amazon announced the soft launch of a virtual storefront on Alibaba Group's Tmall.com online platform, its fiercest rival in the domestic China market.[1]

> 'Amazon.com vies with Tmall for China's online consumers through its own shopping website and has invested in warehouses and logistics to deliver orders to mainland customers. By opening a flagship store on Tmall, China's largest B2C shopping site, Amazon seeks to develop new sales channels, offering Tmall consumers a variety of premium imported brands and a quality life backed by Amazon.

> 'Through Tmall and sister C2C shopping website Taobao Marketplace, Amazon is tapping into Alibaba's e-commerce ecosystem, which has some 334 million active buyers', said Niu Yinghua, vice president of Amazon China, in a statement at the time.

Amazon opened a store within the infrastructure of their main competitor in a bid to reach a larger audience and to boost sales! Many saw this unusual move as admitting to not being able to compete. And those critics were right, as indeed that is how the story ended.

Four years later, in April 2019, Amazon announced it would stop operating its China domestic marketplace altogether:[2]

> 'We are notifying sellers we will no longer operate a marketplace on Amazon.cn and we will no longer be providing seller services on Amazon.cn effective July 18.

> 'Instead of buying products sold locally by Amazon and its marketplace of Chinese suppliers, shoppers at Amazon.cn will be able to buy products imported by Amazon's sites in the United States, Britain, Germany or Japan', Amazon said in a statement.

Having enjoyed a 15% market share in China in 2011[3], the US tech giant's stake had fallen to less than 1% in eight years, leaving it in sixth place in the world's largest e-commerce market by the time it closed its domestic store.

Although it is not unusual to see Western tech companies struggle in the Middle Kingdom, Chinese consumers don't blindly prefer local brands, and foreign businesses do certainly not automatically fail. So how did Amazon get to this stage?

A foundation for success was there early on...

Amazon gained an early entry and foothold into China in 2004 by acquiring local online book e-tailer, Joyo.com. At that time, restrictions for foreign internet companies were still somewhat few. Also, in those early days Amazon had a positive reputation for being a site that had legitimate products and so was trusted by Chinese consumers.

In all, they had a seemingly good basis for success, yet Amazon struggled from the beginning to compete for reasons that are all too familiar to us.

Amazon did indeed face a more competitive and ambiguous legal environment than in many other markets where it is active. For example, prior to 2008 when China entered the WTO, it was legally unclear whether Amazon, as a foreign enterprise was allowed to operate there. It also had to engage in endless price wars that ate into profits and was in a constant battle against knockoffs.

But Amazon did not adapt fast enough.

The US tech giant faced broadly published criticism for failing to modify its online offer to the needs and desires of Chinese consumers and was rapidly outcompeted by local rivals with a better in-depth understanding of how to be successful.

It is often believed that Chinese e-commerce companies copied the operation model of their Western competitors. That was probably true early on, but these companies did not win because they were copycats. They were willing to make significant efforts to deliver a product or service that often far exceeded what Western internet players offered and to rapidly adapt to evolving customer needs.

Pony Ma, the founder of Tencent, one of the largest Internet and technology enterprises globally and the company that among others invented the universal app WeChat, confirmed that view in a 2017 interview.[4]

> 'As computer applications and the internet were invented in the USA, other countries had no other choice initially than to copy. However, here in China the situation and consumers are different, so it was only natural that we quickly launched our own development. And as we work a lot faster in China, we now even see Western players starting to copy many of our features.'

Global HQ and system hampered local success.
Restricted by a global platform that prevented significant improvements to its local user interface, Amazon unsuccessfully competed with the websites of local competitors which were very different. For example, local players had additional product offerings enabling cross-selling opportunities and were a lot more colourful, very unlike the simple, minimalist design Amazon uses around the world.

Most critically, they contained a lot more and often very detailed product information, mostly presented in pictures. This enabled customers to see every detail of the product, a crucial enabler of success. Since they cannot physically touch the product, this more in-depth product understanding is very important for Chinese customers and plays a vital role in driving purchase decisions.

Amazon also didn't adapt well to the unique Chinese market requirement of near instant delivery. It initially controlled much of its own inventory and built its own delivery infrastructure, just like they did elsewhere. In contrast, Alibaba chose to focus on being a platform, hosting a variety of smaller vendors and using local delivery companies, enabling lower prices and faster delivery routes. Over time this approach helped Alibaba outperform Amazon.

Other local players that more closely followed Amazon's model, like JD.com, invested more heavily in their logistics and also outcompeted the American company on delivery service. Rather surprising, given that logistics is at the core of Amazon's global capabilities.

Amazon was not in tune with what consumers needed.
It is well documented how Alibaba gained a massive advantage due to the success of their own payment system, Alipay. While it can be understood that Amazon was not able to rapidly match such a payment system, it is surprising that

Chinese competitors were able to offer their customers still more options to pay. For example, for a long time Amazon did not support a straightforward payment upon delivery service, a crucial 'must have' in a country where consumers are often worried about being cheated and credit cards were not widely used.

Another important driver of a great customer experience that Amazon missed out on was an online customer chat service. Local competitors provided solutions for customers to ask questions, or to facilitate direct communication between buyers and sellers, making it so much easier for customers to get nearly instant support.

Last but not least, the local players outperformed Amazon with clever marketing and sales festivals. China's 'Singles Day' each year on November 11th transformed the marketing landscape in China and is now even gaining traction globally. On November 11th 2021, it delivered sales (GMV) of over US$ 84Billion in one day for Alibaba alone!

All in all, local Chinese e-commerce players were much more consumer centric than Amazon and understood from day one that when consumers go online, they don't want to just simply buy a product, but they want a fully satisfactory shopping experience.

To keep the shopping experience exciting, Chinese marketplaces continue to bring new services and have over the last few years included major content marketing features that barely exist on Amazon global, such as livestreaming.

While essentially there is no major difference between the Amazon shopping experience from ten years ago to today, Chinese players have evolved tremendously, keeping up with, or often driving, the latest consumer experience trends.

Speed and need for local understanding were underestimated.
Not that Amazon did not try to adjust, but they underestimated the speed in which its competitors operate. In a, for us, telling quote, this was well understood by its own disillusioned employees, as cited in China Business Journal[5] after the announcement of the shutdown:

'Amazon's Chinese site has already seen a lot of changes, according to one employee, but getting those changes done was difficult and took a long time.

'That's unlike China's other e-commerce companies,' the person said. 'In those companies, as soon as the boss requests a new feature, the staff burns the midnight oil until it's launched.'

And that may point to one other reason why Amazon failed in the Middle Kingdom. It didn't sufficiently trust the management abilities of local employees. As Richard Liu, founder and CEO of JD.com (a key competitor of Amazon in China), has said on various occasions:

> *To make it in China you need people in managing positions who know the country, its people and their mentality in and out. When Amazon came to China at the beginning of the 2000s, it put foreigners in leading positions who had no experience with China at all. They implemented American — or generally speaking: Western — business practices which proved to be inferior to that of their Chinese competitors.*

The Entrepreneurial company that stopped being entrepreneurial.
So, in the end, Amazon was outcompeted by e-commerce giants like JD and Alibaba, who were often able to offer a broader array of products that came with a lot more relevant and sales-encouraging product information and pictures, that they were able to deliver to Chinese customers faster, with payment options more acceptable to a local audience.

Amazon, an aggressive entrepreneurial firm with many capabilities that has made them a globally feared and insatiable competitor got outmanoeuvred by what we call Dragon Tactics.

To us, both the Amazon and Carrefour developments came less as a surprise. They were simply two more defeats on what was already a long list of businesses that did not make it.

1.2 SUCCESS IN CHINA IS POSSIBLE, PROVIDED YOU CREATE THE RIGHT CIRCUMSTANCES

Many foreign companies that entered China since the country opened up in the late 1980s have failed to become successful. Sadly, the number of failures is much higher than the success stories.

We have compiled a list of often quoted reasons for not achieving business success, arguments given by a variety of business leaders over the years to explain why their business endeavours failed in the Chinese market. We identified two main blocks:

THE 'GREAT RED WALL' - whether intentionally organized or not, it is often claimed that the Chinese government and local competitors utilize their power and control and will go to extreme lengths to preserve sovereignty or win market share. To be more specific:

1. **EXTREME AND UNFAIR COMPETITION** – Competitors offer unfair pricing, copy products, or poach good staff.
2. **POOR PROTECTION FOR INNOVATION AND INTELLECTUAL PROPERTY** – The legal environment in China is less mature, notably in intellectual property. It is often impossible to protect your business model, product, brand, or user interface.
3. **UNCLEAR LEGAL ENVIRONMENT** – China's laws are often vague and not well enforced, leaving a lot of room for interpretation that provides ample opportunity for unfair competition.
4. **CENSORSHIP BY THE CHINESE GOVERNMENT** – Companies need to abide by the rules of a repressive, autocratic government.

THE 'CULTURAL DIVIDE' – There is broad consensus that there are differences in how things are done in China compared to other markets. But from what leaders claim as failure reasons, it is clear they have not understood how to deal with that. Specifically, they state:

1. **FAILED LOCAL PARTNERSHIP** – Misaligned objectives for entering a business partnership or JV. The foreign company getting a license to operate and aiming to learn how to run the business in China whereas the local partner wants to obtain transferable skills and learn the technology from their foreign partner.
2. **LACK OF (LOYAL) CHINESE TALENTS** – An endless but unwinnable fight for capable people that move on quickly when they are offered better terms elsewhere.
3. **NATIONALISM** – Chinese customers prefer local products and solutions.
4. **SLOW DECISION-MAKING AND CENTRALIZED ORGANISATIONAL STRUCTURES** – Not localizing the China business quickly enough, teams that are too foreign and global management that does not 'get' China.

On the surface these arguments are not without merit and have most certainly contributed to the demise of many business endeavours. But when one digs deeper it becomes clear it is not the full story. There is more at play.

For example, Feng Li, a researcher at City University of London, published in 2019 the results of an interesting study held among ex-insiders of various multinational internet firms that failed in China (Why Have All Western Internet Firms (WIFs) Failed in China?).[6] He concluded that many of the same unsuccessful firms, did succeed in dominating many other foreign markets that have radically different political systems and cultures compared to their home markets (for example Indonesia, Thailand, and Saudi Arabia).

Also, the factors listed above have not stopped other Western multinationals from succeeding in China, notably in car manufacturing, consumer electronics, fast-moving consumer goods, and even sectors where culture plays a key role, such as sportswear, coffee shops, fast food, and even the film industry. And the list goes on.

In fact, there are many interesting cases within various categories that demonstrate that success in China is often related to how these businesses are being managed, how much freedom local management is given to optimize their local business model or product offering and how autonomously they can make decisions. And equally important, how well global management understands China and how truly committed they really are to achieving success in the Chinese market to begin with.

In the following section, we highlight three such cases which demonstrate that with the right approach, foreign companies can be very successful in the Middle Kingdom.

These companies were willing from the beginning to compromise global strategy, positioning, or efficiencies to adapt to local circumstances. They created the capabilities needed to operate in an environment dissimilar to conditions elsewhere.

Each case is unique, but for the sake of comparability, we have summarized the reasons behind each success in four areas:

— 'China for China' (Strategic deviation from global strategy)
— 'Adapt to consumer needs' ((Product) offer needed for market success)
— 'Scale, Speed, and Flexibility' (Capabilities that ensure agility and drive efficiencies)
— 'Maintain Global Strengths' (Global capabilities providing a competitive advantage)

KENTUCKY FRIED CHICKEN - FINGER LICKIN' SUCCESS.

Kentucky Fried Chicken (KFC) China is often referred to as the one of the most impressive success stories for a US company abroad. In the early 1990s, after an initially slow learning phase, KFC China positioned itself for the long haul and developed a vision that was radically different from what made them successful in the United States. This strategy not only ensured survival and success in the Chinese market until the present day, it also gave them a lasting competitive edge over various local fast-food players and its key global rival McDonald's, which, for many years chose to stay close to its global positioning and product line-up. KFC opened their first store in China in 1987. McDonalds followed suit in 1990. And they have taken a very different path since. KFC is still market leader and had 6500 locations in 1300 cities, end 2019. McDonald's had 3300 locations nationwide. It is easy to argue that fried chicken is closer to the Chinese palate than hamburgers and thus that KFC had a 'natural' advantage. But that would not do justice to the visionary and entrepreneurial managers behind the KFC success in China. Adopting a strategic direction that took the Chinese business rapidly away from the global positioning and strategy, the KFC team has consistently delivered on the following:

'CHINA FOR CHINA' STRATEGY
- Localized and empowered team, free to pursue its homegrown strategy
- Local vision to 'make China a better place'
- A brand that is seen as part of the local community
- Localized marketing and celebrity endorsements

ADAPT TO CONSUMER NEEDS
- Inviting restaurant ambience where people like to linger and that encouraged group visits instead of a quick take-out
- Variety of foods and traditional dishes that appeal to Chinese customers rather than selling 'regular Western fast food'
- A much broader product offer (initially 50 compared to 29 in the US) to ensure repeat visits and to take local and regional tastes into account
- Innovate: often 50 new products a year compared to two or three in the US

SCALE, SPEED, AND FLEXIBILITY
- Penetrating early into smaller cities
  - To generate sufficient liquidity to compete against McDonald's in the big cities and to grow even faster elsewhere
  - First mover advantage means getting the best locations and the highest free publicity
  - A broader presence also meant a better negotiation position with mall developers
- Deliver a new store from design to opening in half the time vs the home market
- Fully controlled and inhouse logistics network

MAINTAIN RELEVANT GLOBAL STRENGTHS

— KFC kept 'The System', its well-developed set of processes which oversees every detail of the business, from making the product, to service standards, to site development, to staff training and management. This turned out to be a major differentiator in overcoming local competition.

After a multiyear sales slowdown and a food quality scandal in 2015, the global KFC Board decided to spin-off their China subsidiary and create a separate stock market listing in 2016. Yum China has since regained significant sales momentum and has set global standards in digitalisation of their business. For details on this see the Yum China case in Part 2, Chapter 5 It All Starts with Data.

Source: Harvard Business Review [7]

ADIDAS – IMPOSSIBLE WAS NOTHING!

Today, Adidas China is a top market subsidiary for Adidas globally. A business that grew from very humble beginnings, in 1994, out of a living room in Shanghai. Its current success would not have been possible without early strategic decisions that took the brand away from its original roots but that ensured growth in difficult circumstances. Some of these strategic changes ultimately found their way back into the global business vision. An added benefit was that Adidas was able to develop a much stronger competitive position compared to its global rival Nike that still outpaces Adidas in many markets around the world. And it contributed to the brand staying competitive compared to various local players. Adopting a strategic direction that took the Chinese business rapidly away from the global positioning and strategy, the Adidas team delivered on:

'CHINA FOR CHINA' STRATEGY

— Localized and empowered team, relatively free to pursue its homegrown strategy
— Verticalized Distribution. Sales via Mono branded stores; self-owned as well as operated by local franchisees
— Pricing at a premium as opposed to 'for everyone' globally
— 'Sport' as brand differentiator, but casual usage as reason to buy
— Brand focused more on 'winning' than 'participation' globally
— Locally developed marketing campaigns for lifestyle products
— Inhouse production as opposed to 'fully outsourced' globally

ADAPT TO CONSUMER NEEDS
- Product quality and materials where possible above global standards
- Basketball as brand and sales driver rather than football globally
- Running category as volume driver. Not because people would run, but because the shoes were high quality and comfortable for everyday use.
- Apparel products also skewed towards casual, everyday usage, e.g. high share of polo shirts
- Significantly larger number of colour options than the global range
- Creation of a third strategic brand pillar 'Adidas NEO', in addition to global segments 'Performance' and 'Originals'

SCALE, SPEED, AND FLEXIBILITY
- Mono brand store franchise model to rapidly penetrate beyond key Tier 1 and 2 cities
- Low-cost store design (up to 50% less than global), while maintaining global brand image
- Deliver a new store from design to opening in a fraction of the time of the home market
- Fully controlled and inhouse logistics

MAINTAIN RELEVANT GLOBAL STRENGTHS
- Global athletes as brand icons
- Global advertising at brand and technical product level to enhance sports credibility

Source: Authors

STARBUCKS - TURNING A TEA NATION INTO COFFEE AFICIONADOS.

For the first 12 years of its presence in China, Starbucks was a very US-centric company struggling with various typical China issues. As a result, when it celebrated its tenth anniversary in 2009 it barely operated 300 stores, including those of their joint venture with Unipresident, which covered Eastern China. The organisation was matrixed with the entire first line of management reporting to global function heads. The China business was centrally run and controlled like any other foreign market, much to the frustration of the local team. In 2012, a new China CEO was hired. Simultaneously, Howard Schultz, the founder of Starbucks, realized change was needed and 'empowerment' became the new key word. No more matrix. Let China find their way in China. Full local responsibility. The first country within the Starbucks universe ever to see such an organisational reform. Massive growth was unleashed. As of 2020, Starbucks has more than 5000 stores China-wide and 600 to 700 more are added every year. In late 2017, the brand opened its then globally largest Flagship store, in Shanghai. A 'roastery store' designed to turn coffee into entertainment. One of the key features of the store — an almost permanent queue of people waiting patiently to get inside. So, how did Starbucks achieve such a turnaround?

'CHINA FOR CHINA' STRATEGY
— Localized and empowered team, free to pursue its homegrown strategy
— Created Product Innovation and R&D center
— Freedom to create market relevant store designs and formats (e.g., community stores, pet friendly stores)
— Creation of 'Starbucks Now', smaller outlets for quick online order collection
— Selected 'Reserve' store format locations used as a wine bar in the evening
  • China as the global digital business model laboratory. [See full details in Chapter 7.]
— HR policies optimized for local realities (e.g., providing social insurance to employees' parents)

ADAPT TO LOCAL NEEDS
— Menu: Food 100% localized. Beverages only partially localized as global drinks recipes perform well
— Introduction of heated food items
— Consistent stream of innovative products. (e.g., for local occasions such as Chinese New Year, Mid-autumn, Dragon Boat Festival)
— 90% of merchandising items China for China

SPEED, SCALE, AND FLEXIBILITY
— Flat and lean organisation for fast decision making and to empower regional teams
— Creating 'Starbucks University' to support staffing needs for continuous stream of store openings
— Creating local store design and development capabilities
— Internal mobile applications for fast communication and information sharing

MAINTAIN RELEVANT GLOBAL STRENGTHS
— Coffee as a Culture
— A Starbucks location as a 'social space'

Three success stories, one that started in the late 1980s, one originating in the 90s and another more than a decade later. In Part 2, Chapter 4 *Adapt to Change or Die* we will also present a case study about L'Oréal, a company that has very well adapted in today's highly competitive and digital market environment. It is a great example that success is still possible today. In Chapter 7 *It All Starts with Data*, in Part 2, we will further share case studies on the successful digital strategies of KFC and Starbucks.

These examples — and there are many more — in various categories, at different stages of China's market development and with brands heavily depending on faddish and fickle Chinese consumers with different cultural values have one thing in common: they tailored their China 'go to market' to fit local needs and did what was required to achieve success. Just like local Chinese companies, they thought deeply of what their products could bring to Chinese consumers, or how their products could resolve an issue or problem faced by Chinese consumers. In other words, they asked themselves, 'What's in it for China?'.

They accepted significant deviations from the global product offering, global brand values, and marketing approach and built organisations which operated very independently — although not necessarily all based inside China — from the global corporation.

China as 'Engine 2'.

In a blog published in 2018[8], James Allen, a partner at Bain & Co, asks an interesting question: 'Will winning in China transform the whole company?' He goes on to answer his own query with the conclusion that he doesn't see many MNCs answering, 'Yes'. And continues that 'When it comes to winning in China itself, they aren't all in yet'.

He then describes a solution that we very much agree with: Success in China is possible, but it requires the China business to be built as 'Engine 2', a business that is set up completely separately from the main global business. He writes,

You need to reimagine China as your second major engine of growth.

Your core engine, or Engine 1, is the European and North American

markets. These markets are incredibly important in terms of cash and profits generated.

But your Engine 1 still faces fundamental problems. It's too complex for the growth it will deliver. You built vast organisations for these markets, and historically, the complexity of these organisations was justified by the growth you got in return. But this no longer works. Your Engine 1 needs to be dramatically simplified and 'rightsized' for the growth you can expect from Europe and the US.

Your Engine 2 is China — it holds huge growth potential, but you can only capture this growth on a sustained basis by reimagining your firm.

Business leaders never simplify Engine 1 fast enough. Therefore, they never sufficiently invest in Engine 2. Business leaders never free up Engine 2 to compete as it needs to compete, weighing it down with baggage from Engine 1 ways of thinking.

Success in Engine 2 will help redefine Engine 1 and create the next wave of growth.

This last point is important. Rather than think of your China business as unique to China, you should think about China as the model for how you will compete globally over time.

If you can win in China against 'scale insurgents', you can take those capabilities back to the rest of your business.

In particular, the last section of his observation we believe to be profound. *'Think of China as the model for how you will compete globally over time.'*

Whereas the essence of the Engine 2 approach is leaving a lot of autonomy to the team in charge of China, ultimately, you will need to bring China into your HQ. Not to increase global control but to ensure that your HQ fully enables China as your Engine 2. And ultimately to ensure that the skills needed to achieve success in China are adopted also within your Engine 1.

Nike Inc, L'Oréal, and Starbucks, especially through the efforts of their founder Howard Schultz who made it a personal mission to find success in China, are in our view companies that set the direction. Not surprisingly, their businesses are doing very well, both in the Middle Kingdom and globally.

龙之策略

2

DRAGON TACTICS.

2. DRAGON TACTICS.

For many years business success in China depended on how willing a company was to deviate from global strategy, adapt their global offer to match local needs and tastes, and how empowered local management was to make such decisions; in short whether companies created an 'Engine 2' or not.

However, the admittance of defeat and subsequent sale of Carrefour demonstrates that in present day China more is happening that needs to be understood. Carrefour China was once rather successful. They were an early entrant, opening their first store in 1995 in a joint venture with Chinese supermarket chain Lian Hua. Hypermarkets were a new concept at that time and Carrefour became an almost 'overnight' success.

With a management team formed out of expats from France and other Asian markets, they created a formula similar to the global model, but with several adaptations, based on what they knew had worked well in the rest of Asia.

The Carrefour China team implemented a very entrepreneurial business approach. From the start, the management of each store was very decentralised. Each location could optimize its own assortments, choose local suppliers and fully adapt to the needs of the customers in the neighbourhood surrounding the hypermarket. For example, stores catering more to expats would have a much higher share of imported products.

But other stores could have a large share of brands and products very familiar to its local customers. This optimization gave 家乐福 (pinyin: jiālèfú, translated as Family Blessing) as Carrefour was known in China, a quickly earned image of being close to Chinese consumers.

What really helped cement that image was the large offer of fresh produce in its assortment. Vegetables, fruits, meats and (shell) fish were until then almost exclusively available in wet markets. Offering such products in a modern and clean environment really boosted the premium appeal of Carrefour.

With lots of choice, a vast number of products in self-service, a quality that could be trusted, and pricing levels that were acceptable, they met consumer expectations early on. The quality retailing experience that Carrefour offered combined with its great economics convinced millions of Chinese. By implementing very 'Chinese-like values' in its products, services, merchandising, prices, and ambience, Carrefour truly became a household name among Chinese retailers.

What further contributed to their success was great support of local (municipality) governments. Eager to attract a Carrefour branch, they offered tax breaks and help with leasing contracts.

Having been an ongoing success, practically from the moment their first store was opened in Beijing, the next ten years were spent to manage breakneck growth, in some years even opening more than ten new locations per annum.

A decade after entering the Chinese market, Carrefour had grown to nearly 80 hypermarkets with a turnover of close to €2 billion by the end of 2005.

The demise of a successful company.

Carrefour did many things right from the outset and traded profitably. They faced very similar challenges which other foreign business owners often quoted as reasons behind their failure in the Chinese market [see Section 1.2]. But Carrefour made many of the hard decisions needed to overcome these challenges. They even managed to make their JV with Lian Hua work! Carrefour China achieved business success in difficult circumstances. But still, they ended up failing!

How is it possible that a globally successful company can lose its way so quickly in a market they had initially conquered? Why did what worked so well earlier, become obsolete so quickly? How did local competitors out-compete Carrefour so fast?

What is happening in the China market that even a player that had managed to navigate its way in challenging conditions, had figured out a working business model in this so very different marketplace, and traded profitably for nearly two decades was throwing in the towel?

Let's examine in more detail what led to the demise of Carrefour.

Around 2006, a decade after first entering China, Carrefour was a successful company. The fastest growing foreign retailer in the Chinese market, it had so far been relatively free of competition.

Walmart, its main global competitor from the United States as well as Metro Cash & Carry from Germany had entered China in 1996, a year after Carrefour, but had not yet managed to achieve a similar level of success. Tesco, a key European rival, had only just arrived in the Middle Kingdom in 2004.

Local competitors had started emerging, but as was quite common at that time, they had not yet mastered the operational skills needed to efficiently manage large scale and complex hyper markets. Most other local competitors concentrated on supermarket formats with smaller footprints.

Expecting its sales in China to grow by 25% to 30% annually over the next five years it seemed all Carrefour needed to do to remain market leader, was to do more of the same. And so, they did.

But, in hindsight, the company admits that it missed recognizing and acting on massive changes in the market over that brief period. Notably:

1. Market Digitization
2. The trend away from big box hypermarkets to smaller formats and convenience stores
3. The rise of and capability increase of local competitors

Over the period from 2005 to around 2012 Carrefour did not innovate.

While the market was carving two new directions, smaller store formats such as convenience stores and online sales, Carrefour did not invest in digitization nor in new store formats for a long time. Only in 2014 did they open their first Carrefour Easy and Carrefour Express convenience stores in residential areas in Shanghai. They targeted a younger middle-class audience that increasingly avoided hypermarkets, perceiving them to be less premium as the market matured and alternatives developed.

While many retail businesses, in a variety of categories, were creating loyalty programs and by doing so were gaining significant consumer behavioural knowledge, Carrefour failed to start a CRM program until 2012.

While a fast-growing local online player, Yihaodian (founded in 2008), was developing very rapidly and online retailing had really started to take off in 2010, Carrefour China did not take steps toward a digitized business model until 2014 in the form of click and collect. Ensuing digital innovation such as a Carrefour App was too little, too late as the app ran slowly, product variety was limited, and many regions were not able to support the distribution of fresh food.

While local competitors, like Yonghui Superstores (founded in 2000), were building up regional supply chains enabling faster and more cost-effective product deliveries and improved quality assurance, Carrefour China did not implement changes in its logistics model. Even competitors RT Marts and Walmart were out investing Carrefour. The latter buying a stake in Yihaodian in 2011 with the initial aim to speed up the development of their own logistics network.

Various other issues were impeding the competitiveness of Carrefour. The chain did not start any private labels, and with (local) competition growing, had to compete more on price. Neither did it implement assortment efficiencies, further hampering attempts to bring down cost rapidly. Last but not least, it was slow to reduce the number of expats preventing it from building a strong local management team that would have been closer to the fast-changing market.

By 2015, Carrefour China had started losing money. By 2017, despite various turnaround efforts they realized they would no longer be able to compete. Carrefour knew then they would need an alliance to stay relevant.

About a year earlier, Jack Ma, the founder of Alibaba, had announced his vision for 'New Retail'. A truly digital integrated online/offline omnichannel world. As he initially had many doubters, he knew he had to build a case, and nothing fit better than daily groceries to prove the concept. So, Ma founded HeMa, a chain of supermarkets. But operating grocery stores was not their area of competence, so they turned to Carrefour.

Under an initial agreement Carrefour would have managed HeMa and would have merged with Tmall supermarket. However, the global Carrefour Board hesitated to give up so much control and dragged on the approval process. By the time they were ready for a decision, Tmall had moved on and the deal fell through. By acting too slowly, Carrefour lost the chance to manage the most innovative retailing development, globally!

Running out of options, in April 2019, the Carrefour Board agreed to sell 80% of Carrefour China to Suning Commerce Group, one of the largest private retailers in China. The irony being that Suning is majority-owned by Alibaba. Carrefour China is still part of the same conglomerate, but not in the same strong position had they partnered with HeMa. The price of delay!

Within months after deal closure, the digital transformation of Carrefour began and before the end of 2019 Suning announced five long-term strategies for further expansion in the Chinese market:

1. Digitalizing Carrefour's physical stores
2. Improving existing store formats
3. Expanding to lower-tier cities with Suning's Retail Cloud Franchise Store concept
4. Integration with Suning's convenience store chain
5. Opening new (but smaller) stores in existing markets

In all, a strategic plan that Carrefour themselves could have developed and implemented had they acted faster. It is now beyond doubt that Carrefour was outcompeted. It reacted too slowly, did not innovate fast enough, missed the boat on rapid digitalisation and data driven consumer knowledge, and took too long to make critical decisions.

Carrefour was outfoxed by more nimble local players that many outside China may not even have heard off or at best see as companies not to be taken too seriously. That attitude was already on shaky ground a decade ago, but as many better-known Chinese multinationals now show — notably internet powerhouses Alibaba and Tencent, Telecom 5G leader Huawei, home appliances and consumer electronics maker Haier, and investment firm Fosun — Chinese companies are increasingly very competitive global players that have developed and mastered skills to survive in unstable fast-changing market environments.

Their success and that of many others has not relied on simply copying Western management theory. Throughout the centuries, it has been common in China to absorb theories, trends, and technologies from the rest of the world but then build on them with what they know best: their own history and culture. Today's business success in China — and, as we see it, increasingly outside its borders — is based on a set of management beliefs that are deeply rooted in China's thousands of years of development and the environment in which Chinese entrepreneurs and business leaders matured, as well as in the hyper competitive environment in which they operate.

That, combined with a rapidly digitizing society and its inherent increase in scale, speed, and complexities, means successful Chinese companies now rely on a very different skillset. They have mastered management skills needed in today's increasingly competitive, unstable, and digital business environment: flexibility, adaptability, speed, agility, tenacity, and rate of learning.

A skillset we call DRAGON TACTICS, and which comprises the following five Management beliefs and practices:

1. WOLF CULTURE. HUNGER TEACHES LIFE LESSONS.
— The early generations of business leaders grew up during the volatile and turbulent period of the 1960s and 1970s. In the world in which they lived, individuals constantly had to fend for themselves and their families, were sent off to rural areas, often experiencing severe hardship, and literally elbowing their way forward towards the front of food queues.
— Such life experiences left inevitable marks and fostered a highly competitive and risk-taking, survival-driven mindset that shaped the behaviour of the early-stage entrepreneurs that pioneered China's business culture after it had started opening up to commercialism in 1989.
— Business survival was no different than survival in society. Grab any business opportunity. Use whatever connections you have to get ahead. Get knocked down but stand up and keep going. Anything to make sure to stay in the game and out-compete your nearest rival. How is that different from a wolf in the forest?

2. ADAPT TO CHANGE OR DIE.

— Unlike in Western societies (from the Hebrew to the Greek and the Christians), there is no such notion as transcendent gods, eternal ideas, and the essence of things in China's cultural past.

— Instead, Chinese philosophy is infused with the continuous succession of the four seasons and an expectation of permanent change. Transformation is central to the Chinese way of thinking, traditionally as well as today.

— Adapting to change is therefore at the centre of the Chinese approach to business.

— The turbulent and hyper-competitive environment over the past 30 years has further contributed to the need for Chinese companies to manage flexibly. Operating in a large, diverse, and quickly evolving country, companies must scramble to keep pace with fast growth often followed by abrupt periods of slowdown.

— Beyond these specificities of China itself, digitalization is bringing additional disruption, forcing Chinese entrepreneurs to possess a high degree of nimbleness and an ability to adapt constantly to survive.

3. THE EMPEROR DECIDES. BUT AGILITY RULES.

— Most Chinese private companies have simple, top-down organisational structures, with everyone reporting to the top.

— Chinese entrepreneurs often have as many direct reports as needed. But in an unstable business world, where speed of decision making and improvisation are crucial success factors, entrepreneurial organisations with an absolute boss, tend to spread wide rather than go deep.

— In such flat, yet top-down organisations, each team is given enough authority and ownership of their part of the business, enabling them to move as quickly as required. Clear processes ensure the organisation can stay agile, even with the leader making the main decisions.

— Ecosystems ensure not only agility but enable a higher tolerance for risk at lower levels of investment. Teams are assembled and dismantled as projects require. Internal competition is encouraged and often it is survival of the fittest, as indeed, Chinese private companies let 'horse races' between internal teams decide a way forward.

— In a market that requires flexibility and rapid innovation, does it really matter if you spend twice the resource in the short term if it doubles the chance to win against an external competitor?

— When the future is uncertain and competition is strong, adjusting to fast changing realities and thriving in chaos is often the best way to stay relevant.

4. PEOPLE COME AND GO. THOSE WHO FIT STAY LONGER.

— In a society driven by competition for resources and horse races, a 'job for life' is not a certainty. Nor do many people seek one given their consistent quest to better themselves.

— In founder driven companies, loyalty and a cultural fit are often the most important requirements toward success and career advancement. This thinking has significantly influenced how Human Resources are approached in Chinese companies.

— The most-sought-after employees are entrepreneurial, always prepared to work and drive hard, looking and fighting for opportunities. People are hired to be tested. Horse races among hires are not uncommon.

— Staff turnover is not judged to be a negative. Building a team of likeminded entrepreneurial thinkers capable of moving toward the same goal at high speed is seen as much more critical.

— But for the inner circle and the loyal performers, the incentives can be significant. The emperor will look well after his people. Life changing value creation is within reach for many and make the hardship worth it all.

5. IT ALL STARTS WITH DATA.

— China has the massive advantage of enjoying more data than any other market, due to the size of its population, the relative homogeneity* of its internal market, as well as the pace of its digitization.

— Often not hindered by legacy architecture, Chinese entrepreneurs aggressively invest in building the systems that collect, bring together, and interpret various streams of information.

— Favouring speed and tenacity as well as trying and learning rather than sticking to a long-term plan, good data becomes even more meaningful and effective: each trial is proven right or wrong with data. If wrong, a decision to move on to the next trial can be made even faster.

* In the book we refer a few times to the 'relative homogeneity' of the China internal market and its population. We are keenly aware that China is diverse. China is 'more a continent than a country' and as such has a varied cultural heritage, a variety of languages, and a climate that is different in various parts of the country.

However, we refer to its relative homogeneous nature purely from a business perspective. China's internal market has little restrictions for trade beyond province borders. With Mandarin widely spoken throughout the country, marketing campaigns are relatively easy to roll-out country wide and, while considering regional preferences and tastes and the possible need to tweak products to suit these differences, most firms in most categories will find it relatively easy to roll out similar products nation-wide.

Last but not least, the explosion of online commerce, communication, and social media allows consumers China-wide to share the same experiences and tap into the same product offer, regardless of whether they are in a first-tier city or in a small county town, with further benefits that user data sets are built and analysed with an almost unlimited nationwide scope.

— If right, the power of data enables a level of amplification which one could not reach before.
— Chinese entrepreneurs have always been very close to the market and extremely reactive to consumers, but the wealth of data and the advent of artificial intelligence is now even changing business models and turning consumers into users.

Western management theory can easily deride much of the above as leading to chaos, lacking sufficient business sense or worse, lacking a 'business case', and proclaim that will never work.
But yet, as the Carrefour example dramatically proves, much of it does....
In the next section of this book, we detail what makes modern Chinese companies and leaders successful, which of such management beliefs and techniques work and why, and how some of them can be applied in a more Western focused business arena.

PART 2

MASTERING DRAGON TACTICS

狼性文化

3

**WOLF CULTURE.
HUNGER TEACHES
LIFE LESSONS.**

3. WOLF CULTURE.
HUNGER TEACHES LIFE LESSONS.

'In the battle with lions, wolves have terrifying abilities.
With a strong desire to win and no fear of losing, they stick to the goal firmly,
exhausting the lions in every possible way.'

Ren Zhengfei

Founder, Huawei Technologies

3.1 DEVELOPING SURVIVAL SKILLS

Huawei's founder Ren Zhengfei is recognized as the main protagonist of 'Wolf Culture', or as he phrased it once himself:[1]

If Huawei stops its rapid growth one day, it will face death. As long as the main business is still full of vitality, our team will have strong cohesion, and employees will work hard and enjoy it.

Huawei needs to rely on a spirit to unite the team and make the company full of vigour. The factor that Huawei found is the team spirit of wolf nature.

To be a business is to develop a group of wolves. Because wolves have three major characteristics that keep themselves alive: one is a keen sense of smell; the other is an indomitable and relentless offensive spirit; and the third is group struggle. *It is this fierce corporate culture that makes Huawei a 'Wolf' and ensures that even multinational giants can't sleep well.*

Since Huawei Technologies, a global provider of communications equipment, was founded in 1987, the company's performance has been impressive. After just over 30 years, the company achieved 137 bn USD turnover in 2020, representing a more than fivefold increase in the last 10 years alone. With 35% of sales coming from outside China, the company now does business in over 170 countries.[2]

Its ascent stands out even among the rapid development of other highly successful Chinese companies. Although the company has faced international scrutiny for issues surrounding cyber security and alleged close ties to the

Chinese government and has in the past been accused of unfair competitive practices, before the company ventured abroad, it had already achieved an incredible journey of success inside China. A success rooted in a clear vision and a remarkable corporate culture, both driven from the top by Ren Zhengfei.

Huawei's founder was born in 1944 in Zhenning county in Guizhou, which even today is still one of the poorer areas of China.

Ren Zhengfei grew up as the eldest son in a family of seven children. Although his parents were schoolteachers, they struggled financially to support the lives of nine people. After completing secondary school, Ren attended the Chongqing Institute of Civil Engineering and Architecture (now Chongqing University). Majoring in heating, gas supply, and ventilation engineering, he graduated in 1968. As was common practice at that time in the centrally managed country, once he completed his degree, he was assigned his first job.

This was during China's Cultural Revolution, and university graduates were sent for re-education in working-class values. With the military controlling and managing a significant part of business activities in the PRC, Ren was assigned to the Second Company of the State Construction Commission, where he worked as a cook for two years and a plumber for several years before moving to their technology division. While working for this unit, Ren was actually not a soldier.

In 1974, he joined the army Engineering Corps and was assigned to work on the development of the Liao Yang Chemical Fibre Factory in the far north-east of China, a key national construction project which involved advanced technology for processing crude oil and derived chemicals from France. With engineering capabilities within the military not well developed, Ren was selected given his background and experience in technology and construction.

With the Cultural Revolution still ongoing, life was chaotic in China. Food and resources were scarce, and Ren Zhengfei and his comrades lived in tough conditions, in poor quality housing, and with insufficient nutrition.

Meanwhile employed as the deputy director of a construction research institute, Ren retired from the military in 1982, when the PLA was significantly downsized.

Hardship creates a hard driving mentality and a need for survival.
Raised with such family background and having spent over 14 years in a military environment, often in challenging circumstances, Ren Zhengfei has cultivated the spirit of hard work, diligence, and thrift, and has a strong sense of mission and self-discipline. A down to earth, direct but hard-driving personality.

It instilled in him also a strong belief in the collective and personal humility. In the early days of Huawei, he would wear the same dishevelled clothes as his subordinates, looking not dissimilar to all other workers on the production line. Even when Huawei was on the rise, he remained simple and unpretentious, and still often looked like a simple old farmer.

Even now as a billionaire and the Chairman of a Fortune 500 company, he has not changed much. He still dresses simply, often travels in economy class, takes taxis, and still occasionally spends time at the production line. By now in his 70s, he is still working hard and gives his subordinates no reason not to fight.

As is often the case for entrepreneurs with a military background, their management style is equipped with a strong military flavour and Ren Zhengfei is no exception. He always maintained the forceful style of an army cadre. Straight, tough, and unrelenting. Focused on Huawei's efficient execution but singing military songs while doing so.

When founding Huawei at age 44, with most of his experience derived from his time in the army, he looked at the market he was going to conquer through the lenses of a military man.

China had just started its policy of reform and opening up. With no existing market structures, poor planning, and lots of opportunism, resources were limited, while cutthroat competition was enormous.

In Ren Zhengfei's mind, in such a red-hot market, you must create your own chance of survival at the cost of 'eliminating' your opponents. For Ren Zhengfei, the market was a battlefield. Survival of the fittest.

The telecommunication equipment market space at that time in China was very limited with only a few thousand plus county-level post and telecommunication bureaus as possible customers, all using imported equipment.

To enhance the survival awareness and survivability of the company and its employees, Huawei instilled various management concepts and slogans[3]: 'To survive is the last word', 'Everything we do for market sales growth is not shameful', and what is now the most famous: 'The company is to develop a group of wolves'.

> Wolves have three main characteristics: one is a keen sense of smell, the other is an indomitable and relentless offensive spirit, and the third is a sense of group struggle.

Ren Zhengfei believes that ultimately all resources can be exhausted, and only culture can survive. Huawei therefore needs to rely on a spirit to unite the team and vitalize the company. The factor that Huawei found is the team spirit of Wolf Culture. Wolves became the role model for the enterprise to learn from because wolves are the ultimate survivors.

Huawei's Ren Zhengfei is not the only Wolf with survival skills.

Throughout its history, but especially so between the early stages of the The Great Leap Forward (late 1950s), throughout The Cultural Revolution, and even beyond the death of Mao Zedong in 1976, China experienced very turbulent times in which famine raged the country and social instability was high resulting from factional infighting and class struggles.

Just like Ren Zhengfei, the entire early generation of business leaders grew up during this volatile period in the 1960s and 1970s and endured similar hardships. Also, in their world, individuals constantly had to fend for themselves and their families, were sent off to rural areas, often experiencing harsh conditions, and literally having to elbow their way forward toward the front of food queues.

Such life experiences left inevitable marks and fostered a highly competitive and risk-taking, survival-driven mindset that shaped the behaviour of the early-stage entrepreneurs who pioneered China's business culture after the country had started opening up to commercialism following the 13th National Congress in 1987.

Business survival was no different than survival in society. Use whatever connections you have to get ahead, cutting corners where you can. Get knocked down but stand up and proceed. Grab any opportunity to make money, however little it is. Anything to make sure to stay in the game and outcompete your nearest rival. How is that different from a wolf in the forest?

Not all leaders defined the survival mantra as sharp as Ren Zhengfei at Huawei, but even without expressing it so clearly as a Wolf Culture, the majority of successful Chinese companies developed corporate cultures rooted in survival. That is what they knew.

3.2 UNDERSTANDING WOLF CHARACTERISTICS

Having worked for and with a variety of global firms, we both experienced many occasions where global company leaders were unwilling or unable to compromise global systems or processes to reach success in China.

We have never understood such reluctance given the 'size of the prize' and especially as we have barely seen such behaviour on the other side. The will of Chinese companies and entrepreneurs to survive and succeed, even against severe adversity is always larger than the short-term inconvenience or inefficiencies it may create.

Businesspeople in the West often are less opportunistic. They are less willing to take risks or will judge them differently compared to their counterparts in China. Assumptions about what is right or wrong may also differ. For us this is all at the heart of Wolf Culture. The belief you can win against all odds. The belief that your rules can differ from the rules others may follow.

From our research and discussions with leading entrepreneurs[*], we have determined the essence of Wolf Culture and how this approach has driven the success of many Chinese Enterprises.

Adding one additional element to Ren Zhengfei's original Wolf characteristics, we define a Wolf having the following qualities:

1. A keen sense of smell to sniff out opportunities;
2. An indomitable, relentless offensive spirit;
3. A devotion to the collective;
4. An absolute loyalty to the leader of the pack.

3.2.1 The Wolf has a keen sense of smell

The Wolf is always on the lookout for opportunities as he is expected to deliver ideas, deals, or other opportunities. Consistently. Like for wolves in the wild, focus is the key. A wolf does not wander aimlessly in all directions but knows exactly where the low hanging fruit is to be found. Where the weak spots are. And so often the sheep are not aware the wolf is watching.

We have often observed, that when a Chinese businessman or woman looks at the same situation that may come across a businessperson from outside China, the chance is high that two different outcomes are the result. The long list of failed joint-ventures is the best proof of this reality. But it also shows how opportunities are being captured.

A nose for opportunities.
A clear example of sniffing out possibilities is the strategy Huawei used to become a global player to be reckoned with. It's a strategy also followed by many other Chinese companies venturing abroad. A strategy that is firmly rooted in how Mao Zedong first conquered China with his communist army, which in turn was inspired by ancient military thinking: Conquer the countryside to conquer the cities.

[*] In the book we refer a lot to the entrepreneurs, the founders of the companies, but it needs to be understood that in many companies, especially the ones that were founded in the early days, the leadership is broader than the founder alone, or the founder has handed over the reins (e.g., Daniel Zhang who took over the helm from founder Jack Ma at Alibaba). In our view this has however not altered the approach. Even a younger generation still employs Dragon Tactics and Wolf Culture remains part of these companies.

To attack international markets, Huawei applied the same encirclement strategy they had applied to first conquer the Chinese marketplace. From the end of the 1990s, rather than launching in the most popular markets, notably the US and Europe with their high cost of entry, the firm deployed in the most isolated areas of the world. Markets with a hostile environment, difficult conditions, and great political instability — in short, areas neglected by the major international equipment manufacturers.

Huawei executives were strongly encouraged to relocate, not only engineers, but also salespeople and marketing experts. It was even the key to advancing quickly in their careers. This is how the company landed in 1999 in Central and Southeast Asia, then in Africa, Latin America, Russia, and Eastern Europe. The brand was unknown but had the products that made the difference: equipment at unbeatable prices. Complemented with a customer service ready to meet any request, even the most complex and ambitious ones.

When not all notice the same scent.
Sniffing out opportunities or understanding a situation better or from a different angle, can sometimes also create massive misunderstanding or even large disputes as is shown in various major JV failures. Although it happened already some time ago, the Danone / Wahaha breakup remains a good example.

In 2009, Groupe Danone of France resolved a long-running dispute with its Chinese joint venture partner, agreeing to exit the venture by selling its 51 percent stake in the Wahaha Group, one of China's largest beverage companies.

The dispute erupted in 2007, when Danone accused Wahaha of secretly operating a set of parallel companies that mirrored the joint venture's operations with virtually identical products and siphoned off as much as $100 million from the partnership.

On the other hand, Zong Qinghou, chairman of the Group and chairman of all Danone-Wahaha JVs argued that the 'Wahaha' trademark was never officially transferred to the JVs and complained of Danone's lack of efforts throughout the existence of the JV yet reaping significant profits. While admitting clauses in the JV agreement related to non-compete arrangements, Wahaha argued Danone had invested in Chinese competitors, in violation of the same joint venture agreements.

The tensions grew so serious that in late 2007, President Nicholas Sarkozy of France brought the matter up in a meeting with his Chinese counterpart, Hu Jintao in an attempt to resolve the dispute.

As in many other failed joint-ventures, the Danone and Wahaha sides of the story were rather different. This particular case demonstrates an overreliance on the rule of law combined with an underestimation on how a Wolf seeks out opportunities or considers loyalty.

Danone may have assumed Wahaha understood the implications of their JV arrangement that relied on purely technical legal rules, especially on how Danone gained a majority share, but Wahaha felt it had been tricked signing away its rights and took action to correct the situation.

What also played an important role in the fall-out, while perhaps legally correct but a key element in the breakdown of the JV, was that Danone felt it within its rights to start other joint ventures outside the Wahaha partnership. Wahaha had agreed to a non-compete, but it lost faith in Danone as a real partner interested in building a business together when Danone started creating businesses with others and seemingly did not believe a non-compete and partner loyalty was applicable to them.

Wahaha felt betrayed and the emotional relationship was lost. The JV then faced the irreducible difference between the legal and contractual vision of the Westerners and the pack bond vision of the Chinese.

We believe that many of the other failed joint ventures have also fallen victim to a lack of awareness, or at least an underestimation of Wolf Culture. In Section 1.2 we described key reasons frequently quoted for failed foreign business endeavours in China and noted that misaligned objectives for entering a business partnership was repeatedly such a cause.

When evaluating many of the cases, there are often references to contract breach, either side not sticking to what was agreed. Either party accusing the other side of cheating.

While we are certain there are some cases that can be reduced down to pure fraud, we believe that for the large majority of the JV failures, or other deals that have gone wrong, it would be too simple to blame them on a breakdown of the legal framework alone. There is more at play here and both sides have both laid the foundations for the problems they encountered.

Are you smelling the same reality as the Wolf?

Many of the aforementioned business relationship failures resulted from a misjudgement. A discrepancy of terminology. A different interpretation of the same reality. The Chinese have a great idiom for this: 同床异梦 (pinyin, tóngchuángyìmèng), meaning: to sleep in the same bed with different dreams. We believe many problems could have been avoided. If only the dreams would have been the same.

When two parties enter an agreement and it fails, is that a failure of the agreement itself, or was there below the surface never an agreement to begin with? What if an agreement was entered by two parties that did not share a common goal? Who is to blame for that? The person not providing all the information, or the party failing to do the right research, ask the right questions and to understand the situation thoroughly?

And what if the divide is caused by a different cultural interpretation? Which culture is the correct one in that case? Which set of values can be used to judge the failure?

For example, a Wolf will not see pursuing competitive ventures outside of a JV as cheating. Especially when such a new reality was not well covered in the agreement to begin with. If a contract does not specifically stipulate that the Wolf cannot start a separate factory across the street with technology shared as part of a JV agreement, nobody is being deceived when it does happen.

The Chinese JV partner will simply argue that they didn't want to lose a business opportunity and that if they hadn't grabbed it, it would have been lost to another Chinese competitor. The joint venture contract wasn't appropriate for the actual situation, so they just acted according to what they thought was common sense.

Meanwhile, the foreign JV partner will consider the Chinese to be dishonest or to exceed defined boundaries by doing business besides the JV.

So, what we face here is a different interpretation of one possible problem: various conceivable versions based on different value sets. In our view it is too simplistic to merely assume our cultural environment is automatically the one to measure things by. The Wolf would just shrug that off and pounce.

A better strategy is thus needed to fend off a Wolf or better still find a way to get along just fine together, a way that works for both sides. Understand how the Wolf operates. Don't be a sheep but join the pack, on your terms.

Sniffing out the Wolf.

So, what to do when you are confronted by a wolf?

To begin with you will need to understand there is a wolf at your door. And that starts with awareness. Assume nothing. How many of the business leaders that entered those failed relationships really did their due diligence? And we mean, beyond the financials!

To compete or do business in an environment where the person on the other side of the table has a different set of beliefs requires a significant scaled up ability to better understand the framework in which the other operates.

A superior sense of smell takes years to develop, especially when dealing in a culturally different situation. When one studies what happened in fatal joint venture cases where dishonesty was a main cause of failure, it often appears there were alarm bells and signs that were ignored or not picked-up. Or at least, there was critical information that could have been obtained and understood up-front, by conducting better due diligence.

It is also important to recognize that one's cultural frame may not automatically be the superior value set. In our discussions with other business leaders this is always a touchy point to discuss, but can we really expect that when we plan to do business in another territory, our own rules and regulations can automatically take centre-stage?

The Wolf will push the envelope and see how far he can get. This is second nature to the Wolf. Only by developing your own superior sense of smell will you be able to outsmart the Wolf.

Smell the consumer.
The Wolf's sense of smell contributes to one more critical competitive dimension, which in our belief is one of the most fundamental elements of being a Wolf: understanding consumers and their needs and by doing so becoming truly consumer centric. A great example of this is how WeChat Pay became, almost overnight, the standard for mobile payments in China.

They faced a classic chicken-egg problem: how do you get vendors to accept a mobile payment service when there are no users? And how do you get users when there are no vendors? The WeChat team came up with a brilliant solution firmly rooted in observed consumer behaviour:

As part of Chinese Lunar New Year celebrations, an ancient custom is to hand out red envelopes (in Chinese 红包, pinyin: hóngbāo) filled with money, large or small amounts. Launching WeChat Pay in early 2014, Tencent significantly boosted traffic on WeChat's mobile payments platform by creating digital Hongbao. With a click on a red envelope icon, gifts of money could be sent to friends and family. The idea was a watershed moment for China's mobile market, bringing more than eight million users to Tencent's WeChat Payment platform in the first eight days after the Chinese New Year.[4]

In the next chapter, Adapt to Change or Die, we will go much more in depth on how Chinese businesses have built competitive advantages through a laser sharp consumer focus that would not be possible without a real dedication to and ongoing understanding of what the market needs and how to take advantage of it.

3.2.2 The Wolf has an indomitable, relentless offensive spirit
Wolves need to attack but cannot afford to fail. They watch their target while waiting for the best opportunity to strike. And once they do, they pound fast

and don't let go. This tenacious drive is exactly what is needed for a successful business or career.

In his book, 'A Success Called Huawei'[5], Vincent Ducrey describes the bitter battle Huawei had with Cisco over entering the US market. The case is a good example of the unwavering determination of Huawei and of its Wolf Culture in action:

> At the start of 2003, Huawei saw its long-term efforts to expand overseas bearing fruit — notably in Europe, Russia, Africa, and the Middle East. Even though he was still a long way from competing among the world's top three telecoms as he had always aspired to, Ren Zhengfei was seeing his brand gradually take hold and gain recognition outside of China. A year earlier, Huawei reached a new milestone and had entered the United States to explore this huge market where its main competitors originated, and which was critical to become a leading world player. Failure was not an option! It was time to get serious.

> Cisco, the undisputed leader in corporate networks, was the company to beat. Huawei attacked head on with an advertising campaign showing a Chinese branded router and the statement: 'The only difference is the price!', stressing that its products cost twice less than those of Cisco.

> Cisco retaliated and fought back in the legal arena, claiming IP infringements. After several warnings, the American company filed a complaint in January 2003. The indictment included breach of intellectual property relating to software and user manuals for its routers.

> Ren Zhengfei fought back. First by forming a strong team of collaborators, chosen from among the best, in legal, R&D, and marketing, and by turning to the best intellectual property lawyers in the United States. For Huawei, steeped in Wolf Culture as it was, it was clear: Cisco wanted to keep its monopoly at all costs and was trying to eliminate its competitor.

> When initial legal action did not yield the required result, in March of the same year, Huawei announced an alliance with 3Com, Cisco's historical competitor in the United States.

> This move helped reverse the trend in favour of the Chinese firm. Especially when the head of 3Com testified at the trial: 'We spent eight

months authenticating Huawei technologies. They work with talented engineers on ultra-sophisticated software and technology. We would never have taken the huge risk of allying with Huawei if we weren't sure they weren't infringing on intellectual property.

As the facts came out, Cisco softened its tone. In July that year, to move things forward, Huawei agreed to an independent review and ended up making minor changes to its router and switch products. As a result, Cisco suspended legal action. Ultimately, a settlement was reached in 2004. Despite the cost and the reputational impact, Ren Zhengfei kept pushing ahead. Because, in the end, despite the challenges, he had now officially entered the US market and had shown the competition they could match their largest competitor.

This case is a good demonstration of the never give up mentality that we see amongst many Chinese business leaders. A drive to succeed against many odds that expresses itself also in three more quite distinctive 'indominable Wolf' behaviours:

Relentlessly seeking opportunities over efficiencies.
In Western companies 'creating efficiencies' is an ongoing mantra, almost a holy grail and a goal that drives management behaviour, strategic plans, and even the rationale for mergers.

We don't hear much about efficiencies in Chinese firms. In fact, the opposite is often true. For an indominable Wolf the end goal is much more important than how to get there. That does not mean they are unnecessary wasteful, as most Chinese companies are not only notoriously strapped for working capital but also very cost conscious. It does mean however that they are much more willing to put limited resources towards achieving an objective deemed important, at all costs.

An interesting example to illustrate this is how Anta Sports, meanwhile the world's third-largest sportswear company, from Jinjiang, in Fujian province, turned around the fortunes of the Italian brand Fila (for which Anta holds the distribution rights for China), and while doing so, laid the foundation for more group success to come.

Anta acquired the rights to the Fila brand for the Chinese market in 2009. The license was previously held by Belle International, China's largest vertically integrated footwear retailer, which had struggled to make the Italian sportswear brand relevant in China.

Under Anta management, Fila has experienced a dramatic revival of its fortunes, particularly in China, where it now has over 2,000 points of sales and generates a larger share of revenue than the Anta brand itself. Riding the sports inspired streetwear trend, Fila connects seamlessly with the Gen-Z and Millennial generations.

But to get there, Fila had to overcome a lot of challenges that for many other companies would have been a reason to cease operations. Struggling to find a product direction that was accepted by the market, the brand lost money for several years. Not only was the entire management team replaced several times, but the company also tried various product directions.

Where in multinational companies apparel SKU efficiency is often a hotly debated topic, Fila did the opposite, creating a constant flurry of new products, testing the market, learning from its failures until it struck a connection with a younger more fashionable audience. Even while losing money, finding product efficiencies were never part of the discussion. Making Fila successful served a much larger purpose. The future of the Anta Group itself.

Realizing that the Anta brand could face growth limitations within China, Anta knew they had to pursue a multi-brand strategy. Finding market success and a suitable business model for Fila could serve as the example for future brand cultivation. Success could only be achieved with a whatever it takes mindset. A strategy the company has meanwhile copied with the successful development of brands such as Descente, Kolon, and Arc'teryx.

In the next chapter, Adapt to Change or Die, we will home in more deeply on the willingness of Chinese business leaders to remain flexible and change direction until something works that goes far beyond creating an abundance of products. But what certainly also contributes to relentlessly finding success, is how a Wolf perceives and deals with risk.

Relentlessly seeking reward over risk.
The relentless drive to succeed also breeds a culture of taking risks. However, given the speed of change in the China market, a Wolf's observation of a risk is often surprisingly different from what we would envision.

In an environment where expectations of success are high and competition is fierce, the cost of failure is at a premium. Therefore, for a Wolf, a risk is often less about risk but much more about the need to keep up with change, to not fall behind. Doing nothing or shying away from the risk could have a much more severe impact. Risk taking as a result of risk avoidance.

A Wolf's different perception of risk is often also driven by a strong belief in the future. With three decades of economic expansion and its resulting improvement of living standards, personal wealth and even China's place in various global rankings, the Wolf is often a very optimistic creature. Previous hardship has repeatedly paid off. Risks have repeatedly been rewarded. What for an outsider or an opponent therefore may be perceived as too difficult or too perilous, is for the Wolf often still worth fighting for!

An extreme example that illustrates seeking rewards where others see risk is Luckin coffee, a very ambitious barista chain start-up. In fact, the amount of risk taking has sadly led to the company being accused of fraud by overstating up to $300m in turnover in 2019.

However, before the fraud happened, the company achieved a remarkable growth trajectory based on a strategy that perfectly demonstrates a willingness to take outsized risks to beat out competition and to achieve growth at all costs.

Let's open 3000 coffee shops in two years.
Founded only in 2017, Luckin had opened near 3000 locations by the time of its IPO in 2019. Most of its locations are more like kiosks, with little or no seating, as Luckin combines online and offline in a new innovative way. Relying on its mobile app, Luckin uses online customer acquisition to boost offline sales.

Orders have to be placed and paid for with Luckin's app. A strategy optimized to keep costs down and to give Luckin its main advantage: affordability. Its app constantly pushes freebies and discounts to customers, making it difficult to know exactly what it charges, but it's definitely far cheaper than Starbucks.

The company pursued a landgrab growth strategy akin to the early dot-com days: cash over profit. Expansion first, profit later — a mantra common to Chinese firms where customer acquisition is prioritized above all other business fundamentals. As Luckin's Chief Marketing Offer, Yang Fei, noted during the early days of breakneck growth, 'there's no point talking about profit,' because the focus was scale and speed.[6]

The strategy was a wakeup call for market leader Starbucks, which in response strengthened its ties to Alibaba to re-energize growth through a wide-ranging partnership covering takeout via its Ele.me delivery platform, a virtual store, and an app in Alibaba's various e-commerce sites. It also accelerated their rollout of Starbucks Now, a kiosk style store format optimized for online order collection.

Multi-billion-dollar brawl for dominance.
Another interesting example which demonstrates that risk is valued differently can be found in the fight for ride-hailing dominance in China.

Didi Chuxing is China's leading ride-sharing service and was formed after two former fierce rivals, Kuadi Dache and Didi Dache, merged in 2015.

Two years earlier, in 2013, its global rival Uber had entered China. In an attempt to rapidly gain market share, the American challenger took a leaf out of the China playbook and poured enormous amounts into subsidizing fares and driver salaries.

As soon as they had become a united company, Didi fought back, slashing prices in response. The battle heated up quickly. Both companies burned through cash — Uber lost $2bn; Didi likely even more — and raised billions to replace it. As the war intensified, Didi Chuxing struck deals, winning funds from Alibaba and Tencent, China's two biggest tech companies (Alibaba had previously invested in Kuaidi Dache, and Tencent in Didi Dache, before the rivals merged). In May 2016, Didi even unveiled a $1bn deal with Apple.[7]

Not long afterwards, under pressure from its investors to stem losses, Uber threw in the towel. Needing an exit strategy, they agreed to a takeover by Didi of their China operations in exchange for an 18 percent stake in Didi. The deal cleared the road for Didi to become China's leading app-based transportation service company, claiming 80 percent market share in China and more than 550 million users.

A Silicon Valley Wolf was out-Wolfed in China as Didi never took their eye of the final reward and the company and its backers knew they could not afford to lose.

> *'I never expected Uber to win', said Yanbo Wang, a Chinese academic who studies tech start-ups. 'For Uber, burning through $2bn in China was a huge amount. But for Didi, and for TenCent and Alibaba, spending $2bn to win at home? It was nothing.'* [8]

Relentlessly seeking a better future through education and hard work.
In all those years interviewing Chinese staff for all sorts of functions, without fail a question would be asked about what learning opportunities the company would offer. If the organisation would not provide comprehensive training, the firm would not pass the criteria the candidate had in mind.

This respect for learning is intrinsic to Chinese culture and can also be seen in the results of Chinese students around the world. It also shows in the very large number of entrepreneurs in China that — while driving their companies forward — still have managed to find time to achieve MBAs.

There is an inherit need to get ahead, to move up the ladder. Not just a consistent drive to learn but a constant search for opportunities to gain the upper hand. Instilled through many years of hardship and a society that is geared towards survival of the fittest combined with a personal as well as societal expectation of constantly doing better.

Sacrificing oneself for a better future has become the norm. Driven by their strong desire to improve their social status, many Chinese entrepreneurs or people in the workforce, are willing to give up their personal lives for the sake of a better, wealthier future. Long working hours have become a way of life for the many that inherently accept that working through the night regularly to accomplish a common goal is part of their responsibility.

This phenomenon even has a name. It is called '996', a reference to working from 9:00AM to 9:00PM, 6 days a week and it is a common practice in many companies in China. One of the key proponents of 996 is Jack Ma, the founder of the Alibaba Group. Being arguably the most admired businessperson in China, he personifies that a hard charging mentality pays off and as such he has tremendous influence on the work ethic of many.

In Section 1.1. Failure to adapt, the basis for failure, we described the downfall of Amazon and quoted an ex-employee who expressed his frustrations about the tech giant's inability to achieve changes and improvements fast. He observed, somewhat jealously, that the opposite was true for local 996 competitors, where company culture would have ensured instant implementation. 'In those 996 companies', he said, 'as soon as the boss requests a new feature, the staff burns the midnight oil until it's launched.'

The indomitable Wolf Spirit breeds a consistent entrepreneurial drive that ensures ongoing competitive advantages. From the management to all team members a high sense of agility for market development and customer needs is maintained that ensures a rapid response at all costs.

3.2.3 The Wolf has a devotion to the collective

'The tiger is still afraid of a wolf' is a well-known saying, as wolves seldom appear alone and hunt in packs. In an increasingly competitive business world, the power of teamwork and the cooperative is highly valued. Individualism does not exist in Wolf Culture.

Rather surprisingly, in a society that puts the collective over the individual, cohesive teamwork has not always been the norm. Nor does it always yield the required results as can be seen in sports and music where often individuals excel, yet teams or orchestras underperform in relation to such individual success.

In an interesting study,[9] Teamwork in Chinese Organisations: A New Concept and Framework, the author Ying Liu makes a remarkable opening statement:

There is a Chinese saying: 'One Chinese person is as strong as a dragon, while a group of Chinese people is as weak as insects.' This saying suggests that teamwork has always been a big problem for the Chinese.

On one hand, Chinese people would sacrifice their own interests for their teams due to the influence of collectivism and maintaining harmony.

On the other hand, other Chinese cultural values, such as guanxi (a kind of special exchange relationship) among team members, make teamwork very complicated. Maintaining hierarchy and keeping harmony can be important to team cohesion, but it can also get in the way of efficiently achieving team goals.

In another publication,[10] Teamwork in China: Where Reality Challenges Theory and Practice, its authors make a similar point:

The rigid social hierarchy emphasized by Confucian principles could prevent fully autonomous and flexible teamwork; the very elements of Chinese culture that create and sustain group attachment and group conformity also maintain top-down control, which contravenes the principles and practice of true teamwork.

Traditional Chinese cultural characteristics such as filial piety, paternalism and hierarchy and strong pressures for conformity, maintenance of face, and social control have certainly driven group behaviour, but not necessarily true teamwork. All the more so in an environment where factionalization of the workforce, mistrust of co-workers and personalized favouritism was often the norm.

But, for early business leaders competing in white-hot and at times chaotic markets, it was clear from the beginning that only strong team cohesion and cooperation would help them become and stay competitive. Some of this thinking was also inspired by Western management theory that valued and promoted teamwork.

If teamwork does not come naturally, how do Wolf companies ensure that people work together, jointly solve problems, and deliver solutions?

They do so with a clear focus on the collective and with a reward system that remunerates the pack, and by driving a culture that requires a high degree of unity and cooperation, with teams expected to act with the 'intensity of a wolf pack' that some have described as 'hyper-intense teamwork' or giving a team 'combat capability'.

Teamwork with Chinese characteristics.

And so, within Wolf Culture a strong focus on teamwork became the norm. However, it has to be noted, teamwork the Chinese way: more the output of a collective than teamwork in the Western sense. More like a clan, with the cohesion of a pack. Later in the book, we will see the same characteristics at play in the creation of ecosystems.

Chinese companies often refer to themselves as an army of ants; a group of people working towards a common goal with shared means, under a central direction; a military team working towards one objective, with a strong emotional bond built around the pack leader, as can be found back in Huawei's corporate culture:[11]

> *Share happiness and sorrow. Share prosperity and disgrace. Unity, cooperation, and collective struggle are the soul of Huawei's corporate culture. Success is the result of collective efforts. Failure is the responsibility of the collective. We do not attribute achievements to individuals, nor do we regard failures as personal responsibilities; we are all the same. Except for differences in tasks, Huawei people are equal in work and life.*

A lofty goal perhaps but keep in mind the military thinking that lays at the foundation of Huawei's corporate culture, and it gets easier to put it in context.

Teamwork that suppresses the individual but amplifies individual talent.

In general, Chinese society greatly values harmony and tradition and tends to frown upon overtly aggressive, self-promotional, and excess individualism and that attitude found its way seamlessly into Wolf Culture through a strong focus on group thinking.

An interesting dynamic that almost automatically limits individualism within a Chinese group, is the role of competition among individuals within such a team context.

Whereas cooperation and competition within groups are viewed as opposite to each other in Western thinking, in the more harmonious Chinese society the two concepts are more likely to be perceived as coexisting, concluded a team of researchers from the University of Washington and Peking University.[12]

The benefits of competition within a group are perceived differently also. The study concluded that the more collectively minded Chinese scored significantly higher on vertical individualism, a drive wanting to be better than others; but significantly lower on horizontal individualism, an orientation to maximize personal interest, when compared to individuals abroad.

Diametrically opposite to findings among Western individuals, in China, competition within the group indicated cooperation and no competition within the group indicated team non-cooperation. This means that trying to do better than other people in the group is not seen as a negative as long as that does not come at the expense of the group. Competition between individuals makes the entire group stronger.

Real competition therefore is more likely to happen not within but between groups or teams. How entrepreneurs turn that insight into their advantage, we will describe in later chapters.

So, while pure individualism is not acceptable, it does not mean however that in Wolf Culture individual talent and achievement do not matter. The opposite is true: individual creativity is encouraged and companies give individuals plenty of room to maximize their talents. The norm here being to respect individuality but strive and celebrate collectively — the individual in support of the collective.

It also does not mean there is no individualistic behaviour at all. There is, but given the top-down culture in Chinese organisations [see Chapter 5 The Emperor Decides. But Agility Rules], that is mostly at the top of enterprises. Lower down, collectivity rules. The army of ants fights without too many individualistic antics.

Teamwork through clear and continuous boundaries for the pack.
When teams don't work together naturally but still need to deliver collectively, it becomes imperative to have a KPI driven approach or a process of managing collaboration and ensuring that individuals are constantly in line with overall goals and direction to optimize team output.

This ensures that everyone understands their responsibility to the collective, and that they stay connected to oftentimes fast-changing realities and priorities [see next chapter Adapt to Change or Die, for more on fast-changing realities].

Whereas in Western companies the trend is to move away from annual performance reviews, such evaluations are a critical part of Chinese management systems and are taken further than the yearly process of setting objectives and a subsequent performance review.

Not only is great emphasis placed on communication, so all company staffers understand their work within the larger picture of shared group goals, but clear procedures are also in place to ensure everyone knows, understands, and delivers towards these goals.

When Aldo first joined the Fosun Group, one of China's largest non-state-owned conglomerates, he was very impressed by how the system worked. Although the exact process differs from company to company, the overall approach has many similarities and tends to have a clearly defined and focused methodology that relies on three core elements. For example, within Fosun the process was as follows:

PHASE 1 – RIGOROUS TARGET AND WORK PLAN DEFINITION

At least twice a year, strategic alignment sessions are held with a wide span of (senior) leadership in attendance in which a very ambitious strategic direction is newly set, updated or finetuned. In the next chapter, Adapt to Change or Die, we will describe the role of a vision and the use of strategy within Chinese firms. But here we want to note already that such an aforementioned high-level strategic direction is exactly that: high level.

These lofty company goals and objectives are then boiled down to clear and actionable personal objectives for each individual within the company on an almost ongoing basis. They are set, reviewed and updated each quarter and turned into quarterly work plans and priorities. It is expected that such plans are created in full consultation with superiors to ensure they reflect the high ambitions as well as the latest directional developments, since priorities can change rapidly inside Chinese organisations.

PHASE 2 – COLLECTIVE STRUGGLE

Daily, weekly, monthly, and quarterly reports and corresponding periodic assessments ensure a continuous delivery toward the goals and the growth of the business. It also creates a sense of urgency and aims to create eagerness toward periodic achievement evaluation among employees.

Such a rigorous performance management establishes a mechanism of self-motivation, self-management, and self-discipline. Through the continuous setting of goals, coaching, evaluation, and feedback between managers and employees, performance and capabilities are improved, and results achieved.

Understanding collective struggle is not complete without noting the strong reliance on joint solution development. Chinese companies rely heavily on brainstorm sessions. These often happen daily and are aimed to swiftly solve problems when they arise. It is worth noting that these brainstorms are quite different from Western companies where brainstorming is mostly used at the onset of a plan, to release creativity rather than to resolve (daily) issues. Also, from personal experience, such sessions offered great room to freely express ideas and opinions, without hindrance of seniority levels, and were always very solution focused.

The assessment process is also comprehensive and systematic: quarterly reviews and an annual overall assessment of work attitude, work quality, and work goal completion are adopted and follow standardized procedures and evaluation criteria.

As is common in other parts of Chinese society, these evaluations have a strong focus on self-evaluation and self-criticism aimed at each individual employee to push themselves continuously, to look for ways to improve, do things differently or better and keep people honest about how they contribute to the team goals.

Teamwork through rewarding success and achievement.
Benefit management and the distribution of staff perks, wages, and bonuses does not seem to have as many common threads among firms as their methodologies to align the entire company behind a clear direction and goals. Best practice seems to have less similarities. Yet, in true Wolf Culture companies, remuneration systems ensure that a significant share of the pie is distributed.

In Chapter 6 People Come and Go. Those Who Fit Stay Longer, we will dive much deeper in remuneration systems and provide examples of how they benefit and impact people throughout the organisation. Chinese entrepreneurs are expected to look after their people, and many take that role very seriously. Making and keeping staff happy in China goes often far beyond financial incentive schemes such as year-end bonuses or share options.

But one thing is clear: a wolf pack can only be kept happy with lots of meat. Money and incentives which can be truly life altering, in Wolf Culture companies it is very rewarding to deliver, especially for the highest contributing employees. Connecting long-term economic value creation to those who support creating it, is a win-win model that therefore many Chinese entrepreneurs have embraced.

3.2.4 The Wolf has an absolute loyalty that is more important than ability
Strict organizational discipline and team spirit keeps a wolf pack strong, but their survival depends on their loyalty to the leader and the group. Once the head of the wolf pack is determined, all members will be loyal until death.

Ren Zhengfei originally highlighted three characteristics of a Wolf: a **keen sense of smell**, an **indomitable, relentless offensive spirit**, and a **devotion to the collective**. However, there is one more critical quality to being a true Wolf: *an absolute loyalty to the leader of the pack*.

Loyalty to the cause is the prerequisite for gaining the trust of leaders and colleagues. The development and growth of many Chinese enterprises is maintained by the fidelity of its employees. In fact, such loyalty and its implications are so pronounced, that in the chapter, People Come and Go. Those Who Fit Stay Longer, we will explore the role of loyalty within Chinese companies in more depth.

3.3 CHALLENGES FACING WOLF CULTURE

A discussion about Wolf Culture would not be complete without understanding the downside. Even in China nowadays there is much debate whether or not a company should adopt or even maintain this form of corporate culture.

The approach has certainly contributed to enterprises maintaining a clear focus and creating incredible sales momentum, and has led to remarkable development speed, but there are increasing signs it has limitations, especially when it consistently ignores the feelings of employees.

A wolf is cruel and ruthless by nature, so when leadership turns a blind-eye, and company culture spirals down into 'cruel competition' and even behaviour of 'life and death', Wolf Culture will have run its course.

With Gen Z and even younger staffers joining the Chinese workforce, we start hearing more and more criticisms of certain aspects of Wolf Culture. These younger generations have not gone through the same hardship as their parents and grandparents and are less willing to work so hard. They lack the same sense of sacrifice as their elders, have grown up in a more prosperous environment, and think more individualistically.

In a 2017 study[13] done among users of Big Canton Internet (大粤网), a Guangdong province focused portal website with a broad audience, it was laid bare that Wolf Culture has its limitations and certainly is not for everyone.

Among others, the study concluded that if too much emphasis is placed on cruelty, such as punishment for underperformance, this will lead to internal pressure and even disgust among employees.

996 facing increasing criticism.

The voices against the 996 work ethic are also growing louder. After Jack Ma, the founder of Alibaba, in May 2019 publicly defended the practice and credited it for creating personal and business success, it triggered an exceptionally vivid online debate on whether it is the price to pay to get ahead in the booming Chinese economy, or it is a symptom of a work hard culture that has simply gotten out of control.

Websites such as 996.ICU ('Work 996 and End up in the Intensive Care Unit'), full of quotes from frustrated workers like 'we are human beings' and 'we don't all want to end up without hair on our head' are a tell-tale sign that the practice is increasingly under strain.

It even sparked a free to play internet game My Office 996. While poking fun, the game challenges the inherent demand for long working hours and personal sacrifices.

Set in the office of a technology firm, the game requires you to make hard choices and impossible decisions with the aim to further yourself within the company. Do I work extreme long hours to please the boss, protect a colleague likely to be fired, surf the internet, have something to eat, agree or disagree with someone in the company that is clueless but that could mean I will have a future in the company...? Decisions, decisions and all of them have consequences. They all impact your stress level, income, health, and people's trust in you. Office life, ruling your life.

In China, despite a strict labour law, workers have often tolerated long work hours and a sometimes-gruelling working environment. But one of the My Office 996 creators, Fang Hang from Evil Wind Studio, hopes 'the game encourages people to confront reality and ultimately achieve a better work-life balance.'[14]

Efficiency vs. opportunities in a slow growth environment.
Although China continues to show an impressive growth rate, it is no longer growing exponentially. The country and its economy are maturing and changing focus away from expansion at all costs. Opportunities are naturally becoming scarcer and potentially less rewarding, especially outside of the tech industry.

In such an environment, Chinese companies will inevitably need to revisit the opportunity/efficiencies equation. Seeking out new possibilities will certainly keep the upper hand as that is wired into the mindset of so many businesses and their leaders. They will remain opportunistic, but initial work toward efficiencies is starting. Digital transformation will lead the efficiency drive.

Reputational risk that may jeopardize expansion outside of China.
All in all, some of the unforeseen damages — on people, on returns on investment, on reputation — created by Wolf Culture when left unchecked, are now more scrutinized and less accepted, especially for Chinese companies that want to expand outside of China.

For example, Huawei (though they are not alone in this) has in the past been accused of unethical behaviour and although various measures have been taken inside the company, ingrained behaviour seems not so easy to change.

In 2019, the New York Times published an article[15] in which they outlined some of the company's legal wrongdoings. And they quoted the founder Ren Zhengfei — who at various occasions had said that Huawei had toughened its safeguards against employee misconduct — acknowledging that many workers did not pay attention to internal rules and controls, perhaps, he said, 'because Huawei used to evaluate staff solely according to how much business they won.'

It is clear to us that blindly promoting Wolf Culture is a non-starter. And yet, employing characteristics of a Wolf into a company ethos can have merit when it breeds competitive behaviour and a sense of belonging. The challenge is to capture the right elements.

3.4 HARNESSING THE POWER OF WOLF

While some aspects of Wolf Culture would appear too militaristic for a Western environment and could lead to unwanted conduct, there are still lessons to be learned from it for Western companies.

First, to be able to compete with their local competitors in China, when competing against a Wolf, being a Wolf is often the only way to survive. Any foreign business that operates in China will benefit from being or thinking like a Wolf.

It also has merit in today's increasingly volatile and increasingly digital international business world. Wolf Culture is well suited for unstable markets, fierce competition, and when relentless changes happen.

The offensive spirit, the relentless, never-give-up attitude within Wolf Culture, breeds a consistent entrepreneurial drive that ensures ongoing competitive advantages.

A Wolf-like spirit can add an upbeat and upward drive to energize and unify employees. When executed well, employees can feel the company's motivation, see and understand the ambitious goals and plans set, and constantly spur themselves on, and align themselves toward the same goals as the company.

But it can only be successful as part of a strong corporate culture. Publishing work systems on the wall, reminding people of performance goals at any time, holding fixed review meetings at standard times in the morning and evening, and occasionally shouting a slogan or two will not cut it.

For a business to decide what elements of Wolf Culture could be acceptable as part of the company culture, the first thing to remember is that any corporate culture comes from the top, not from a few processes.

The essence of a successful corporate culture is to reflect the style and personality of the leader of the company. If the company leader is not a Wolf, its culture never will be. But also, if middle management does not possess the same qualities, the spirit can never reach the work floor and the effort is doomed.

Leaders must first understand what kind of corporate culture they want to shape and how that relates to the actual needs of the company and its future plans. It also needs to be instilled top to bottom.

It is for the leader to define how far to push. What boundaries to set from the onset. A Chinese proverb says that 'the fish will rot from the head' and the risk for the leader to push too far and unleash behaviour that is difficult to change or control is real.

Wolf Culture as energizer. For the right people.
We see a way forward for the implementation of what is good about Wolf Culture into the modern organisation, and we distil three important elements:

The FIRST is very well defined by Zang Longsong, an educational expert involved with the Big Canton Internet study mentioned above. He provides a clear guide to which elements to implement[16]:

'Wolf Culture should emphasize discipline, career pursuit, and teamwork, a force behind taking responsibility.'

In this view, Wolf Culture is the driver of positive energy with the following core values to be instilled into the corporate culture. Values that nowadays we notice too little of in many Western organisations:

— Dedication to hard work
— Never. Give. Up. mentality
— The competition as *the enemy* to be beaten
— The Team over the individual
— And a remuneration system that reflects the efforts of the pack.

The SECOND element is proper management of where in the organisation Wolf Culture has its place and what its rewards are.

Wolf Culture does not make sense in all parts of a corporation, but it has clear merits in some departments. People engaged in Sales or Business development will benefit a lot more from Wolf Culture, provided the right people with the right mentality are hired.

Recruitment and talent selection must ensure that the right people are placed in suitable positions; not everyone is fit enough for working in the wolf's den. In Chapter 6 People Come and Go. Those Who Fit Stay Longer, we will home in on the phenomenon that people are hired to be tested, evaluated on how well they can fit in, and encouraged to move on if they don't.

And THIRD, it needs to be clear that wolves need to eat. Implementing a Wolf mentality must be supported by a value-based evaluation system that ensures there is enough upside for all participants. As Ren Zhengfei sees it: In a true Wolf enterprise there needs to be enough meat, and naturally there will be a true wolf pack.

Implementing elements of Wolf Culture certainly is not for every company. It may not sit well with every millennial in the West and may be frowned upon by many a business leader. However, we are convinced that reinjecting the essence of Wolf Culture, a more entrepreneurial management style and behaviour, into companies that have become too bureaucratic will be highly beneficial.

In the more digital, more complex, and faster business world of tomorrow, one that globally will look more like what China experiences today, such values will become the differentiators between success and failure and will become the difference between a successful and failed career.

适者生存

4

**ADAPT TO
CHANGE OR DIE.**

4. ADAPT TO CHANGE OR DIE.

'Become as flexible as water, which always finds its way
forward by adapting to the ground.'

Lao Tzu

Ancient philosopher and writer

4.1 CHANGE IS AS OLD AS HISTORY ITSELF

Rooted deep in Chinese culture, there is the view that the world around us never stands still and that all that is happening on it is changing continuously.

Unlike Western societies (from the Hebrew to the Greek and the Christians), there is no such notion as transcendent gods, eternal ideas, and the essence of things, in China's cultural past.

Instead, Chinese culture is infused with expectations of permanent change. It is central to the Chinese way of thinking, traditionally as well as today.

Chinese are the heirs of three millennial traditions: Taoism, Confucianism, and Buddhism and over these vast swaths of time a different form of thought has developed, not linear and rational but circular and intertwined. Chinese thinking is based on the realization that in reality, things are woven together like the weaves in a carpet.

In the 'Yijing' (易经, sometimes stylised 'I Ching', and also called 'The Book of Changes'), one of the oldest Chinese texts that first originated during the 1000 to 750BC period, the Chinese character 易 (Yi) as a noun means 'Change', and as an adjective, 'Easy'. The combination of the two meanings gives the idea that nothing is easier than change.

Confucius (孔夫子, meaning Master Kong; 551-479 BC), one of China's most revered and influential scholars was crucial in further developing this philosophy. Master Kong strongly rejected preconceptions, categorical assertions, and stubbornness. His teaching aims not to get an idea about things but to put fluidity in and between things: Why get attached to ideas while reality is in continuous transformation?

This thinking is also underlined by Buddha: 'The only law which does not change is the one which states that everything changes. To refuse this ontological law is to be narrow-minded.'

A mind must be sharp to deal with change.

Knowledge is the path to coping with change. All Chinese wisdoms consider that it is through vision and not through speculation that man gains knowledge. Studying, however, is not just accumulating book knowledge but also sharpening your mind, so that you always have the right answer for a given situation.

Lao Tzu (老子, meaning 'Old Master'; likely 6th century BC), another prominent Chinese philosopher and the founder of Taoism, was the leading force behind the notion that learning is critical to gaining an edge: 'He who does not know, always sees opposing forces. Those who know, see the necessary complementarities in the contradictory aspects.'

It is in the same spirit that Confucius advocates study. He constantly brings his teachings back to the realm of the concrete: 'Knowing is nothing, knowing how to live is everything.' As described earlier in Chapter 3 Wolf Culture, this respect for learning is still highly valued in modern Chinese society and can, for example, be seen clearly in the results of Chinese students around the world.

While in Western philosophy the important thing is to think well, for the Chinese the important thing is to observe well, and all the more so since luck does not fall from the sky: it is not the result of chance or Providence, but it is the fruit of the potential of a situation that has been detected, here and now, with its benefits to be exploited.

Time stops and starts.

Time, in Chinese wisdom is also interpreted differently. In the Chinese scriptures, time appears as a spiral, an eternal restarting but never with a similar restart, like the four seasons that will always follow each other but are not alike. There is no beginning or end in such a view of time, only change.

And such eternal restarting has profound consequences beyond the realm of time itself. It is at the basis of what is often erroneously termed as 'lack of vision or lack of a clear goal'. But in Chinese reality, it is seen as maintaining full flexibility. The Western fixation on a specific objective presents two major drawbacks in traditional Chinese wisdom: (1) It is a source of tension which squanders the vital energy of man; (2) It does not allow you to see what is happening at ground level and therefore to seize the opportunities that arise. Chinese thought is concerned with always being in tune with reality, an adequacy all the more successful when the object of aim is forgotten.[1]

The gap between our two thoughts is illustrated in the conception of genius: in Western philosophy he is a gifted being of exceptional creative thinking; Chinese wisdom would describe him as quite simply the one who is able to seize the opportune moment which escapes any plan conceived in advance.

Lack of aim is certainly NOT stupid.

Chinese thought is concerned with always being in tune with reality and thus, opportunism is a virtue in China. Because it meets the demands of the moment. We usually criticize an opportunist for not hesitating to take advantage of the circumstances by compromising, if necessary, rules and principles. But there is nothing to compromise when you don't lock yourself into those rules and principles to begin with.

Inflexibility, that is to say loyalty to principles or pre-agreed arrangements, is for Lao Tzu 'a stupidity'. In an ever-fluctuating world, changing attitudes and behaviour means showing adaptability, and therefore intelligence. Since reality is in continuous transformation, the Chinese thinker does not strategize toward a goal.

And lack of aim does not mean lack of vision.

The aim here relates to a specific objective to be reached as quickly as possible based on a pre-defined strategic plan. The vision, on the other hand, has a much broader scope, is long-term and anticipates the future based on the potential of the situation here and now.

In the West, strategic planning is seen as critically important. But in China, with so many ongoing changes in the here and now, it is considered difficult to consistently execute a fixed plan. Strategy is merely the middle ground between vision and tactics. It is vague and ambiguous. It is particularly unimportant. In China, one only needs vision and tactics.

While working towards a long-term goal, the short term therefore can be as flexible as the here and now requires. After you have a clear vision, you can start to act. But you don't need a pre-determined roadmap to get there.

Think of it as Chinese calligraphy or better still a water colour painting. A Chinese master will create his painting without an initial sketch. While he knows clearly in his mind he will produce a misty landscape, he just starts with a first brush and sees where this initial stroke may take him.

A master painter creating a Western style oil painting often starts by first sketching the outlines of the image he wants to create and then uses his colour palette and brush to fill it with the desired hues until the end result is close to what he had set out to create.

Do nothing does not mean nothing is happening.

And this gets us to a third element of critical difference. Traditional Chinese thinking does not believe in the power to change the course of events; man can only follow the flow.

This belief is rooted in Taoism and called 无为 (pinyin: wúwéi) directly translated as inaction. This interpretation however is somewhat confusing because it seems to evoke passivity, to just let things happen. It would therefore be more appropriate to speak of non-interference. Wuwei literally means empty (wú) action (wéi), that is, scarcity of activity. It really is about doing just what it takes to make things happen on their own.

Any situation can evolve by exploiting favourable factors, detected here and now. Evaluating is therefore more important than planning. If nothing is successful, one waits for the situation to turn favourably. When one intervenes, it is always upstream, where the change begins.

Upstream, in fact, the situation is more flexible, as here one can intervene without attracting attention or arousing resistance. Once a direction has been committed and all can see it clearly, the situation downstream will have hardened and there is likely to be resistance and opposition. When nothing is set in stone yet, anything is still possible.

For the Chinese thinker therefore, there is only indirect, invisible and progressive effectiveness. When he waits, we should not think that he is doing nothing: he will discreetly arrange the conditions upstream such that the consequences flow by themselves downstream in his favour. A situation cannot be changed but the conditions responsible for the situation can be adapted.

Upstream rearrangements.
An interesting example to explain this phenomenon is the suspension of the initial public offering of the Ant Group, China's premier fin-tech. The Chinese banking regulators pulled the IPO shortly before it should have taken place on November 5th 2020.

Days later, Jack Ma, founder of Alibaba and Ant vanished and was subsequently not sighted for nearly two months.

Ma's ordeal started shortly after he had criticized authorities in a speech given at a financial conference, the Bund Summit in Shanghai, where senior leaders such as Wang Qishan, China's vice president, and Yi Gang, the central bank governor, were also in attendance.

Although we are not in the position to know what happened during the period Ma was not seen, to us it seems a great example of 'upstream' rearrangements.

While for the outside world, the IPO remained suspended and no news about possible next steps was being communicated, Ma suddenly reappeared in public in a video released in January 2021[2] in which he was interacting with 100 rural teachers via a video link.

Showing devotion to uplifting China's rural poor, it was clear things were now different, as he proclaimed, 'My colleagues and I have been learning and thinking, and we have become more determined to devote ourselves to education and public welfare', he said, addressing teachers at a rural school.

Although Ma has a track record of supporting rural causes, going — within two months — from roasting financial authorities at their own conference to a public statement full of self-criticism gives sufficient reason to assume that invisible to the outside, the situation has been adapted.

At the time of writing this book, there is no conclusive update about the future status of the Ant Group IPO, but we would be surprised if it is not a matter of time for it to be rescheduled.

Conditions surrounding the IPO will most likely have changed by then. Regulations governing online financial lending will probably also have been amended. We may even see that state-owned banks have had time to catch-up on their digital strategies and will need to rely less on the Ant ecosystem for revenue. Even the ownership structure of the Ant Group could possibly have been changed.

In the here and now the Ant Group may seem stuck. But certainly upstream factors are being addressed to change direction.

With time that restarts constantly, flexibility is seen as a virtue and a notion that while doing nothing a lot can be achieved, adapting to constant change is at the core of Chinese philosophy. Naturally this thinking has found its way into the Chinese approach to doing business. And so Chinese companies have become masters at adapting to changing realities.

Turbulence and hyper competition.
The turbulent environment over the past 30 years has further contributed to the need for Chinese companies to manage flexibly. Operating in a large, diverse, and quickly evolving country, companies must scramble to keep pace with runaway growth interspersed with dramatic slowdowns while dealing simultaneously with massive urbanization and huge rural markets. Succeeding in such a complex and shifting environment requires businesses to possess a high degree of nimbleness and an ability to adapt constantly.[3]

Surviving against hyper competition, price erosion, and endemic corruption means not many companies have reliable sources of long-term profits and so firms are forced to be agile, able to transform themselves and seize opportunities even outside their own fields of expertise.

In general, Chinese entrepreneurs are positive thinkers and are often optimistic that they 'can get it done', as they have succeeded before; but operating in such unpredictable circumstances also creates anxiety and the need for rapid results. In such an insecure business environment, company leaders feel enormous pressure to reap their gains as quickly as possible, because they really don't know how the world around them is going to evolve. The rules of the game change often — what worked last time may not work again in the same way.

HYPER COMPETITION - THE BIKE SHARING CRAZE.

Fruit. Flowers. Apparel. China seems to go through periods with commercial trends that grow exponentially, until the next opportunity comes along. Bike sharing was the most recent example of how a great idea turned into hyper competition that made it near impossible for any of the market participants to make money.

A GREAT IDEA...

Ofo, founded on the idea of five members of Peking University's cycling club in 2014, started it all. Although bike sharing itself was not new, making a bike available anytime and almost anywhere via an app was novel. And it proved to be a great idea, initially.

The service, first offered at top universities in Beijing, expanded quickly to a city-wide bike sharing model. In 2016, Ofo expanded to other cities in China, and had a fleet of 85,000 bicycles by the end of that year and had started attracting attention.

By 2017, the race was on and other bike sharing companies started developing.

...LOVED AND HYPED BY MANY...

A euphoric optimism ensued, spurred on by the dream of dock-free bikes that allowed travel in an environmentally friendly and affordable way and government officials who, eager to reduce carbon emissions, provided a near regulation-free environment to experiment in.

...WELL-FUNDED...

In a relatively short time, more than 30 bike-sharing competitors to Ofo sprung up in China, with Mobike and Bluegogo leading the pack of copycats. Each picked a different colour, until every shade of the rainbow carried a logo.

With a business model requiring significant capital and with a land grab mentality toward being the leader in this supposedly profitable new business arena, investor money poured in by the billions in the belief that money was to be made from the endless user data that would become available. With the success of the industry and the hope for future expansion, Xinhua News labelled dock-free bike sharing as one of the four great innovations of China in 2017.

...UNTIL COMPETITION KILLED IT.

But as early as 2017 the first realities had also started to set in. The seemingly not well used colourful sea of bikes all over many cities were early warning signs that not all was well in bike sharing. Fierce battles raged for market share, led by Ofo and Mobike, its strongest rival. Just like in the ride-sharing industry for taxi rides, consumers were lured with massively subsidized prices by both competitors, funded on each side with money from investors who had been told that profits would eventually follow.

Bluegogo was the first victim, going bankrupt end 2017. In 2018, four years after Ofo was founded, the company came close to bankruptcy also and Mobike was acquired by Meituan-Dianping, a Chinese giant that had started to build a 'super app' offering consumers everything from restaurant reviews to online retail and hotel bookings, taxi rides — and now bike rides. In 2020 Ofo was still going, albeit barely, extending its life as a shopping app.

YOU ARE NOT WINNING IF YOU ARE NOT THE FASTEST OR THE BIGGEST.

'Ofo can serve as a metaphor for the overall market in China', according to Michael Pettis, a professor of finance at Peking University. 'Investors are very speculative here and the ingredients for rational investment patterns are still in short supply'. It is, others say, a form of high-stakes gambling.

What happened with Ofo is not unusual for Chinese businesses. Especially in the internet and business-to-consumer (B2C) space, investors zero in on two or three companies in emerging industries and then equip them with mind-boggling amounts of cash to quickly acquire customers and grab market share. Then the race is on. 'If you are not the number one or number two in your space, you quickly die', states Pettis's former colleague Jeffery Towson, previously professor of investment. 'While this kind of "vc2c-investing" [venture capital to consumer] that subsidizes the customer acquisition of loss-making companies, is also seen in Silicon Valley or elsewhere, what makes China stand out is the "ferociousness" of competition', says Towson.

'These Chinese companies are out to kill each other. Spending lots of money is necessary, and if your competitor gets a billion dollars and you don't, you fall behind.'

Source: Roland Berger, 1421 consulting [4&5]

Innovation, nothing more than something new.
Market changes are often consumer led and Chinese buyers are notorious-ly faddish and fickle. Resulting from the rapid development of consumerism since the economic opening up, several generations have grown up with an endless string of 'new' and have come to expect no less than continual different

and improved products. In our view, this has given a different meaning to (the role of) innovation.

From the late 1980s onward, a completely new consumption culture was established and with it a consistent string of previously non-existing or highly underdeveloped categories was developed. Each competing to be noticed and appreciated by consumers with very little disposable income.

For Chinese citizens who grew up during the turbulent years prior to 1987 it was often a baffling experience. Imagine people using shampoo for the first time in their life, buying their first ever pair of comfortable running shoes, eating out in a fast-food burger restaurant, or drinking a first coffee after having grown up with tea. Imagine the impact on a society that switches from bicycles to cars in less than 15 years or going from an abacus almost directly to a smart mobile phone, skipping practically the entire personal computer experience in the process. When we came to China in the early 90s, the only way to pay was cash, often in very old and crumbled notes. Today China has the highest rate of digital payments using mobile applications, globally, exceeding 80% of all transactions!

In many ways, Chinese consumerism went from the 19th century to the 21st within 30 years, often faster, depending on the category. And during this time Chinese consumers were continuously exposed to entire new product lines and endless new and competitive launches and consumer experiences. Imagine the impact such a development had on the expectations of shoppers.

In China's rapidly expanding consumer market, this has created customers that are increasingly confident, increasingly rich and sophisticated, and ever more willing to experiment. This is further amplified by the fact that in China power and money is with the younger generations. For example, a recent survey conducted in cooperation by the BCG and Tencent concluded that consumers aged below 30 were responsible for 47% of luxury spending in China in 2020, a much larger share than in Western markets. And the contribution of this age group continues to grow. Money is with young people who are less set in their ways![6]

Faddish and fickle, the enemies of brand loyalty.

And therein lies the next challenge for companies operating in this environment. There has historically been little brand loyalty in China. Although over time this has improved somewhat and can also differ by category, a vast majority of pragmatic Chinese consumers place a strong focus on functional attributes. Emotional brand connections do exist but are often volatile and subject to the buzz of the moment.

This means companies must adapt faster to changing needs and desires to stay appreciated. Or better still, demonstrate to consumers they deserve their attention and money by creating a constant stream of new and desirable alternatives. Such constant craving for 'new' has given a novel meaning and purpose to innovation and product development. One that is very different from how innovation is perceived in Western markets, which move and develop more slowly and where brands are more resilient.

The need for innovation is often misunderstood or outright dismissed at global HQs. In our discussions with global colleagues at headquarters or when interacting with global leadership teams of companies we have consulted for, we were always surprised how poorly understood this phenomenon was. It was often extremely difficult for them to understand that China could be in need of more innovation. More often. Or even simply more choices, colours, or varieties than consumers were expecting in their own established home markets. Failure to deliver sufficient innovation and newness has often been the reason for global companies to struggle, or worse, fail in the Chinese market.

ADIDAS NEO - THE €200M BUSINESS THAT WAS NOT ALLOWED TO EXIST.

Today in China, Adidas relies on three brand pillars for its growth.
1. Adidas Performance   'Sports'
2. Adidas Originals   'Sports Fashion'
3. Adidas NEO   'Sports Casual'

Prior to 2006, Adidas NEO did not exist. Here is why and how it was created.

A CLEAR MARKET NEED WAS IDENTIFIED.
The casual market was significantly underserved as many mass-fashion brands (local and foreign) had either not yet been launched or were still very small in country. Demand for such casual product for daily use was high and opportunities for retail space — particularly beyond a pure sports environment — was abundant.

EXISTING ADIDAS PRODUCT OFFER AND DISTRIBUTION WERE NOT ABLE TO FULFIL THIS DEMAND.
Adidas Sport Performance already had a very high share of the casual products market. Increasing this further would seriously risk its sports credentials.

Adidas Originals (or Sports Heritage as it was then called) was a higher priced product, out of reach for most consumers. Also, the brand was deemed more 'fashionable' and for a trendy audience. Broadening the range with casual product and lowering pricing would damage its 'must have' brand-enhancing appeal.

THE INITIAL SOLUTION...

Standalone stores with 'Adidas Casual' products, branded with the generic 'adidas' and three stripes logo.

Initially, these stores were stocked with products from both Sports Performance (casual/daily apparel and lower-end basic footwear) and Sports Heritage (lower-end, more basic apparel and footwear).

THE JOURNEY – TENACITY AND BELIEF:

— Summer of 2006, five test stores were opened by local management. They were an enormous success.
— September 2006, the business idea was first pitched to global leadership. They said no.
— In response, the pilot was increased to 50 stores, mostly in lower tier cities to keep the pilot as low profile as possible.
— March 2007, the idea was pitched again to the global board. They again said no.
— The number of 'test' stores grew to 100.
— June 2007, a multiyear business plan was presented to the global board, with a €200m (20%) difference between a scenario with and one without the Casual opportunity.
— Finally, the Board agreed.

At the end of 2020, this casual business segment had nearly 3000 POS in China. It was renamed Adidas NEO in 2008, targeting teenagers and young adults with product that is priced up to 50% lower than Adidas Originals.

Benefitting from dedicated design and supply chain, the brand still helps the company penetrate lower tier cities, and still provides Adidas China a clear competitive edge.

Source: Authors

Innovation is not going away.

With its economy maturing, China is seeing a slower growth rate and has stepped up economic restructuring. The country is transforming from high-speed growth to high-quality growth, increasingly less driven by manufacturing but by consumption and the service sector. This repositioning does not mean, however, a diminishing role for innovative products and the need for constant adaptation. The opposite is true. With growth slowing, it gradually becomes a market share game, and this calls even more for constant newness and innovation.

This transformation is driving more investment into innovation and technology and so the rapid market development remains, ushering in a new phase of market turbulence and an ongoing need to adapt. This digital transformation is also increasingly reaching out beyond China's borders.

Adapt or die. What would you choose?

When things change as fast and fundamentally as they do in the modern and digitalized world, adapt or die will become a more acute question for more businesses around the world. It will be imperative for brands to stay current or risk losing out to more digitally savvy and more nimble rivals. Carrefour can attest to that.

One could argue that in Western markets the business environment is more stable, perhaps more predictable with less change or at a lesser pace. But we are actually living in a time of unprecedented transformation.

The interconnectivity of people, businesses, and markets has never been as strong and pervasive. Disruptive technological advances are transforming the way we live, work, and consume. The unprecedented acceleration of emerging digital trends driven by the global Covid-19 pandemic is providing further hints of what our future may look like.

Brand loyalty is also under threat worldwide. In an increasingly digitized world, this trend is exponentially amplified by the power of social media and its characteristic faddish behaviour as well as a growing reliance on digital platforms and online opinion leaders. The latter themselves depending on a consistent stream of new and exciting products to promote, to remain relevant. What we see in China is a blueprint for what is to come also in so-called developed markets. Especially among a Gen Z and Millennial audience which will determine a brand's performance and commercial success in the decades ahead.

Additionally, new global value chains are forming. For example, where it was more difficult for Chinese companies to sell to a Western audience only a few years ago, digital solutions (e.g., via Alibaba's international presence) are making this increasingly possible.

Going the other way, by using cross-border e-commerce solutions into China, foreign brands and businesses are more and more able to target China-based audiences directly through an online presence that reduces risk and the cost of doing business with Chinese consumers.

Although in the last few years there has been somewhat of a slowdown, significant Chinese outbound investment will continue the export of Chinese capabilities and methodologies as Chinese company owners will infuse their invested companies with what they know. And they will compete with the way they are used to doing things at home.

4.2 LEARNING ADAPTATION SKILLS

The difference between either successfully adapting in this changing environment or fading away depends on skills that many Chinese companies have already mastered:

1. Extreme focus on consumer needs;
2. Innovation by experimentation;
3. Adhering to the 80/20 rule;
4. Thrive in chaos.

4.2.1 You are not in the game without really observing the consumer

As described in the first section of this chapter, in Western philosophy the important thing is to think well, while for the Chinese the important thing is to observe well. As a result, the Chinese have a surprising flair for detecting underlying trends. They are very skilled at understanding signs.

With their antennas always on, understanding the markets and the consumers they serve is second nature for a Chinese business leader and his team.

In our chapter It All Starts with Data, we will dive much deeper into the strategic advantages that Chinese companies have developed based on growing digital capabilities and the ever-expanding data connectivity. But apart from the data analysis, here are some interesting examples of how Chinese companies have become so customer focused and how they are using the internet toward a rigorous consumer understanding:

TENCENT is one of China's leading digital players. Nowadays, more and more companies call customers 'users', but Pony Ma, the founder of Tencent, one of

China's most successful firms, always thought this way. His 10/100/1,000 rule reinforces Tencent's user-first philosophy. Each month, product managers run 10 end-user surveys, read 100 users' blogs and collect user-experience feedback from 1,000 people.

XIAOMI CORPORATION, a multinational electronics company that describes itself as an internet company offering smartphones and smart hardware connected by the Internet of Things (IoT), has a similar dedicated consumer devotion. As Liu De, a founding partner and vice-president phrases it:[7]

> *The Internet era is good for companies that are totally transparent in what they are doing and what they are selling. The Internet is more than just a tool and should be regarded as a new way of thinking, and that implies respecting customers. When the customer comes across a problem, you fix it right away online.*

Xiaomi has more than 110 million registered users, about 90 million of whom are very active online. Most are men in their 20s who are studying or who studied science or engineering at university.

> *'These people are different from others', Liu says. 'They understand products, have a good education, and can discern the good points about products, and usually they can reflect a whole group of consumers. If some of them like it, the whole group is very likely to like it.*
>
> *'So, with our products online, tens of thousands of people could take part in a discussion, and you could see what good points are being made and where the differences of view are.'*

The company has a team of more than 40 staffers who collect feedback about Xiaomi phones every day.

Also, there are over 15,000 employees, and everyone is considered a customer service representative, expected to monitor social media such as Weibo and WeChat and pass on feedback within the company.

Uniquely, each Xiaomi employee, including the founder, has contractual responsibility to directly deal with a certain quota of customer requests. A sophisticated digital problem distribution system allocates questions to any suitable employee.

At HAIER CORPORATION, a world leader in home appliances and well known for its business innovation, for many years they have been going a step further: Pioneering the development of product in direct cooperation with its future users, even if that was not initially understood and accepted by all its employees. But egged on by their visionary CEO, Zhang Ruimin, who is known for his entrepreneurial acumen and consistent drive for change and innovation, they experimented and saw the advantage. As Zhang Ruimin recalls:[8]

> We put forward some new concepts. For some appliances, we designed a group of various modules and invited users to select, for example, the colours and designs they wanted. In one day, we sold more than 10,000 television sets online. This made us realize that our old ways of thinking and conducting business needed an overhaul.
>
> Many employees, especially those in management, had a hard time accepting this approach. When we started requiring that products be developed in cooperation with users participating in the front-end design, employees felt like they didn't know how to go about it. Some flatly refused, whereas others were [passively] unwilling.
>
> We told our employees that it wasn't a big deal if they failed, that it was meant to be a process of trial and error. The employees accomplished it successfully. As a result, we now require that all products be developed in this way, with users as interactive partners.

PERFECT DIARY – an online cosmetics sensation, which emerged from the Chinese digital ecosystem. Targeting women aged 20–35 with relatively high spending power, the company was founded in 2016 and shot to fame on the 2018 Singles' Day, when Perfect Diary ranked first among Chinese makeup brands.

A year later, on November 11th 2019, sales reached RMB 100 million in 33 minutes on Tmall[9], overtaking global brands like L'Oréal and Maybelline in the makeup category. And in 2020 again they ranked first with RMB 600 million (GMV).

Fully leveraging the digital lifestyle of its key targets, China's Gen Z and Millennial young adults, Perfect Diary meshes its consumer understanding, interaction with its users, and sales in one streamlined and combined approach [see separate box for details on their leading digital strategy as well as Section 7.2.2 in the chapter It All Starts with Data for an analysis of their use of Artificial Intelligence].

Here is an interesting example on how being close to consumers led to instant business success during the Covid-19 pandemic:[10]

'When consumers wear face masks, they need to fix their makeup more often as the mask wipes off the makeup', according to David Huang, founder. 'We learned this from our users and we immediately carried out research on products they want, citing an example of data gathered during the coronavirus pandemic that resulted in a new pressed face powder.'

PERFECT DIARY - THE DIGITAL MARKETING SENSATION.

Almost out of nowhere, Perfect Diary shot to fame on 2018 Singles' Day, ranking first among Chinese makeup brands. A year later, on November 11th 2019, sales reached RMB100 million in 33 minutes on Tmall, overtaking global brands like L'Oréal and Maybelline in the makeup category. And in 2020 again they ranked first with a total of RMB 600 million (GMV).

Perfect Diary targets women aged 20 to 35, with relatively high spending power. Promoting itself with the concept of 'Unlimited Beauty', the brand encourages its users to challenge themselves to explore more of life's possibilities, which highly resonates with its target audience. The products are of good quality and very attractively priced, but this is not their only reason for success. Their innovative, interaction based, digital marketing approach is what made them famous.

MIXING CONSUMER UNDERSTANDING WITH MARKETING.

Fully leveraging the digital lifestyle of its key targets — China's Gen Z and Millennial young adults — Perfect Diary meshes its consumer understanding, interaction with its users, and sales in one streamlined and combined approach. Pioneering the use of new social media platforms such as Xiaohongshu (lifestyle sharing), Bilibili (short video sharing) and Douyin (short video sharing) and maximizing the possibilities that WeChat offers, Perfect Diary is permanently present on the platforms where its target market gathers, creating real communities that are simultaneously their source of inspiration as well as their marketplace.

Interaction with 'private traffic', away from the big platforms. In China, large e-commerce platforms (e.g. Tmall and JD) control the 'last mile' between the brand and the consumer. The platforms possess unlimited consumer data, but brands are only given limited access. Another downside is not being able to interact and learn directly and regularly from customers. Perfect Diary has cleverly managed to get around that. Attaching promotion cards to products sold on a marketplace and using lucky money and personal invitations to encourage consumers to enter its own online channels, Perfect Diary has managed to build its own pool of 'private traffic', equivalent to a

'VIP customer emailing list'. Mainly on the WeChat platform, Perfect Diary now has hundreds of directly managed private traffic groups enabling it to interact with well over one million users directly.

ARTIFICIAL INTELLIGENCE THAT GROUPS LIKEMINDED PEOPLE TOGETHER.
A fictional, AI driven avatar 'Xiao Wanzi', a girl modelled on its target audience, gives customers access to their lucky money on WeChat and distributes personal invitations to specific groups, where customers can interact with likeminded girls.

In these myriad groups, Xiaowanzi acts as a reliable friend, is their beauty consultant, and provides exclusive services for all consumers in the group.

FOCUS ON KEY OPINION CONSUMERS AND MICRO-INFLUENCERS.
In addition to more standard cooperation with Chinese celebrities (e.g. Zhu Zhengting) and with celebrity cosmetics KOL, Li Jiaqi, on platforms such as Tmall, the Chinese beauty brand cooperates on platforms like Xiaohongshu with less well-known, but often more authentic key opinion consumers (KOCs).

For example, when Perfect Diary launched Daydream, a new product for 2020 Chinese Valentine's Day, they collaborated with over 150 KOCs. The majority of these KOCs have less than 10,000 followers.

INNOVATIVE DIGITALLY, BUT THEY DON'T NEGLECT MARKETING BASICS...
With light, playful collaborations and campaigns with unexpected brands such as the Discovery Channel, National Geographic, the British Museum, and the New York Met, Perfect Diary's approach is spot on. Art and nature, two of Gen Z's key interests.

...AND MAKE FULL USE OF 'NEW RETAIL'.
Having started out as a pure online player, Perfect Diary today seamlessly blends in offline via pop-up stores and a fast-expanding, highly digitized retail presence, with no efforts spared to move offline customers into their private traffic pool online.

Source: Beijing Review, Daxue Consulting [11&12]

NEIWAI – a lingerie company that very successfully connects with Chinese women. Founded in 2012, the brand first appeared online and has now widened its distribution to physical retail in over 70 stores. A key reason behind their success is a continuous interaction with their users which has enabled them to understand and benefit from shifts in consumer attitudes at the right time.

Building a brand based on female empowerment, it literally puts its consumer understanding in its advertising and in documentaries, tapping into the need of their users to express their hidden desires and aspirations.

Its most talked about campaign, launched in 2020, featured real women who spoke about the ways in which they were pre-judged and devalued by society for their perceived deficiencies. Each representing stereotypes such as 'Big Boobs with No Brains', 'Mom', 'The Aged', 'Muffin Top', and 'Scars', the campaign celebrated body diversity and was one of the boldest examples China had seen of inclusivity and female self-empowerment.

> *'Nothing is more beautiful than freedom of the body', Neiwai founder, Liu Xiaolu said.* [13] *'Only when women wear clothes which celebrate the freedom of the body, can they celebrate the free life choices of their own. That's how we combine the brand philosophy with product design.'*

Neiwai consistently demonstrates true user understanding, in a changing society with a rising consciousness among Chinese women about their own bodies and expressed with subtle feminism and sensuality.

'Private Traffic' – the source of consumer knowledge.

What all these companies have in common is that they listen and observe continuously. They make understanding consumers and users part of the fabric of the entire organisation. Not just the market research department or the R&D team. But a continuous cycle of checks and double checks with the people who use their product and who expect a continuous string of new products.

And they go one step further. Moving away from communicating via the large marketplaces and their increasing cost of traffic retention, they are creating pools of Private Traffic. Free from the algorithms of large e-commerce platforms, the brands are taking control of how consumers see their products.

They morph research with commerce. By creating communities through hundreds of WeChat groups, they increase the granularity of segmentation, collect data on an ongoing basis, and sell the products developed based on such knowledge directly in the groups where the insights originated.

Another interesting conclusion is that for them a rigid consumer segmentation does not exist. Targeting is much more based on an ongoing observation of behaviour, rather than thinking in specific groups that are set for a longer period of time. The Perfect Diary case above is a great example.

In Chapter 1, in the section China as Engine 2, we refer to the success of L'Oréal in China. One of the Dragon skills L'Oréal has mastered to stay competitive, even against fast movers such as Perfect Diary, is to also cater to a much more fluid audience.

Rather than segmenting based on income or age, they now focus their targeting on a woman's lifecycle, with the product need of a student being both different but also having some overlap with a girl that has just started her first job. A subtle difference perhaps, but one that is commercially significant.

How L'Oréal competes successfully in China and is spreading what they've learned around the organisation globally is detailed in the box on the next page.

L'OREAL - A LEADING BEAUTY.

L'Oréal entered China in 1997 and is today the number one beauty group in this market. Still growing by double digits every year, the company is one of the most successful Western businesses in the Middle Kingdom. The achievement of L'Oréal in China is a demonstration of how adapting to a changing environment is a winning strategy, even for bigger corporations. In this rapidly changing market, the company has remained agile and has learned to become extremely consumer focused.

Adapting to new realities started early. The first move was to relocate operations from Hong Kong to Mainland China in 1997, recognizing earlier than many others that this is where the centre was. Since then, the organisation has continued to adapt, staying relevant and competitive, even in today's highly digital market environment with growing local competition.

CHINA STRATEGY AND PRODUCTS FIT FOR CHINA.
— As early as 2005, L'Oréal built an R&D centre for China in Shanghai. Their main mission was to conduct and support scientific research to better understand the structure and behaviour of Chinese hair and skin.
— L'Oréal was quickly able to create region-specific products such as anti-aging serums, whitening creams, and pollution-fighting cleansers.
— Skin reconstruction technology, developed in the Shanghai lab, further helped L'Oréal create customized make-up and skincare for Chinese customers.
— A flatter and younger organisation enables faster decision making and agility.
— L'Oréal has benefitted from a stable China management that ensures continuity of knowledge and strategy.

GLOBAL ORGANISATION FULLY ADAPTED TO WORK FOR CHINA, LIKE CHINA, AND LEARN FROM IT.
- 'All of L'Oréal works for China' [see above about China as your Engine 2] instead of trying to make China work within frameworks designed for other markets.
- 'The rest of the L'Oréal world' is learning from China as it addresses a younger and more digitized consumer, which brings new perspectives to Western markets.

EMBRACING THE DIGITAL CONSUMER, EARLY AND CONTINUOUSLY.
- Being truly consumer centric, L'Oréal created a Chief Consumer Officer position for the China market.
- Adopted a segmentation strategy enabling rapid reaction to shifts in the Chinese market (as based on smaller lifestyle-based clusters (covering a span of three to four years compared to longer, age-based cycles in the West)
- They fully embraced digitization and developed social listening skills to keep track of brands' performance and discover new opportunities.

Consumer centricity and digitization are the two main drivers of continued L'Oréal success in China. This focus would not have been possible without adaptation skills: observing, listening, and seizing opportunities without compromise.

With a strategy and organisation that fully supports the essence of the global brand **('To offer each and every person around the world the best of Beauty')** to satisfy all beauty needs and desires in their infinite diversity, L'Oréal China is well equipped for continued success.

Source: Interviews, authors

4.2.2 Innovate by experimentation

Another method that many Chinese companies have mastered is to create innovations utilizing a step-by-step approach. Instead of developing a product completely, it is battle tested early to gauge possible success, to learn more about ways to improve it, or to determine what products to mass produce. Launching innovations while actually learning from and about consumer behaviour and feedback speeds up competitiveness at a much higher level of efficiency.

In Section 1.2., we described a research project done in 2019 by Feng Li from City University of London. This study was among employees at internet firms and was aimed to understand why companies originating from the West failed so clearly in China.

In this study, Feng Li also drew the conclusion that the Chinese firms were much faster at innovating:

> 'Unlike Western Internet Firms which have established procedures for developing and implementing innovations, Chinese Internet Firms are often more result-oriented and more prepared to innovate by experimenting', Li explained, 'If a new idea works, then scale it up rapidly; if not, move onto other ideas.

> 'Chinese consumers are generally more tolerant of such product development processes than in the West, which enable Internet players in China to test and refine many new ideas very quickly at low cost, with significant cumulative effects.'

This method is not limited to internet companies alone. Making products that are 'good enough', but not sophisticated, has long been the approach across many Chinese manufacturers. Here is another interesting example:

Perhaps not the most practical product for the majority of users but one with a market among households with a limited budget, appliance maker TCL developed a dual screen television in close cooperation with its future users. [14] The unique selling point of the product is that it enables two people to watch different programs full screen on the same television, which caters to the viewing styles of many Chinese residents.

The TV is receiving and displaying two different signal sources. Playing a Blu-ray blockbuster while displaying the racing game of PlayStation 3, two users only need to wear all-left or all-right 3D glasses, and they can watch their respective pictures without affecting each other.

This novel approach required TCL to carry out intensive research and development that involved a trial-and-error approach before the product was perfected.

Xiaomi follows a similar process for new product development that focuses on getting prototypes to market early in the cycle, creating good-enough products by actively involving users in fine-tuning and updating the technology and design. This results in products largely co-developed by the community and are thus closer to the market need, with a more efficient R&D process and a higher success rate.

An interesting example is the Mi Laser Projector. The team under co-founder Liu De debated for a long time the idea to give the world a home theatre that would be budget-friendly, but qualitative and innovative in image reproduction. The development was even put on hold for a while because there were still doubts if the Xiaomi ecosystem required such a device, as the market price for laser projectors was high and these items were large. But the team persisted and went ahead with a true let-the-customer-decide mentality, as explained by Liu De:[15]

> *After two years of experiments and user testing, we managed to create a product worth not more than $1000. We then decided to only launch 2,000 units to see how the broader market would react.*

The Mi Laser Projector was a hit and sold out within a day! And so, the product was ramped up and is now a key bestseller of their home-based smart devices.

Quickly, develop more products!

There is widespread evidence across multiple industries that the speed with which Chinese companies develop new products from existing technologies and ramp up large-scale production is often impressive. For example, it is a key reason why the Chinese have come to dominate the global silicon-based solar-panel business, forcing U.S. and Japanese producers to focus on more-exotic thin-film solar technology.

Another interesting example is Goodbaby International, China's market leader in baby carriages and child car seats. They beat rivals by introducing 100 new products on average each quarter. And as described in the case study in Part 1, Section 1.2, KFC China introduces more new products each year than their U.S. counterparts, because local variations in taste demand it.[16]

Actually, the basic skills needed for a fast-paced and stage-by-stage innovation cycle are not unique to China. In fact, a lot of this thinking could have come straight out of the annals of IDEO, one of the world's leading innovation firms, based in San Francisco, California. They termed it 'design thinking', being 'a set of both mindsets and design-based activities that foster the collaboration required to solve problems in human-centred ways.'[17]

Many global firms already apply a designer method of work processes to systematically extract, teach, learn, and apply these human-centred techniques to solve problems and create products in a creative and innovative way.

The core of such design thinking is recognizing a problem or a need. Then design early-stage solutions or prototypes and test and improve your way forward in cycles until the solution meets its demands, rather than trying to attempt to leapfrog to the ultimate solution in one step.

Although the skill is universal, in our view Chinese firms master the process better for three reasons:

1. EXTREME COMPETITIVE PRESSURE drives them to launch quickly and early then build and improve later. To survive, it is better to be first, lead consumer interest, and stay ahead by improving the product based on such initial feedback.

2. RISK AVOIDANCE: In the chapter about Wolf Culture, we explained that Chinese entrepreneurs have a different approach to evaluating risk. Launching a product that is not 'ready' but is first to market ultimately brings less risk than not being able to launch before others. The price of being late could be a lot higher!

3. TENACITY: Chinese entrepreneurs possess incredible capabilities for not giving up. Try. Fail. Try again. Fail again. Keep trying until you succeed. Survival all depends on how many problems you solve. And how you get yourself back up again after failures. In an environment where you need to adapt or die, only a desperate need to succeed and a never-say-die attitude will keep you going. A persistent mindset, a powerful work ethic, plus the ability to make sure things happen are key weapons in the arsenal of Chinese entrepreneurs.

We realise that innovation for many firms can be a complex- and resource-intensive activity. But it is also evident that in our increasingly digital world, the cost of not innovating fast enough is going up. Accordingly, many companies need to review the ways they innovate, and many leaders still have lots of opportunity for improvement. In their book, 'Payback, reaping the rewards of Innovation', James P. Andrew and Harold L. Sirkin say it very well:[18]

> *Innovation is not a black art, a roll of the dice, or a creative free for all. It is an act, not an idea. It requires continual change, an agreed process, and a combination of deliberate risk taking.*
>
> *Lack of ideas is rarely the issue. Thousands of good ideas exist within every organisation, even among those that don't think of themselves as innovative. The real problem these companies have is how to turn their ideas into cash. They don't have a process for collecting the ideas, screening them, nurturing them, and ultimately commercializing them.*

Given the increasing speed of innovation nowadays in China, business leaders there are improving their game and taking advantage of creative thinking within their organisations.

In the next chapter, The Emperor Decides. But Agility Rules, we will show how Chinese companies further improve the innovation process by creating internal competition. Through encouraging rivalry among teams for resources and with a 'first to reach the post' reward system, they are able to significantly improve the speed and results of innovation. They then make the cost and risk of the efforts more manageable by combining this with a go-to market structure that enables early-stage innovation being launched and marketed, and ultimately earned back earlier.

Upgrade your engine while it is running.

Another method Chinese entrepreneurs have mastered is to innovate by simply starting something and see how things develop. As described earlier in this chapter, a significant difference between Chinese management and what is more common outside its borders is the use of detailed long-term planning.

The only time you see Chinese companies create a five-year plan is when they're about to IPO or sell themselves to a Western firm. The market is moving too fast for companies to be under any illusions that they can anticipate sales five years out.

That does however not mean that they don't think ahead. Quite the opposite. But, instead of spending endless hours debating five-year plans, Chinese companies regularly discuss how they envision the market will evolve over a ten-year period while they think about what they can do immediately to win in that future.[19]

As a result, many successful companies in China operate in two timeframes, executing today's business while preparing to double in size in three to five years. This involves not just adding resources but incubating new business models and launching new brands.

In the United States or Europe, the business unit head would normally handle both timeframes. But Chinese founders usually appoint two managers, each autonomous and responsible for one timeframe and effectively competing for resources.[20]

In the digital space, the ongoing development of WeChat is a good example, and even a good metaphor. When WeChat 1.0 was launched, it was very basic: mostly a replication of what was available in the market. In functionality it resembled WhatsApp: essentially a messaging app.

But look at it today. WeChat is an ecosystem all by itself, far more sophisticated than the simple app it was when launched and now more resembling an operating system. Upgraded over time into the unique and diverse product it is now through incremental innovation. The red packets invented to drive acceptance of WeChat Pay we described in Section 3.2.1. was only the beginning; today WeChat has morphed from a messaging software into a portal, connecting a user via their smart phone to myriad services ranging from games, social networking, ride hailing, payment services, and, especially via the WeChat mini programs, an unlimited offer of e-commerce.

While envisioning the future and upgrading software with the existing product in the market is certainly easier to manage, one of the most famous examples of how well the thinking works and how it can even change an entire country was given by Deng Xiaoping, 'the Great Silent Transformer', as described by Hesna Cailliau in her book 'Le Paradoxe du Poisson Rouge: Une Voie Chinoise pour Réussir':[21]

> *In 1978 Deng launched his great movement of reforms and openness without a specific objective, without presenting a five-year plan but by adopting a simple slogan: 'Test the stones while crossing the river.'*
>
> *This was an old popular expression understandable to all, but that Deng elevated to a political motto. It reflects the absence of a route mapped out in advance to guide the future of China: two steps forward, one step back. We will see as and when the opportunities arise what should be done.*
>
> *Starting a complete rethink of the country by 'simply' opening a special economic zone in Shenzhen, with the idea that if it works, others would be opened elsewhere, and change would be on its way.*
>
> *Had he come up with a precise and irreversible plan, it would have sparked violent opposition from Mao's supporters, who were still numerous at the time.*

Deng tested the stones while crossing the river and made it safely to the other side to unleash the largest transformation in the history of the Chinese continent. A remarkable result achieved by following 'a poor model', according to Western thinking. It was highly successful however, in a Confucian way 'to act without preconceived ideas, without a fixed plan, if need be, without necessity', Cailliau writes.

4.2.3 80% will do just fine

Highly correlated to the speed of innovation, but worth describing in a standalone section, is what is called the 80/20 rule.

One of our key lessons from living and working in China is applying this 80/20 principle: value timing over perfection.

If 80% of a project or activity is completed, working on the last 20% is very often not worth it. Perfection is quite frequently a loss of time and opportunity. The last 20% is likely to take as much resources as the first 80% and delays launches without significantly improving the rate of success.

We have witnessed the process many times over where — in our multinational company environments — it was mandated to cover all bases, to do that extra bit of research to have all the answers to questions that might be asked, to make sure the PowerPoint presentations were slick and convincing enough to get everyone to sign off, just to make sure that all interests were aligned and everyone within the power structure was on board and the business case was solid.

But while working for local firms we were constantly being challenged because things were taking too long. We were being urged to share initial thinking. PowerPoints deliberately not required! Instead, we were urged to sit down and talk with the most senior leaders to give them an initial feel of where our ideas were going. We would then be inundated by advice, ideas, and most importantly, we would receive on the spot WeChat introductions to people inside and outside the firm to talk to and solicit for more early feedback or direct support in getting started whatever we were working on.

Each of these leadership conversations were always concluded with an encouragement not to just keep going but to find ways to do things faster and to start thinking about execution. Rather than planning endlessly, proceed with rough plans and mobilize resources rapidly once it is better understood how to deploy them.

Perhaps not many people know this, but the first major chat app in China wasn't WeChat; it was MiUI which was produced by Xiaomi Technologies. Their founder and CEO Lei Jun admitted that WeChat eclipsed his product because Tencent could release one or two versions every week.[22]

> 'We could only release one version per month', Lei Jun noted. 'Even for software as complicated as theirs, the WeChat team still maintained the speed of releasing two to three versions every month. And consumers accepted it!'

For Pony Ma, the founder of Tencent, that was simply the result of 80/20 thinking, as he wrote on WeChat's internal platform in April 2017:

'A service [or product] starts with the satisfaction and needs of its users in mind and is solely defined by those two things'.

Ma goes on to say that developers often undermine their own products by over-developing them to the point of losing their original basic intention.

'Spending core resources and time repeatedly on the optimisation of the obvious characteristics is basically the mania of novice entrepreneurs.'

According to Pony Ma, no product is ever perfect from the beginning. It is a process of fast and continuous iteration and in fact perfection is never reached.

As a result, Tencent can achieve an executional speed that gives it an early launch ability that leaves its rivals envious.

Another good example of how 80/20 works is to compare livestreaming in China with teleshopping around the world. Livestreaming is the teleshopping for the digital age. Or better, livestreaming is teleshopping 2.0.

Nowadays, we see some of the leading livestreaming hosts creating larger productions. Likewise, main platforms such as Alibaba and JD.com are even organizing large scale live shopping shows to support 11/11 and other sales festivals. However, the essence of livestreaming, and certainly its origin, is an individual with a mobile phone, selling products in real-time.

Whereas teleshopping shows in the West are much more staged and often produced in custom made studios, most livestreaming in China is artisanal, meaning low-cost production that could be done anywhere by anyone, bringing together entertainment and commerce.

While in the West the target audience of teleshopping channels is mostly older, in China, teenagers and young adults frequent various teleshopping channels hosted by bubbly presenters trying out products and responding in real-time to consumer enquiries. It is often more the simplicity and perceived honesty of the host that draws the buyers, rather than a slick, overly commercial environment.

Livestreaming in its 80/20 format depends on and promotes interaction with consumers. You can click and buy as you watch the people you trust, like rural live-streaming host Chen Jiubei. She is known for helping farmers in her hometown sell and clear two million kilograms of unsold oranges in 13 days[23]. There was nothing slick or over-produced in her livestreaming show, yet it has proven to be successful in reaching consumers and achieving commercial success.

COVID-19 TECH RESPONSE - FAST IS JUST SO MUCH MORE IMPORTANT THAN COMPLETE!

Not surprisingly, China's response to the Covid-19 virus has been decidedly high tech and the pandemic may well be the catalyst to get the country ahead globally with technological innovations. We realize that the Chinese legal environment provides a broader frame of reference than might be possible in other parts of the world, yet this example is worth sharing. That is precisely because the tech response to the Covid-19 pandemic is a perfect illustration of the Dragon Tactics we describe throughout this book, particularly the 80/20 principle.

The public sector worked hand-in-hand with the key private companies of the Chinese digital landscape — the BAT (Baidu, Alibaba, Tencent) as well as the rising stars of artificial intelligence, SenseTime and Megvii — to develop solutions in a record time that managed all aspects of the crisis.

— First came the health QR code within only a few weeks after the beginning of the outbreak.

Initially developed by Alipay, with and for the city of Hangzhou, it used data collected by mobile operators, mobile payment APPs, and other mobile service providers to assign people a health code (green, orange, or red) that they show at the entrance of buildings or public transportation. This was put in place all around China.

— Soon this was followed by various extensions of existing apps to manage life during a pandemic and lockdown.

Most of these innovations were pragmatically built upon the basis of existing technologies and developed in a surprisingly short time. Instead of spending months to develop the 'perfect app' for the general public, major Chinese tech companies progressively built new Covid-19 layers and functions into their existing multi-functional apps, already in use by large parts of the population.
Messaging tools, payment options and video platforms, the multitude of data collected on almost the entire population enabled them to offer a range of services around two critical Covid-19 hot buttons: safety/reassurance and contactless services.

FOR EXAMPLE:
• AMap, a leading geo-location application in China and part of the Alibaba ecosystem, developed a detailed information service indicating the precise

location of contamination cases in real time.
- The Tencent ecosystem (WeChat, Qihoo 360, and Sogou) launched its online maps, which located nearby residents who are carriers of Covid-19. Available in more than 170 Chinese cities, the map also showed the location of confirmed cases.
- Instead of disclosing the names and personal information of patients, the maps used data from the Chinese Ministry of Health and indicated the distance between people infected with Covid-19 and the user.
- Progressively, in the various competing apps, additional services were provided to the user, from medical advice, hygiene tips and hospitals nearby to where to buy (online or offline) masks and sanitizer, or videos to keep people entertained at home during the lockdown.

— Meanwhile, the pandemic has also been an opportunity for other significant digital advances that, without a doubt, will lead to many innovations for years to come:
- Artificial intelligence and big data were used extensively in diagnosis and treatment and in the search for a vaccine.
- 5G technology, only in its test phase before the outbreak, was scaled up to geolocate cases and transfer medical files and data.
- Acceleration of the use of drones, autonomous vehicles and robots, be it to deliver food and other products to confined citizens or to perform necessary tasks in hospitals like cleaning or the distribution of medicines to patients.

In contrast to the approach used in many countries in the West, these examples illustrate Chinese business pragmatism, the 80/20 rule, as well as the idea that it is always better to launch a first version, be it rough, of a new product and improve it through innovation while it is already running.

Source: Authors

4.2.4 Thrive in chaos

In the first section of this chapter, we concluded that adapting to constant change is at the core of Chinese philosophy and that such thinking naturally has found its way into the Chinese approach to doing business. And so Chinese companies have become masters at responding to rapidly shifting realities. We then continued by describing methodologies that enable them to react quickly.

In the next two chapters, The Emperor Decides. But Agility Rules and People Come and Go. Those Who Fit Stay Longer, we explain in detail how they have built the needed organisational structures and people skills to manage it. In uncertainty there is a fine line between finding value and uncontrollable madness. Not much separates innovative chaos from disruptive chaos.

Chaos can be positive, as it can be fertile ground for improvisation, creativity, and innovation. Unpredictability can create interesting opportunities, if one is equipped to capture them. Whether to benefit from chaos or not is a matter of leadership.

Chinese management is very top-down. We explain why that is in detail in the next chapter. But here it suffices to state that the founder or leader in many Chinese companies can often be compared to being an Emperor. If the Emperor is enlightened, then dealing with chaos will bring many advantages.

If the Emperor is more absolute, it will work against him and the entire organisation, as he is likely to leave less room for creativity and empowerment of the team below, especially at more junior levels. In such environments, the Emperor himself can become a source of the chaos, especially when his whims get in the way of everything — something that happens very often in Chinese organisations.

But if his thinking is shaped by Taoism, his organisation will thrive in chaos, especially, if the organisational structure is kept flat and agile. For, the enlightened leader knows he should not consistently impose his view only. Instead, he should ensure that things are allowed to happen as they arise. Following the quote from Lao Tzu at the beginning of this chapter, the Taoist leader merely follows the flow, shapes the here and now, and naturally grasps the opportunities that cross his path.

An organisation that is open to learning from its surroundings and has a high degree of flexibility built into will find ways to shape the situation, observe and use the new information straightaway in the here and now, apply the new knowledge instantly to the new reality, and be opportunistic and secure quick wins.

For foreigners who work or have worked in Chinese organisations, including the authors, it can be quite daunting to deal with what often looks like chaos. Between Aldo being hired at Fosun and his first day at work, part of his presumed job responsibilities had disappeared. Fosun had in the meantime acquired a company that could cover the same tasks he was assigned. He was simply expected to deal with the situation and find other ways to become useful. Priorities can change quickly based on progress (or lack thereof) in various entrepreneurial ongoing activities.

Chaos is not a problem, if you don't let it surprise you.

Chinese organisations are well equipped, however, to deal with changing circumstances and bring order to chaos. In Section 3.2.3, we described a clear procedure that ensures that everyone in the organisation knows, understands, and delivers toward lofty company goals. Such a process is well suited to deal with fast-changing circumstances.

If everyone is aware that their surroundings are fluid and are given the right tools to deal with it, sanity can be found within presumed insanity. A great example of such a tool is the re-planning process being used inside Alibaba.[24]

To deal with ever-changing surroundings, Alibaba adopted a continuous process of 'replanning'. Rather than meticulously executing a fixed, detailed annual plan, the company keeps revising tactics as circumstances change.

Alibaba does have a regular planning cycle, in which business unit leaders and the executive management team iterate on plans in the fourth quarter of each year.

However, it's understood that this is only a starting point. Whenever a unit leader sees a significant market change or a new opportunity, he or she can initiate a co-creation process, in which employees, including senior business leaders and lead implementers, develop new directions for the business directly with customers.

At Alibaba, co-creation involves four steps:

1. Establishing common ground. Identify signals of change (based on data from the market and insights from customers or staff) and ensure that the right people are present and ready to work together. This typically happens at a full day working session.
2. Getting to know the customer. Now participants explore directly with customers their evolving needs or pain points and brainstorm potential solutions.
3. Developing an action plan based on the outcome of customer discussions. An action plan must identify a leader who can champion the opportunity, the supporting team (or teams) that will put the ideas into motion, and the mechanisms that will enable the work to get done.
4. Gathering regular customer feedback as the plan is implemented. This can, in turn, trigger further iterations.

The co-creation process highlights the self-directed nature of self-tuning enterprises. Alibaba's business units can initiate co-creation sessions whenever they see a relevant market stimulus without any central mandate or oversight.

And although the process follows a successful pattern, each co-creation initiative is tailored to the situation at hand.

By creating a forum for regular exchange with customers, Alibaba is able to evolve synchronously with the market. The approach leaves more room for innovations to bubble up from the market, as opposed to being pushed down from the top of the organisation. Alibaba has found a way to thrive in chaos.

4.3 MAKING ADAPTING POSSIBLE

One can argue that in more established markets with lower growth rates a long-term plan is needed to maximize strategic advantages or a competitive position. Another reason for requiring longer term planning is when companies are listed and stock markets and investors, by law, need to understand the future direction of the company. While the latter is certainly correct, we believe the first can be achieved even with a more flexible approach.

Quickly adapting to change and learning from it may at times work better than rigidly following a plan. Successful Chinese companies demonstrate that you can lead without detailed plans. Summarizing observed best practices of such leading firms, here are thought starters on how to make a less rigid business approach work:

— ADOPT A VISION THAT ALL PEOPLE CAN *RELATE* TO. They keep it simple and focussed on the end-user. It gets their employees and business partners excited about a future they can believe in. For example, Fosun's vision is: *Rooted in China, creating a global happiness ecosystem fulfilling the needs of one billion families in health, happiness, and wealth.* This is bold, simple, yet inspiring and leaving plenty of room for various entrepreneurial endeavours in diverse parts of the company.
— ADOPT A RE-PLANNING PROCESS. Build more flexibility into yearly planning. Rapid change of reality does not need to equate chaos if well managed.
— BRAINSTORM, BRAINSTORM, BRAINSTORM. Brainstorming sessions are daily reality. Group problem solving and new opportunity development is part of business culture. They don't require long alignment sessions. Instead, meeting time is used to jointly find solutions giving many people the feeling they have the opportunity to be heard and to contribute.
— SIMPLIFIED INTERNAL INFORMATION EXCHANGE. The amount of information sharing inside Chinese firms is significant. Apps like WeChat and DingTalk allow for a fast and flexible set-up of groups where people

consistently post interesting articles and ideas for all to see and build on.

— **TESTING AND EXPERIMENTING IS CRITICAL.** (Parts of) the organisation is given the flexibility and freedom to find out where and how new growth can be ignited. Ideas are tested early and often. Opportunities are evaluated on merit more than efficiency.

— **SYSTEMATIC LEARNING SKILLS.** Short cycle times provide fast opportunities to learn and to embrace failure. Then Chinese companies observe, adapt, and try again.

— **CREATION OF ECOSYSTEMS.** Chinese entrepreneurs are masters in creating and leveraging ecosystems. Internal and external co-creation processes, networks, and alliances significantly contribute to idea development, speed to market, risk mitigation, and cost control. In the next chapter we will go much deeper into the topic of such value system creation.

There are many reasons not to do a lot of the above, but many organisations in the developed world are too complex and rigid for the business environment of tomorrow.

And while we recognize the downside of needing duplicate or potentially large additional resources to execute adapt or die tactics, in our view, it is worth it. Experimenting toward a more nimble, agile, and flexible way of working can and will prove the difference.

Test the stones, while crossing the river!

令行禁止

5

**THE EMPEROR
DECIDES. BUT
AGILITY RULES.**

5. THE EMPEROR DECIDES. BUT AGILITY RULES.

'When the Generals are fighting in the fields,
they do not have to obey each order from the King.'

Sun Tzu

Legendary general, military strategist, writer, and philosopher

5.1 A SOVEREIGN HAS ALWAYS BEEN IN CHARGE

The emperor of the Xuantong Era (宣統) was forced to abdicate in 1912. Also known by his personal name Pu Yi (溥儀), he was the last Emperor of China, but not the last Chinese absolute leader.

Throughout most of its history, dating back as far as 2852 BC, China has been ruled by demi-god, Chinese sovereigns. With a past stretching so far back, it will come as no surprise that not a single system nor a single title has been used to describe the leader of its time. But whether called King (王, pinyin: wáng), Son of Heaven, (天子, pinyin: tiānzǐ), or, most commonly known outside China, the Emperor (皇帝, pinyin: huángdì), most of the rulers that have been in the position at some time over these thousands of years have wielded tremendous powers and were treated and acted like living gods.

Whereas in Western philosophy, most notably among Greek thinkers such as Cleisthenes (born around 570 BC) and Socrates (470-399 BC), early democratic thinking was developed that argued for decision making based on the majority principle, Chinese philosophers have mostly adhered and supported absolute leadership.

Heavenly Mandate.

This stemmed from the ancient belief that the legitimate ruler was given the Mandate of Heaven. The leader owed his position to the Heavens, the highest entity in the natural order. It was not required that the ruler was of noble birth, as the mandate depended on how well that person ruled and demonstrated a just and able performance.

The Mandate of Heaven does not provide an unconditional rule. Intrinsic to the concept was the right of rebellion against an unjust ruler. Throughout Chinese history, times of poverty and natural disasters were often taken as signs that heaven considered the incumbent ruler unfit and thus in need of replacement.

Without an automatic birth right for a leader and with the inherent acceptance for the people to revolt, there was enough belief among China's most important thinkers that the system provided safeguards against abuse of power.

Confucius supported this thinking, albeit with an important twist. Absolute power in his view is only legitimate under absolute moral principles. Submission to authority was only taken within the context of the ethical obligations that a ruler had toward his subjects. In particular he was required to show compassion and generosity. He could expect loyalty as long as he ensured his underlings would not starve.

Confucius suggested that those who want to be rulers have to, first of all, be principled leaders having virtuous characters and attitudes to make themselves acceptable. In his words:[1]

If a man manages to make himself correct, what difficulty will there be for him to take part in government? If he cannot make himself correct, what business has he with making others correct?

A leader must therefore always do their duty, do their best, ultimately, to 'achieve moral self-actualization and to build a harmonious socio-political order'.[2]

Confucius subsequently argued for harmonious interpersonal relations in social organisations, more specifically, a mandatory two-way relationship based on a hierarchical liaison. In essence, the leader was allowed to rule from the top but with the obligation to look after his people. In return he could expect loyalty.

Confucianism advocates putting the interests of the collective over that of the individual. This emphasis on hierarchy combined with a diminished role of individuals means that decision making tends to be centralized at the top of the entity. In turn, such thinking has had a large impact on the structure of organisations, turning them into centralized command structures.

WHEN AN ABSOLUTE BOSS IS ALSO A VISIONARY – HUAWEI ORGANISATIONAL SHAKE-UP.

Huawei experienced exponential revenue growth from the mid-1990s onwards. However, the telecom and IT giants were still far ahead. How to further accelerate development, and what levers to use? Ren Zhengfei was worried that the motivation of employees was weakening. Huawei's recent successes in the home market were causing teams to relax too much and even show a certain self-satisfaction.

The former soldier could not stand this. He then made a decision at the end of 1995, which would be seen as an earthquake in the company. On December 26, he asked each manager of the sales division, including the president of the department, to simultaneously draft an activity report on the past year as well as a letter of resignation. For a month, this massive resignation campaign rocked the organisation and at the end one in three managers was dismissed. The method was radical and risky, but it fulfilled its four objectives: to bring new blood with a new generation at the helm; to prevent the installation of bad habits; not to depend on the network of a few alone; encourage self-criticism.

More generally, it is this feeling of permanent crisis that Ren Zhengfei wanted to instill internally: he himself was deeply aware of Huawei's vulnerability and wanted everyone in the organisation to have this awareness that nothing is ever acquired in a market in perpetual motion. This episode also created a strong sense of belonging for those who stayed and gave them that urge to fight back.

This event became the starting point for two draconian and founding decisions of the management of the company: each year, all employees are evaluated on objective criteria and the less performing ones are reoriented. Furthermore, an employee cannot occupy the same position for more than three consecutive years and must progress whatever happens to higher or lower functions if his results are not there. The whole idea is never to settle down in one's comfort zone. Another example is Huawei rotating management: For almost 20 years, Huawei has adopted a principle of rotating management at the head of the company, where three CEOs simultaneously occupy the management of the company, each for 6 months. This original principle aims to ensure fair representation of the main departments of the company.

Source: A Success Called Huawei, Vincent Ducrey[3]

Top-down organisations still rule...

Whereas in government and in many state-owned enterprises this has resulted in more rigid organisations with more layers that slow down the decision-making process, in more entrepreneurial, founder driven companies the opposite has happened.

A foreign lawyer we know well who works in a leading Chinese law firm told us half-jokingly that within his firm there is a rule of 'one man, one vote'. So, it is very important to understand how that one man (the founder, of course) votes!

Just like the law firm, most Chinese private companies still favour top-down organisational structures. But in an unstable business world, where speed of decision making and improvisation are crucial success factors, organisations with an absolute boss tend to spread wide rather than go deep.

...but are embedded with agility.

Instead of building a huge hierarchical organisation with layers and layers of professional managers, they're keeping structures flat and flexible.

Chinese entrepreneurs quite often have as many direct reports as possible or rather as needed. They encourage teams to mobilize and demobilize as they take on specific strategic initiatives. They are building in flexibility, not rigidity. As a result, at least at the top, there are no long consensual decision-making processes needed.

The law firm chairman is universally respected and has the final decision-making power. He is not aloof from the (daily) operations of the law firm and is kept well informed of all aspects.

There is a group of partners who are responsible for managing the firm, but the founder sets the vision, encourages and selects partners to lead an initiative, and if the initiative does not go in the right direction the founder himself will intervene and either new people will be assigned to the initiative; or the initiative will be quickly discarded, without much discussion. No feelings are hurt.

Fosun demonstrates that this approach also works at a much larger scale. The conglomerate is officially organized in three 'ecosystems': Health, Wealth, and Happiness. These three pillars are then officially further divided into nine subgroups, ranging from Pharma & Healthcare to Tourism, Fashion, or Investment, etc.

These groups are made up of at least 50 business units and individual companies either fully or partially owned by the Fosun Group. And a majority of the leaders of these companies or units report directly to both the Chairman Guo Guangchang and co-Chairman Wang Qunbin. Where not, both leaders are still on a regular basis involved in very detailed decisions within these units. In fact, it will be near impossible for any smaller unit, whatever its size, to make critical decisions without them having been discussed in detail with the Chairman or co-Chairman.

And the speed at which this happens is astonishing. From Aldo's own experience, whenever a decision was needed, a meeting with the chairman or with the extended leadership was possible, often on short notice. What was even more remarkable is how well prepared and knowledgeable the leadership was, even for businesses that, turnover-wise, only made up a fraction of the group revenues.

The speed at which Chinese founders can move was also demonstrated when Sandrine wanted to sell her business. It all started with a Saturday morning conversation with the founder and CEO of the company that ended up acquiring her company.

He immediately stated his interest clearly and set his timeline: a term sheet signed in two weeks and a full closing in one and a half months. This step was the necessary trigger from the top.

From there, a thorough due diligence had to be conducted (the company is listed in New York and Hong Kong) and all legal preparation work finalized. Mobilizing large teams that worked around the clock and across the Western New Year holiday, his plan was never in doubt and the CEO's timeline was respected.

5.2 DRIVEN FROM THE TOP, YET MOVING AT HIGH SPEED

Given the relatively short existence of a market economy in the Middle Kingdom and the ensuing explosive growth of the business world in just over 30 years, the vast majority of Chinese enterprises, even the very large companies operating today, began as a start-up.

When a company has few employees, a flat organisation is the logical structure to build. In a more hierarchical environment — as the company grows — more layers of management would normally be added.

However, as described earlier in this chapter, Chinese entrepreneurs have resisted such layering and have kept their structures flat while maintaining strict control.

Traditional organisational thinking and even plain common sense would say that placing so much decision-making power centrally would slow down an organisation, especially when it grows significantly in size. Yet we have observed the opposite. Even large organisations such as Fosun remain nimble and entrepreneurial.

The work ethic and hours worked in Chinese organisations, including their leaders, is high, which would partially explain their ability for speed. However, the fact that Chinese companies can move as fast as they do is clearly a derivative of how they are organized.

We identified five areas that enable such agility despite a central command:

1. Decentralisation is the secret of a centralised organisation;
2. Think in projects not in departments;
3. Compete internally as hard as you can;
4. Build ecosystems;
5. Flat is not just for the small.

5.2.1 Decentralising is the secret of a centralised organisation

As described in the previous chapter, *Adapt to Change or Die*, to keep pace not just with a rapidly changing market but also with differences in the level of development across the country, Chinese companies need constant adaptation.

To allow for such a high degree of agility while maintaining control, Chinese entrepreneurs have therefore created organisational structures that, while keeping power firmly at the top, simultaneously grant business units significant autonomy to keep them nimble and their individual contributors involved. Dating back to imperial China, and even nowadays as reflected in the management of the People's Republic of China, this type of organization has always been favoured and therefore a natural source of inspiration for Chinese entrepreneurs.

Chinese leaders are well aware that hierarchy discourages ownership. There is even a Chinese phrase for it: 本份 (pinyin: běn fèn, lit. one's duty) or put in context, dutifully sticking to one's role. But, in Chinese organisations, more is expected from individuals. One is expected to contribute to the output of the team and the success of the enterprise. Individuals that can hide under layers of hierarchy and by doing so skirt their responsibilities and do not add value.

While a large number of decisions have to pass the founder or the leader, in such decentralised, flat yet top-down organisations, each team is given enough authority and ownership of the part of the business it is in charge of.

A good example is how at Tencent, the WeChat team, is organized.[4] It is a top-down driven decision structure but with significant freedom to explore and innovate. The organisation of WeChat is very flat. Allen Zhang, the creator of WeChat, one of the largest internet products globally, serving over 1 billion users, has 20 senior managers reporting to him, and each manager is in charge of a team of 50 to 150 people.

Although final decision-making sits with Allen Zhang, the WeChat management approach still relies on the joint work of many small autonomous teams. And the top-down approval of core product features doesn't prevent freedom and innovation at the team level.

In WeChat, each team has its own R&D members, developers, product manager, and testing group. Each team can independently complete a project without asking for help from another team.

This is very different from the traditional function-oriented team structure. This agile approach unavoidably creates duplicate resources. But it maximizes the ownership and speed of creating a new feature. Each team can build, and all teams are allowed to try new approaches and make mistakes. It also creates a healthy dose of internal competition, something that we will explore in more detail in Section 5.2.3 Compete internally – as hard as you can.

The high level of autonomy, the simplified reporting structure, and the need for fast decisions means that the approval process is kept simple. In the chapter *Wolf Culture*, we described how Chinese entrepreneurial organisations create consensus around what needs to be achieved and how progress toward targets is kept on track.

The result of such a process is that between the leader and the team there is already a high degree of shared knowledge about the many issues at hand. And with a disdain for long presentations, leaders are brought up to speed on the key elements of the decision needed to be taken, and a go or no-go often follows almost immediately.

5.2.2 Think in projects, not departmental silos

Traditional hierarchical organisations are shaped like a pyramid. A command structure relies on a vertical chain of authority, with the CEO at the top, several layers of management underneath, and consisting of distinct departments each with a specific function.

Such a configuration enables large numbers of employees to work together and clarifies reporting relationships. But such a model is also prone to create bureaucracy, is likely to result in departmental silo behaviour, and slows down approval processes because decisions need to pass upward through the hierarchy to be approved.

Xiaomi Corporation, a maker of smartphones and smart devices, is proving that foregoing such traditional structures is possible, both organisationally as well as in terms of profits. While management now realizes, as they grow larger and their business gets more complex, that some elements of a more traditional organisation are needed, they still maintain a very agile organisational model.

Founded in 2010, in 2020 Xiaomi became the third largest smartphone maker in the world.[5] Four years after their first phone was launched they outsold Apple in China. The company then went on an innovation spree with the aim to reduce pain points for Chinese consumers, launching an array of products, most of them successful. By 2018, they had created over 40 internet connected devices, ranging from smart rice cookers and air purifiers to robot vacuum cleaners and even fitness bands and power banks.

What makes Xiaomi stand out, however, is its organisational model. Prior to 2019, with already over 15000 employees, the company was not organized in business units or departments and only had three organisational layers consisting of the seven co-founders, departmental leaders, and its employees.

Today however, its structure is more reflective of the harsh reality that bringing products to market, especially at the speed of Xiaomi, requires strong business basics such as a stable supply chain and sufficient business support.

Starting in 2018, Xiaomi therefore restructured itself and is now a networked, ecosystem-based organisation arranged around core competencies, each led by a co-founder, such as e-commerce, hardware, routers and cloud, UI, and internet TV. This ecosystem is further strengthened by several strategically important supporting departments that together cover IP, internal and external affairs, finance, legal, and international expansion.

Xiaomi Organisation (after December 2019)

Source: Bo Mingdun

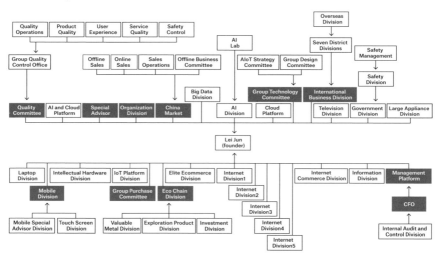

Please note: the red Divisions are overseen by a Group Vice President or higher levels.

However, despite now having a more structured organisation, Xiaomi is still a highly versatile and exceptionally flat company where they approach product development as cross functional projects, just as it did with only three organisational layers. Xiaomi may be creating products in diverse categories; all products are linked to the same internet ecosystem and as such have high interdependencies between the various competencies across the organisation. And so, capabilities are brought in as needed.

The co-founders are also still required to be directly involved with new product development directly. Each new product is still treated as a project that can be achieved by mobilizing resources inside and outside Xiaomi.

Laser-focused on getting prototypes to market as soon as possible, Xiaomi relies on its key competences: customer interaction, technological prowess, and design. They emphasise project-driven product development and marketing rather than manufacturing.

Such customer-driven projects gain speed by leveraging external resources within its ecosystem. After its three initial designs — the smartphone, TV set top box, and router — all subsequent Xiaomi products were developed as projects in collaboration with other companies or entrepreneurs [for more on this, see Section 5.2.4 about ecosystems].

5.2.3 Compete internally – as hard as you can

For a country founded on communist ideals, its society has perhaps somewhat surprisingly long relied on more primal instincts. Survival of the fittest is a concept that is common in the Middle Kingdom.

The need to win, or rather the fear of losing, is an important part of life and is fittingly expressed in a well-known Chinese paradigm: 胜者为王，败者为寇, (pinyin: shèng zhě wéi wáng, bài zhě wéi kòu) which translates as The victor becomes a king, and the loser becomes a bandit.

In present day China, competition is at an all-time high, a direct result of China's massive population of 1.4 billion and its drive to modernize, develop, and create wealth. To get into a prestigious university or obtain a well-paying job, individuals must compete against hundreds (and often thousands) of other people vying for the same position. When in 2006 we launched the first Adidas China Trainee program we had seven positions available. Yet we received over 16,000 applications! The numbers have come down a bit since but were still well over 12,000 for 16 positions in 2020.

Competition and the need to win thus comes naturally to China's entrepreneurs and business leaders. And this drive to win is not limited to external competition only.

In survival driven, high stakes Wolf Culture type environments, everyone is expected to contribute ideas. Internal competition is therefore encouraged, and, in the end, it is survival of the fittest. Intuitively making sense in a winner takes all market requires rapid innovation. Yes, this agile approach inevitably creates duplicate resources. But it maximizes ownership and speed. Ultimately, does it really matter if you spend twice the resource on the short term if it doubles the chance to win against an external competitor? When the future is uncertain and competition is strong, embracing chaos might be the best way to move forward.

And where there are winners, there will be losers. But a typical Chinese entrepreneur expects people to bounce back from losses, pick themselves up, and start over — because it is precisely what he or she did to get where he or she is.

Organize horse races.

Chinese private companies often let horse races between internal teams decide the winner. These are internal battles, where two teams can (sometimes unknowingly) work on variations of the same product lines. Or they can be open, for all to see head-to-head internal battles between two individuals to determine who will be employed or promoted.

When Aldo was first hired at Fosun he was up against another candidate. Not because his future direct boss was considering two alternatives, but because one of the leaders his future boss reported to was considering his own candidate. The internal proposal was to hire both Aldo and the other contender, let them race for six months against each other, and keep the winner and terminate the loser. A practice fully accepted and widely used.

The use of internal competition is also well established for new product development, with WeChat being a notorious example. This highly successful product is the result of a famous horse race between three internal teams at Tencent: Two teams within the wireless business unit (the Q letter team and the team of QQ mobile, at the time one of the leading Tencent products) and the upstarts that ended up winning the race, led by Allen Zhang.

In 2010, mobile usage was skyrocketing and this surge was a new opportunity to be exploited. Allen Zhang, who had previously developed an email client system called Foxmail (subsequently acquired by Tencent and branded QQmail)[6], was at that time a mid-level manager with some time on his hands. He used this time well to stay up to speed on internet trends, and while doing so had come across Kik Messenger, a product launched in 2009 by a group of students from the University of Waterloo in Canada.

Zhang was concerned that Kik or similar products could rival Tencent's QQ and he asked the founder of Tencent, Pony Ma, for permission to create a competitor to Kik. Ma agreed to go ahead despite other teams, including QQ, plugging away on similar products.

Zhang set up an autonomous unit in Guangzhou, away from the Shenzhen headquarters. By giving the project the green light, Ma in effect gave Zhang full license to cannibalize the existing QQ product. He delivered. Riding the wave of increased mobile use, WeChat soared and today has more than 1 billion users worldwide.

Another interesting horse race example comes from Xibei Oat Noodle Village, a restaurant chain founded in Linhe, in Inner Mongolia, in China's northern region.

One of the largest restaurant chains in China, it specializes in the hearty and richly flavoured food of China's northern Shanxi Province. It is also known for its entrepreneurial drive and internal competition.

To motivate store employees and to stimulate growth, Xibei Oat Noodle Village has created a system of entrepreneurial divisions complemented by a competitive gaming system called the 'Xibei-style partner plan'.

The restaurant chain is divided into thirteen entrepreneurial divisions. To emphasize the unity within each of these operational entities, sub-branches are named after the main unit and each entrepreneurial team within each of the divisions is a partner in the plan and has the right to collect dividends from its operations.

Although the units cover separate geographical areas, this territory allocation is not exclusive, and two entrepreneurial divisions can conduct business at the same time in the same region.

Xibei headquarters will coordinate the location selection of entrepreneurial branches to ensure that divisions are in healthy competition, rather than harming the company's interest; but beyond that, it is game on among the stores controlled by each division.

In a system inspired by sports, there are various competitions between employees. Not only is there significant prize money to fight for, it is a fight for survival. Each store team is ranked based on key performance indicators such as profit, customer evaluation, store environment, and menu innovation, etc.

Each store team that finds itself in the bottom 30% gets their operating license withdrawn and the team will be broken up. Their members will then be reassigned to other teams, so that employees can still prove their personal abilities in the next grouping. To avoid losing good employees, Xibei will pay all salaries as usual when the team is in the transition period.

This system gives top-ranked teams the control over store expansion. And for most stores, the quality of food and service will continue to improve incentivised by the possible loss of license.

Go Amoeba Style – run your business in units of three.
Internal competition does not stop with horse races. There is another rather unusual organisational model, one that in our view embodies a lot of other elements of Dragon Tactics, too: 'Amoeba Style'.

Pioneered by Zhao Yingguang, the founder of Handu Yishe, an online fashion company and Tmall store operator based in Jinan in Northern China, the model has gained devotees among Chinese business leaders, and not just among pure digital players.

The core of Amoeba Style management is that an organisation is split into units of three people who, while competing with each other, ultimately all contribute toward the overall company goals through their joint output.

In a highly competitive business environment, the 'unit-of-three system' can stimulate rapid growth with agility and customer focus. This will even be the case in larger organisations. The model ensures that products are highly relevant to their target audience. But if not, the enterprise will fall behind, or worse, be out of the game.

If it is good enough for the army...

The amoeba model has been used successfully outside China as well, notably by legendary Japanese business leader Kazuo Inamori, who among others founded Kyocera (a producer of industrial ceramics, semiconductor components, electronics devices, and information and telecommunication equipment) and turned around Japanese Airlines when it was close to bankruptcy.

Inamori is credited with the invention of amoeba management in business. He initially developed the organisational methodology to make it easier for ordinary employees without an operations or finance background to see how they can contribute to the success of the business, and he went on to make it the core of Kyocera's management model.[7]

In China however, the model's origin can also be traced back to the Chinese military. As described at the beginning of Part 2, in Chapter 3 *Wolf Culture*, China's modern history, and subsequently its business management thinking, is substantially shaped by military strategy. Such philosophy is also at the basis of this unit-of-three, or Amoeba model.

During the Chinese civil war in the aftermath of the second world war, Mao Zedong's Communist forces ultimately achieved victory over the huge, modernized, American-equipped armies Chiang Kai-shek had sent to fight the Communists for control of China's Northeast territories, Manchuria.

To overcome this vastly superior force, the military leadership instructed their troops to fight in the three-three system. Under this system, a platoon would be organized into three or four teams of three or four men each.[8]

While it was essential to concentrate superior troop strength at the strategic and operational levels, at the tactical level of combat manoeuvre, they dispersed troops, spreading them out and giving them sufficient flexibility to make the best situational decisions toward their survival while overcoming the opposing army.

Having lots of soldiers did not mean they all had to charge at the same time in the same direction. The three-three system sidestepped herd behaviour and maximized operational effectiveness and survival.

...it can work in business too!

Survival and efficiencies were exactly what Handu Yishe's founder, Zhao Yingguang, wanted to find. Avoiding herd thinking was another benefit.

Through his work as a translator in a state-owned Sino-Korean trading house, Zhao realized that Korean fashion was increasingly trendy in China. Wanting to start a fashion business but lacking the resources, he started offering products available from websites of Korean fashion businesses and brands on his own website for sale in China. But he soon realized it was hard to select the right products from the thousands of possible items. And he was facing operational challenges with all the original product information available online only in Korean language, which had to be translated for his own site.

His response was to recruit 40 students. Half of them studied fashion design and were keenly aware of the latest trends in fashion. The other half studied Korean and could develop the necessary product information for his website. Immediately, the business took off.

Generating steady revenue, Zhao's next step was to start his own production, adding a third responsibility to his mini teams. The original buyers now became responsible for design and product images and the translators continued online marketing support and customer interaction with the third member of the cell responsible for production and inventory.

With workloads often being shared and people gravitating to the colleagues they worked with best, the amoeba seed was planted. Linking the income of each unit directly to its own sales and profits, the amoeba model was in place.

In the process, Zhao created a highly competitive organisation. The ultimate proof of what is fashionable is based on what sells well, so early on he gave his frontline teams the responsibility to create and develop their own products in competition with each other. Zhao Yingguang built his organisation around permanent horse races, while still being mindful that internal competition is not detrimental to overall company success.

To enable growth and stability and to avoid unnecessary battles for available resources, Zhao realised that a structure was needed to hold his amoeba organisation together. He went on to create a planning and coordination department, set up company logistics, and created digital systems for all to use. Contracts between the departments and the amoeba keep the structure firmly in place and working in sync.

Handu Yishe organisational philosophy

Before: pyramidal management structure

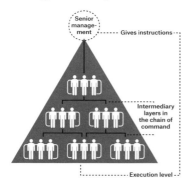

After: customer centered management structure

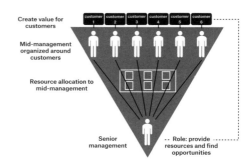

Internal competition / Flat sharing of resources / << just a job >> mentality / Company centered processes

Open and win-win culture / Resources and income according to performance / Autonomy at work / Customer centered processes

Source: Handu Yishe

The advantages of the model are clear: Employees work with the same dedication as when they are their own boss and it lets everyone in the company consider on a personal level the company and its needs. The model increases the speed of overall enterprise development while reducing overall cost because waste is kept to a minimum. Company money equates own money.

The model also helps to attract and keep talent. Being entrepreneurial and the dream of having one's own company drive many employees in China. In a market with a gradual shortage of labour, the talent market scale is tipping even farther away from the enterprise and toward the talent. An amoeba model gives them the best of both worlds: to be entrepreneurial while still having sufficient access to the needed resources to grow.

A third advantage, in particular in digital environments, is that it brings data management much closer to product development. Rather than collecting large stacks of information centrally with the risk that analysis and usage of the data become disconnected or biased, in the amoeba model where small cells are responsible for their own output, the use of market and consumer data is kept close to where it brings the most benefits.

Can the model work for other companies? Why not? In Western business organisations, for example, a product development department would be structured in three distinct teams, one responsible for design, one for development, and another one for sourcing, dividing responsibility for the end result over various teams and reducing individual accountability for the final products in the process.

In a three-unit system, a mini team is directly responsible for the financial results of the products they create, significantly increasing their exposure and contribution to overall results. May the best team win! And they often do!

In a business world that is increasingly digital with large online product offerings on various platforms, where target audiences are less brand loyal and where brands have a weakened ability to build brand coherence, is top-down design and development really still the superior method?

Would it not be more beneficial to have very agile teams that not only are able to move fast, but also represent the various thoughts and opinions of each team, exposing them to market pressures in real time to find out what works?

Yes, the model will have inevitable effects on how a brand is built. Full consumer centricity and opportunism will put pressure on a brands' consistency, but in a fast-moving digital world developing towards platform-based economic models with high frequency consumer contact, this is not by definition all bad.

And it does not mean building a brand and business in a three-unit system is a free-for-all. Product and brand guidelines and parameters can still be set. Yet, they are debated in an annual cycle and adjusted based on what has worked best over the most recent six months — agility at its best.

Outside China, Kyocera and many other companies also prove that a decentralised management system like amoeba management drives Dragon Tactics. The model is designed to spur market agility, customer focus and team empowerment. It can reinforce performance management processes, human resource selection, and training and it will drive the successful implementation of an organisation's strategy. Last but not least, you can expect an amoeba organisation to fully explore opportunities for new innovations.

5.2.4 Ecosystems – *The* solution for scale and agility
Covering approximately 9,600,000 square kilometres, with a population of over 1.4 billion, the scale of China is unique. 300 cities with a population of 1M or more, 14 with 10M+, the People's Republic of China is the world's most populous country and the 4th largest country by landmass.

Yet, although China consists of a large number of governmental entities (34 provinces split into 2,851 counties and nearly 40,000 townships) and has vast differences in culture, landscape, climate, religion, and language, the internal market is surprisingly homogeneous [See comment on page 41] with limited restrictions for expanding beyond provincial borders.

The competitive power of scale.

For a business operating in China, this scale is both a challenge as well as a great opportunity. Once a product works somewhere, conquering the rest of the country is often a matter of time and money. But in a market known for hyper competition [see Section 4.1], the speed of achieving sufficient size is of the essence. With often razor-thin margins and a winner-takes-all mentality, Chinese firms believe that scale means survival. The larger the roll-out becomes, the greater the profit and the chance to invest in that survival.

But that is where the challenge begins, not just for the entrepreneurs that started out in the early days of China's market economy, when a large part of the business infrastructure did not yet exist, but still today when either owned or internal resources are insufficient to scale up fast and access to bank resources is very limited to become for private companies. The practical solution: Scale through ecosystems.

With cashflow limited and risks high, many businesses are able to grow fast by outsourcing many parts of the business cycle. From department stores or home appliance retailers such as Gome or Suning (that never owned stock but rent out square meters to independent suppliers which display and sell the goods), to franchise networks that span the vast country, to intricate digital ecosystems that enable multi apps like Meituan Dianping, alliances and cooperation is everywhere.

In the Chinese business environment, it has always been important for the players in the community to both compete directly with one another and to interact and cooperate. Since the beginning of commerce, and all over China, concentrations of sellers of the same products have grouped together, ranging from the multi-story 'light market' or 'glasses market' in Shanghai that respectively house hundreds of sellers of light fixtures and glasses frames and lenses, to the world's largest tea market in Guangzhou with 6,000 tea shops next to each other.

Internationally better-known examples would be the world-famous Yiwu Small Commodities Market, which is in essence an entire town made up of small and medium sized traders supplying almost anything globally, or digital platforms such as the original Alibaba B2B suppliers' platform, and Taobao, the B2C/C2C shopping platform for sellers and resellers of a variety of products and goods.

Such platforms not only help small scale operators attract customers, but they can also provide payment and credit check services, user-generated feedback and rating information, shared logistics, and so forth. The large-scale markets have become mega-brands in themselves that draw in the crowds.

No Ecosystem. No Future.

In a business environment where scale ensures future, one of the most interesting business model concepts that was pioneered by Chinese business leaders is the creation of ecosystems. They think partnerships, not assets.

All Chinese entrepreneurs, big or small, believe they have to create their own business support networks. This started when China first opened its market economy. Chinese founders often needed to build almost everything from the ground up since not much existed back then: basic business skills in recruitment, supplier networks, government ties, capital sources, and even at times dormitories for employees. Often lacking time, money, and resources to do it all by themselves, they looked around for help. Although the market has matured a lot since, the idea of ecosystem has remained, while evolving over time.

As an organisational form, ecosystems have developed beyond internal structures but are still used to maximize limited resources, manage risk, and stay agile while growing. Also, rather than retaining full control over all elements of the ecosystem, entrepreneurs have accepted that building alliances without full power can be equally beneficial.

With the rise of digital platforms, organisational boundaries are blurring further as companies like Alibaba, Xiaomi, and Haier are clearly demonstrating. Leadership is no longer defined by the assets you own, but rather by your role in the ecosystem that surrounds you.[9]

Today, a business ecosystem is a dynamic network of entities interacting with one another, creating and exchanging value. Some companies in the ecosystem can be 100% owned subsidiaries, minority investments, or simple commercial partnerships. Business ecosystems offer firms unprecedented access to more resources and talents. And the larger the ecosystem, the more competitive it will become in efficiently and rapidly addressing evolving market needs.

The endless Alibaba ecosystem.

Alibaba Group is today one of the world's largest retailers and e-commerce players. But it is not one company. Nor does it have just one specific business model. Its success can be largely attributed to its innovative organisational form, a business ecosystem, which has enabled the rapid growth and transformation of its businesses since the company was founded in 1999.

According to Jack Ma, any empire can fall, but an ecosystem can be endless. Enabling multiple simultaneous bets in non-core activities, the Alibaba ecosystem allowed the company to pursue new opportunities while minimizing distraction in existing fast-growing parts of the business.

Letting new ventures run as separate units also allows horse races and lets the market decide winning concepts without financial risks to the overall company. And it brings a self-perpetuating force to growth and earning ability. The more the members of the ecosystem earn, the more the builders of the ecosystem earn.

CAINIAO – AN ECOSYSTEM WITHIN AN ECOSYSTEM...AND BEYOND.

Alibaba never planned to be a logistics company. From its earliest days, Jack Ma Yun, its founder, believed instead that Alibaba should make use of China's existing logistics infrastructure, rather than build a complete fulfilment system by itself. As he once remarked, 'it is impossible for a company to manage more than 1 million employees to do express delivery'.

And yet, today he probably directs triple that number of couriers. But Alibaba is still not a logistics company. Instead, it owns just under half of the Cainiao Smart Logistics Network, an Alibaba-led consortium founded in 2013. Cainiao, which means 'rookie', sees itself as a 'newcomer to the logistics scene'. But it is a beginner with a clear ambition to shake up that scene completely.

Cainiao's aim is to create a single ecosystem for all logistics firms across the world. Just as numerous smartphone makers operate on Google's Android, Cainiao envisages thousands of independent logistics firms operating within its system, sharing everything from labelling standards to customs information and allowing for the seamless transfer of goods between companies and jurisdictions.

'What they're doing is bigger than it appears to be', says Jeffrey Towson, a professor of investment at Peking University in Beijing. 'It might be the single most important thing happening in China's digital space.'

Cainiao is far from a typical logistics firm. It is **an open platform** that allows for collaboration with thousands of logistics partners, including 70 carriers covering over 150 countries, encompassing the top 15 delivery firms inside China. The data platform drives real efficiencies in China's logistics industry and beyond by connecting e-commerce companies with players along the logistics chain to enable end-to-end solutions.

The network allows merchants to choose the most cost- and time-efficient delivery option, based upon real-time data crunching of optimum firms and routes. And, by putting sensors in everything — along with cameras in every warehouse and GPS on every truck and package — Cainiao aims to digitize the logistics process from top to bottom.

Just as Google's Android has millions of software engineers around the world creating products to operate within it, so Cainiao's system offers an incentive for builders of apps and logistics infrastructure — such as the self-driving robotic delivery vehicle Xiao G — to create products up to the Cainiao standard, knowing that they can be sold to any of the thousands of firms tied to it.

Alibaba took a collaborative approach to logistics. Cainiao is a consortium — an ecosystem within the Alibaba ecosystem with in-house capabilities and enlarging its big data competences with every delivery, but without the investment in logistics hardware.

Source: Time, Inc & Medium.com[10 & 11]

Today, the Alibaba business ecosystem consist of hundreds of companies, ventures and projects across at least 20 different sectors. Alibaba is a dynamic system of companies, ventures, and projects all enabled by digital technology. Instead of directing the development of new products and implementation of all projects top-down, Alibaba now often functions more as the gravity provider and network orchestrator.[12]

Giving up some level of control is imperative in such a system. Many ventures are independently run operations, neither part of strategic business units, nor subject to reporting structures. And yet, Alibaba remains a cohesive platform driven by a shared vision of the future and a highly flexible business planning process.

The interdependence is maintained in collective growth strategies, investment approaches, and resource sharing. Entrepreneurial projects in this ecosystem are allowed to fail without severe consequences for the sustainability of the whole ecosystem, or the careers of top management. The consequence of such a value-driven approach is encouragement toward taking risks, a strong organisational culture, and internal competition.

A set of strong principles guide the employees to operate in this highly dynamic environment. They can initiate any project they like without regard to their current company or department. In fact, the ecosystem of Alibaba provides a safe marketplace of resources in which project initiators can execute without the limits of corporate hierarchical boundaries and complex vertical reporting structures.

Alibaba has made considerable efforts in keeping its business ecosystem entrepreneurial. It has been, by far, the most active generator of new chief executives in China. By the beginning of 2016, over 450 individuals had emerged from Alibaba to start their own ventures.

In total, over 250 start-ups have been established by former Alibaba employees, many within the ecosystem of Alibaba, leveraging its rich resources and opportunities.

The Xiaomi MiOT Ecosystem.

In Section 5.2.2 above we already featured Xiaomi's organisational model that allows it to work in projects. This flexible system is supported by a network of businesses that enable and support its overall corporate activities.

Xiaomi's core competence is customer-focused product design and development, rather than manufacturing. As a result, the enterprise is able to deliver good-quality user-centric products fast by leveraging external yet connected resources without the investments in production and R&D that a traditional organisational model would require.

As we mentioned in Section 5.2.2, all Xiaomi products created since their three original designs (smartphone, TV set-top box, and router) were developed as projects in collaboration with other companies or entrepreneurs. This ecosystem is responsible for some of Xiaomi's greatest successes, such as the smart air-purifiers or its connected home ecosystem MiJia.

Xiaomi sees itself as the builder of the Internet of Things (IoT). Named MiOT, their vision was first described in the 'Xiaomi Ecosystem Plan', launched in 2013. In this blueprint, the foundation was laid toward leveraging its core technologies to promote the development of IoT platforms and become the leader in the IoT industry.

Today, Xiaomi's IoT platform covers many household areas, and has become — in the company's own assessment — the world's leading consumer IoT platform. As of 2020 Xiaomi Corporation has invested in over 300 ecosystem partners, with more than 100 focusing on the development of smart hardware and lifestyle products.

Around the world, increasingly more people are aware of the brand and company Xiaomi due to its global success of its smart phones. However, not many people know that all their products that are not either a smartphone or a smart TV are not truly Xiaomi products in the sense of having been developed and produced fully inhouse by Xiaomi.

The reality is that Xiaomi invests in small satellite companies and sub-brands. These stakes are often a minority investment, which leaves the businesses autonomous. While Xiaomi does not control these companies, they share corporate culture and positioning. Quality control, marketing, and sales will also involve Xiaomi. Last but not least, Xiaomi has complete patent and marketing rights for these products.

By sharing technology and development resources and by creating a central marketing platform under the trusted Xiaomi brand, 'millet' (as 小米 xiaomi translates in English) has managed to create an ecosystem that makes it look much larger on the surface than it is underneath. Xiaomi provides a brand platform and distribution opportunity for many smaller entrepreneurs that otherwise would have had many more difficulties getting attention for their products. A win-win for both parties.

Xiaomi even has its own crowdfunding platform — a starting point for up-and-coming companies that want to make a difference in the world with their innovative inventions.

MIOT and the ecosystem that was derived from it have turned Xiaomi into one of the most versatile tech companies globally. This Xiaomi ecological chain now even cooperates with foreign enterprises such as Philips for desk lights and Honeywell for fire alarms.

In the mind of Liu De, one of the co-founders of Xiaomi, smart gadgets today live in the third era of their evolution. First came computers with internet connection. Then the internet landed on our smartphones. But now, practically all electronic devices, home appliances, means of transport, and a lot of little gizmos are hooking up to the internet, which allows them to interact with each other. Xiaomi has been one of the driving forces that is making that happen. Their ecosystem is turning it into a reality.

Fosun: The health, happiness, and wealth ecosystem.

Fosun International is another interesting example to highlight. As a diverse non-digitally native conglomerate, they are turning themselves into a digital ecosystem.

Fosun was founded in 1992 by five graduates of Fudan University in Shanghai, one of China's top universities. Having started out providing market research services, over its 28 years of operations, Fosun has developed into a diverse conglomerate with assets under management of nearly 700bn RMB (approx. 99 bn US$).[13]

The company initially followed a similar approach as many other early-stage Chinese entrepreneurs, opportunistically capturing whatever prospect they could find to make money. With close ties to the biogenetics department of Fudan, Fosun—复星 (pinyin: Fù xīng), or Stars of Fudan, as the five enterprising students ended up calling their company—evolved from market researchers into the developer and supplier of Hepatitis B diagnostics kits. From there, growing rapidly into a biomedicine technology company, they became in 1998 the first listed enterprise in Shanghai. They then used their IPO proceeds to invest in ailing state-owned pharma enterprises and the real-estate market.

This sparked their move toward becoming an investment firm, and over the following two decades the group evolved rapidly, investing beyond pharma and real-estate in various other industries such as insurance, banking, manufacturing, retail, fashion, and even sports and entertainment. Driven by a very opportunistic investment culture and a penchant for great deals, the group became so diverse that it was hard to understand its business focus.

Having had a strong emphasis since the founding of their company on technology and research and development, Chairman Guo Guangchang and the remaining co-founders set out to redesign the group they had built, using technology to drive not only synergies, but in the long run, become a truly digital platform organisation.

Following their company vision to create a global happiness ecosystem fulfilling the needs of one billion families in health, happiness, and wealth, Fosun today aims to create a multiplier effect through synergies between various industries. Fosun aspires to combine all the strengths and fruits of innovation for its health, happiness, and wealth ecosystems to provide comprehensive, one-stop solutions for its customers worldwide.

The key to the creation of this business ecosystem lies in a strong digital backbone, equipped with advanced information technology and smart systems: a digital mid-layer combining Big Data and AI that will enhance both the efficiency and connectivity of Fosun's ecosystem.

Companywide, everyone now thinks in synergies and digital solutions. To fully connect the various membership programs within Fosun's many independent assets, they have started linking up these businesses through the Youle Customer Loyalty Program (有乐). Other platforms, such as the IDERA property development platform enables the sharing of knowledge.

In 2018, Fosun Cloud was launched. It empowers several dozen companies within Fosun's ecosystem by providing them cloud computing and various smart technologies. Moreover, the company rolled out several smart management sub-systems, such as intelligent finance and HR platforms and other online platforms, to enhance the efficiency of management and operation of both the mid and back offices.

In addition, Onelinkplus, a centralized purchasing platform, has been developed to enhance Fosun's procurement and supply chain management capabilities, the latter being the springboard toward their long term C2M (Customer to Maker) vision linking consumers directly to Fosun's intelligent manufacturing capacity in various industries.

Fosun's self-incubated Fonova is helping its tourism, culture, commerce, and retail units to digitalize and intelligentize their operations with smart technologies such as Big Data and AI.

In their health unit, Fosun has also developed specific programs, such as the Xingqiao Program, which enables the application of Big Data analytics to its health businesses. With diversified products and services, Fosun is able to integrate its various businesses and form a closed-loop health ecosystem.

In the words of founder and Chairman Guo:[14]

> *Investment is in Fosun's genes and is a very important component of our business success. However, investment is not our ultimate goal, rather, it should serve to complement the development of our industrial businesses, oriented towards the demands of families worldwide for 'health, happiness, and wealth' products and services, Fosun is now building a global ecosystem that brings happiness to everyone!*

5.2.5 Flat is not just for the small

As the idea of speed driven by flat organisational structures and ecosystems gained traction in China, even large enterprises started transforming themselves. As has been the case for much of its existence, the world's largest home appliance giant, Haier Group, is leading the way, with their so-called Platform Organisation. Haier is arguably one of the most agile large companies globally.

The conglomerate now comprises thousands of mini companies, all reporting to the chairman. There are no pure cost centres; even the finance department functions independently, providing financing and advisory services for a fee.

This extremely innovative and daring business and operation model has yet to fully prove itself. Nevertheless, it remains one of the most interesting initiatives of the last few years and a perfect illustration of the audacity of Chinese entrepreneurs in terms of business models and organisation innovations.

Haier Group is today the world's leading home appliance brand. It reached a revenue of over 200 billion RMB (=€25B) in 2019, and in 2016 even acquired General Electric's appliance division, a feat unimaginable three decades ago, considering its humble beginnings.[15]

As summarized in an insightful article about the Haier Platform by Michael Greeven, a Professor of Innovation and Strategy at IMD, Haier is reflected as a truly innovative and consumer-focused company and has many examples of products that satisfy special needs: washing machines with quick, 15-minute washing cycles, or extra-large washing machines for Pakistani robes, and durable ones with large hoses for washing vegetables on Chinese farms, for instance. Many of the product ideas come from the front-end of the company, such as repairmen and salespeople.

Run by a visionary CEO, Zhang Ruimin, since its very early days, Haier has been experimenting with new organisational forms to reduce hierarchy and control and increase autonomy with self-organizing work units and internal labour markets. But it was not until 2010 that Haier put a unique project organisation platform in place throughout the company.

HAIER PLATFORM ORGANISATION

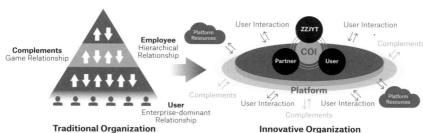

Traditional Organization	Innovative Organization
Managers give orders to employees	Managers support their teams and provide resources
→ Distance between decision and customers	→ Each unit manages a customer group
→ Dysfunctional behavior of employees	→ Decision-making power among employees

Source: http://www.haier.net/ / DETECON

Haier's first step to create such a platform organisation was to fundamentally reorganize the company's structure. First, the company eliminated business units and managerial hierarchies with the purpose of removing any distance with the users of its products. The company reorganized around projects with specific focus, such as on new product development, marketing, and production. These three work units, or small project organisations, are the core of Haier and closest to the user.

A second set, or level, of project organisations is organized around corporate support functions like HR, accounting, and legal. The highest-level work unit is the executive team.

Yet the third-level work unit is the smallest and positioned at the top of the pyramid. Its role is redefined as a support function for the customer-facing, self-organizing project organisations.

All self-organizing teams act as independent mini companies.[16] They make transactions and contracts with each other as if they were in an external market. Because of this, teams interact in a more competitive manner. Monetary rewards for individuals are more closely tied to the performance of their team.

How does this work in real life? Imagine you are a member of such a mini company. And let's say your team is delivering HR services to other mini companies in the network. But you don't only deliver services to other teams. You need to sell them, and they need to buy from you. If you don't sell enough, your team can go bankrupt, and you and teammates will lose your jobs.

Plus, your team needs to deliver competitive services because yours is not the only team offering HR services. Several teams in the network are permitted to offer HR services. This creates a competitive environment. Every team needs to add enough value to internal or external customers to survive.

Haier now has thousands of work units, more than 100 of which have annual revenues in excess of 100 million RMB. More recently, the platform has evolved further to allow work units of non-core products to spin-off.

After 2014, external investors were allowed to invest in promising new products, jointly with Haier's investment fund. For instance, a furniture-maker invested in one of the e-commerce platforms (youzhu.com) that a work unit developed for house decoration.

To date, 41 such spin-offs have received venture capital funding, of which 16 received in excess of 100 million RMB.

Haier has become a platform-based business, every part of the organisation has its own financial statement, makes autonomous decisions (including which other parts of Haier to work with), and can reach out independently to customers, potential employees, and collaborators. Research & Development projects now often reach beyond Haier's walls to include academics, independent designers, and even competitors.

One example is Haier's COSMOPlat, a world-class industrial IoT platform that was originally created for its own use but later opened up to third parties. Small and Medium Enterprises (SMEs) can use the platform to tap into supply chain and logistics resources. Outsiders' use of the platform has increased to the point where around half of orders placed are for non-Haier clients.

The Haier vision is making the enterprise truly borderless. Using digital technology to connect everyone. There is no longer 'inside' the company versus 'outside'.

Visionary Zhang Ruimin accepts that in such an ecosystem-like structure, giving up control in favour of individual independence is inevitable and even encouraged. He sees this form of organisational structure as a natural evolution for all major companies, particularly those focused on business innovation in the Internet age.[17]

5.3 THE AGILE ORGANISATION OF THE FUTURE AND THE CULTURAL CHALLENGE

Chinese entrepreneurs are very adept in leveraging scale and although there is lots of room to grow within China still, Chinese entrepreneurs will be eying global markets and will expand their ecosystems abroad.

Simultaneously, disruptive technology is leading to unprecedented change and uncertainty in many markets forcing once stable and established businesses to compete with younger, more nimble players.

Digital developments are also providing increasing access to consumers in other parts of the world. This opens up more opportunities for building scale beyond existing borders, and with it the risk to be outcompeted by larger, yet more adaptable companies.

Meanwhile, most Western corporations have been organized in the same way for decades. Their layered structures have become one of the main obstacles to speed, innovation, and growth.

Firms based in Western markets also tend to be more internally focused. To become firms of the future, they'll need to improve their business models and to provide new services, products, and customer experiences.

Meanwhile, Chinese entrepreneurs are leading the way toward modern methods of organizing companies for this more unstable world. Their flexible ecosystems and partnership-based organisations are very different from the structure and chains of command used in most Western corporate organisations. And they are even able to make it work in large enterprises.

The examples we have described provide clear methods that could also be applied in Western companies. Adjusting the structure, shifting power, and breaking the traditional management models is the only way forward. Yet, to achieve it, will require sacrificing the old individual-driven mindsets for the common good of the organisation.

And herein lies one of the main challenges for enterprises originating in the West attempting to adapt to more agile forms of organisation, as well as for Chinese entrepreneurs venturing outside China to maintain the qualities that made them successful. The main barrier will be cultural and will hinge around managerial style differences between the East and the West.

In the West, the ideal manager is a 'resourceful democrat'[18] who sets the vision and strategy for the business, and delegates and empowers others to execute within the agreed strategic boundaries — a leader who encourages two-way communication with his employees and supports bottom-up input in decision-making. But once the plan is agreed, the strategy cannot be challenged.

However, what often makes more loosely built and flexible organisations work in China is the group-oriented culture. Except in alliances and more ecosystem-like organisations, where control has been surrendered in favour of autonomy, top-down but agile organisations don't provide much room to do things independently, a view often reflected by foreigners working in Chinese organisations (including ourselves) who sometimes feel they are not fully trusted to manage their own work.

Chinese agile organisations rely a lot on strict and often changing priorities that are then executed without much pushback. It is driven by teams that adhere to processes that enable speed of execution without too many questions about direction and that encourage self-reflection to ensure individuals stay on course. There's not much room here for two-way communication and individual expression.

For the Chinese Emperor herein lies a clear challenge, also. Too rigid a top-down culture has limitations. Chinese bosses venturing abroad need to learn to be more open for feedback and pushback. Avoiding too much 'ben fen', where people just execute regardless of what happens around them, will help their companies to stay more agile and in sync with the here and now.

Flat structures, or ecosystems with a lot of autonomous teams where innovation is encouraged, will inevitably generate mistakes and redundancies. It will therefore require a tolerance for error and acceptance of some inefficiencies, the latter often difficult to accept in a lean business culture. To us, however, that seems a price worth paying to achieve a faster and more innovative business.

Last but not least, another challenge that needs to be overcome is the inevitable limitation of career growth for individual contributors in flat structures. Chinese leaders and many of their people have accepted this. It is the core difference between corporate careers and a more entrepreneurial view of success.

In a Chinese company you will not necessarily go up the ladder. But, as the Alibaba example demonstrates, you can have a shot at 'doing it yourself' and become part of the ecosystem or, equally important, you can succeed financially through your loyalty.

In the next chapter, *People Come and Go*. Those Who Fit Stay Longer, we will dive deeper into this phenomenon.

大浪淘沙

6

PEOPLE COME
AND GO.
THOSE WHO FIT
STAY LONGER.

6. PEOPLE COME AND GO.
THOSE WHO FIT STAY LONGER.

'In Chinese society, no one is an end in themselves; you are a means to an end. The view of personhood is that the person is valuable in so far as they are in a relation to others.'

Jerusha McCormack

Professor, School of English and International Studies, Beijing

6.1 FAMILY CHARACTERISTICS

Family culture is at the core of Confucianism*. And with Confucian thought at the centre of traditional Chinese society, family culture equates to Chinese culture. Or stated differently, Chinese culture is family culture.

As we described at the beginning of Chapter 5 *The Emperor Decides*. But Agility Rules, Confucianism promotes social harmony in human relationships, a principle thus naturally applicable to family relationships as well. Achieving harmony within the family relies on the combination of a parent's authority, conformity to the rules, and the role and responsibilities of each individual.

Conventionally, in Chinese family culture, respecting the old and loving the young is the most prominent feature. 孝 (pinyin: xiào) translated as filial piety is highly valued. Xiào is rooted in China's feudal social structure, in which land was held by large clans whose internal life was structured hierarchically and patriarchally. Traditionally, Chinese people obey the hierarchical relationship between the previous generation and the next. Children are not willing to contradict their elders. Obedience is an expression of respect from the child toward parents and the elderly.

In Confucianism, this virtue is directly associated with a person's citizenship and leadership in society. Confucius said, 'To put the world in order, we must first put the nation in order; to put the nation in order, we must first put the family in order; to put the family in order, we must first cultivate our personal life; we must first set our hearts right.'

---

* For nearly 2,000 years, Confucianism has shaped the social, ethical, and political aspects of Chinese cultures. Developed by the greatest Chinese philosopher, Confucius, Confucianism is a philosophy that focuses on the conduct and practices of people in daily life. It is a complex set of ethical and moral rules that dictate how a person relates to others. It plays a key role in forming the norms of social morality that influence the culture in personal, familial, and social relationships.[3]

It is believed that children who respect their parents will become good citizens and leaders. Rebellion against parents' authority is unacceptable and will result in harsh consequences. Being 'unfilial' was considered a crime in traditional Chinese society. It even could result in death as a punishment.[1]

Family culture is the moral bond that holds the family together and improves its fortunes. It brings cohesion and requires mutual support. While children are expected not to rebel, the patriarch is expected to expand the prosperity and vitality of the family, which explains the extraordinary determination of most Chinese families to do better than the previous generation in education, job prospects, and wealth. Cohesion is also the driver of mutual trust among family members.

Trust in the family.
American Japanese scholar Francis Fukuyama believes that culture can be divided into high-trust culture and low-trust culture.[2] High-trust culture refers to a society where trust exceeds blood relationship, while low trust culture equates a society where trust only exists in blood relationship.

China (and with it for example France and Southern Italy) in his view is a low-trust culture, where people trust others more when they are related to them. The family is the circle of dependence.

This base for trust is the reason why the large majority of businesses in China is generally family-based; even when the corporation is publicly held, the family is often still in control. No wonder then, that family culture has entered the thinking and behavioural rules of Chinese enterprises.

In China's businesses, the corporate culture is often an expression of traditional Chinese family culture, which can even determine property rights and organisational forms.

The family members generally take a hands-on approach in the affairs of the business. Decision-making can often be informal and may even occur at events such as family dinners. The organisational chart does not necessarily provide information about who actually holds the power; often a person with an influential-sounding title may only be a figurehead.

When the family is a clan.
Beyond the inner family culture, China has a long history of organized groups of descendants of one common ancestor, known as clans: autonomous organisations with broad social and economic functions and important providers of public goods and social services, and sometimes even a substitute for the state.[4]

The Chinese clan was traditionally a social organisation that had, in the pre-modern era, a well-organized hierarchy, with the clan heads having strong authority in managing clan affairs and dealing with disputes within, between, among, and outside the clans.

A traditional clan was typically organized around an ancestral temple in which sacrifices to ancestors were offered. They also had a code of conduct to direct, guide, and constrain clan members; an elder board to administer clan affairs; and common properties used to assist members in need.

Although, since the ascent of Communist rule, the role of clans in society has declined, clan culture has persisted even after more than 30 years of state-power suppression. In fact, it has helped the country in its initial stages of economic development and has formed the basis of China's entrepreneurial prowess. China's clan culture is highly associated with entrepreneurship.

Chinese economic organisation in the 1990s and early 2000s, was to some degree the re-emergence of traditional social structures and behavioural patterns. Clan culture helped privately-owned enterprises overcome financing constraints and, by doing so, stay out of reach of eager local governments.

The 'Wenzhou Stirfry', in which groups of wealthy friends in Wenzhou, China's freewheeling city in Zhejiang Province at the forefront of capitalism, pooled millions of dollars' worth of Chinese yuan and put it into hot investments like Shanghai real estate, where it was stirred and then flipped for a hefty profit, is a high-profile example.

Beyond clan action for pure speculation, the rise of ecosystems (which we described in the previous chapter) is a more lasting proof of the power of the clan; early ecosystems were built within the (extended) family of most founders.

Although in this book we will not examine in more detail the role of clans in Chinese business, their history has profound implications because clan culture is significantly related to values that are very relevant for private businesses.

The business as a family.
In the previous chapter we also detailed the role of the patriarch, or the Emperor, while emphasizing how his central control still enables high levels of agility within organisations. In this chapter we will look deeper into the role of members of the (extended) family around him and the dynamics that foster relations and behaviour and that ensure the family stays together, even if members are not direct, blood-related family.

According to Chang Boyi, former head of Asia at consulting firm Roland Berger, enterprise management can be divided into three levels: knowing, doing, and being.[5]

'Knowledge' means that managers need to know their theories, frame-works, and common sense that constitute the 'core understanding' of management. For example, knowing the 4P theory of marketing.

'Doing', also phrased as 'Action', means that managers must have the practical ability and skill. Such as executing a project, conducting performance reviews, public speaking, selling products, etc.

The 3rd component 'Being' in the meaning of 'Self-realization' includes values, attitudes, and beliefs. It is the practice of integrity and justice, and how they view the strengths and weaknesses of themselves and others, how they treat others, and the organisation.

Professional managers trained in Western management pay a lot of attention to 'knowledge' and 'action', but they are not very concerned about the self-realization of managers.

Chinese leaders subconsciously think that they are playing the roles of 'father' and 'emperor', and they have an 'emperor complex'. The emperor needs to protect his people and subordinates, which creates a strong emotional bond and connection between the leader and his followers.

Leaders manage business just like elders and parents manage the family. Founders stay in control based on the family members they employ, the leadership teams they build, and how they incentivize. Chinese leadership is the absolute boss with a closely held and tightly knit inner circle. The BOSS decides. The trusted inner circle makes sure things are done. And the loyal performers are rewarded very well for their efforts.

As a result, it is striking to see that most successful entrepreneurs — from Ren Zhengfei (Huawei) to Jack Ma (Alibaba) or Ding Shizhong (Anta), and with them many others — mention their company culture as the main success factor of their enterprise, what they take most pride in, and what they often dedicate most of their efforts to.

This is mirrored in the behaviour of employees. We will not forget the weddings where we would see more members of the staff than family members of the bride and groom. If an employee gets a serious disease or encounters difficulties in his private life, other employees will go to great lengths to help him or her, as they would for a brother or sister.

From our own experience at Adidas and other businesses we were involved in in China, as well as based on input from various other foreigners working for multinationals such as L'Oréal, Bestseller, and Starbucks, the creation of a 'family feel' atmosphere contributes significantly to the loyalty of the staff and ultimately the success of the Chinese business. Not surprisingly, in these companies the leadership teams were very stable over a very long period.

In our view, this warrants an adjustment to people management in markets such as China. Many multinational corporations rotate top managers on a regular basis who, as a result, cannot build a stable long-term relationship with their teams.

6.2 WHAT HAPPY FAMILIES CAN TEACH US

In a society driven by competition for resources, internal strife and horse races, a 'job for life' is far from certain. Nor do people necessarily seek one, given their consistent quest to better themselves.

In founder-driven companies, loyalty and a cultural fit are often the most important requirements toward success and career advancement or stability. They are also, beyond financial incentives, key reasons for employees to stay.

This inherent contradiction provides an interesting dynamic in Chinese companies. On the one hand, there is an inner circle that is close to the leader. This inner circle enjoys high levels of trust and protection, is loyal to the founder and the organisation, and tends to stay a long time. On the other hand, at lower levels in the company, there is often a very high turnover rate, with people that come, get tested, or judge for themselves whether they fit in and then either stay or (are being) move(d) on.

To explain this phenomenon, we have identified three elements that influence human resources management in Chinese companies; behaviours that enable Chinese entrepreneurs to build tight and loyal organisations that stay agile and entrepreneurial.

1. Entrepreneurs seek entrepreneurs;
2. Rely on the inner circle;
3. Real incentives keep many happy.

6.2.1 Entrepreneurs seeking entrepreneurs
The most-sought-after employees are entrepreneurial, always prepared to work and drive hard, looking and fighting for opportunities, and well rewarded for their contribution and loyalty.

An interesting example of a constant search for, and development of, entrepreneurial talent is hotpot restaurant chain Haidilao, founded in Jianyang, in Sichuan province in 1994.

Hotpot (火鍋, lit. 'fire pot'), is a popular form of Chinese food and there is a vast availability of restaurants in China offering a range of this hearty simmering pot of soup stock, filled with a variety of foodstuffs and ingredients.

Currently suffering, like many other restaurant chains around the world, from the effect of Covid-19 related drops in traffic, it remains a remarkable example of staff management. Haidilao has consistently outperformed its competitors through a combination of very innovative management approaches[6] pioneered by its founder Zhang Yong, who started work as a welder, and did not eat in a restaurant himself until he was 19!

The competitiveness of the chain depends on what can only be described as the ultimate customer service combined with a highly motivational incentive system.

It's a potent combination that turns employees into entrepreneurs with a laser-sharp focus on customer needs. Or rather, that ensures that entrepreneurially minded employees are identified and enabled to maximize customer satisfaction in a way that maximizes benefits for the customer, the employee, and ultimately the company.

Examples of the Haidilao customer service are legendary around China. Most of them are small tokens of appreciation, for example a customer getting a button sewn back on a coat, getting your hair washed while you have to wait for a table, the gift of a free watermelon when it is too cumbersome to create a doggy-bag for the leftover half watermelon, or a bottle of sauce delivered to your home after you mentioned you really liked it. But all these small gestures are consistently, yet unexpectedly, delivered in all restaurants, all year round and keep bringing back customers for more.

The mostly small benefits offered to customers could easily be copied by other restaurants, but what makes Haidilao stand out is the consistency in which it is able to deliver them at scale. And that in an industry that — worldwide — is known for employing people with often low levels of education or even sophistication. And an industry with very high levels of staff turnover.

In Section 6.2.3 we will have a closer look at the employee incentive system that Haidilao utilizes, but here we first describe the level of entrepreneurship that is sought and expected at the hotpot chain and that clearly embodies the belief in nurturing entrepreneurial talent.

When Haidilao entered its scaling up phase and needed more people fast, the company began to recruit high-end talents from outside the company to join the management team. But it quickly became clear that external people did not fit in well culturally nor were they well equipped to deal with the details required to manage a restaurant.

Haidilao went back to solve the problem internally and developed a mentorship system with an entrepreneurial twist. A method that also solved the challenge that often prevents staff to train newcomers properly for fear of being outperformed.

The solution: an incentive sharing mentoring mechanism.[7] Any top-rated employee who is able to pass Master certification (after participating in various trainings and passing theoretical and practical examinations), is allowed to choose up to 12 apprentices to train and develop.

The wages of the master will subsequently be increased depending on the performance of each apprentice. The apprentice passes on to the master all incentives they earn based on customer feedback, for as long as the apprentice has not passed all qualifications.

In return, the master will pay bonuses to the apprentice based on how fast the apprentice reaches specific performance levels and how long they stay at the company.

A similar system exists at store manager level, where a store manager as a master is given the option of profit sharing. A store manager/master can choose between a larger percentage share of the profit of its own restaurant, or a smaller share of profit of its own restaurant but additionally a larger share of the profit of an apprentice's restaurant, once they have been deployed elsewhere.

Think entrepreneurial and your future will be great!

This intricate system safeguards that master and apprentices think like entrepreneurs. It not only ensures a great level of ongoing basic customer service, but it also stimulates inventing innovative ways to surprise customers frequenting the restaurant. And happy customers will continue to provide positive feedback fuelling performance and incentives.

It further encourages the master and his apprentices to look for opportunities such as opening a new restaurant, even in an often-overcrowded market.

It also ensures an ongoing identification, training, and development of the best likeminded people. Staff turnover is not judged to be a negative. Building a team of compatible entrepreneurial thinkers capable of moving toward the same goal at high speed is seen as much more critical.

Hai Di Lao's Chairman, Zhang Yong, drives this entrepreneurial spirit. Known for his ability to spot, recruit, and retain teenagers capable of growing into store managers by the time they are 21, he likes to test trainees by assigning them tasks above their responsibility level, such as negotiating the takeover of a rival chain. That allows him to weed out those with low potential.[8]

In Chapter 5 we described horse races as a tool to compare abilities and judge the contribution of people. To find the most entrepreneurial candidate, it is common to hire two or more people, test them and see who survives. The winner may stay. The rest will be let go with not too much concern about high staff turnover.

Hopping is actually not bad.

Among companies in Europe and the USA, it is frequently argued that it is a challenge to find good people. Yet in China, one can really say there is often a lack of skilled talent. We also hear that when foreign enterprises hire people in China, they balk at resumes that show a lot of job-hopping. But what if hopping is actually good?

Chinese entrepreneurs ensure they have people with the right cultural fit. If you want your company to move fast, your people need to be able to move fast. If you want your organisation to be constantly hungry for opportunities, you need the right type of person for that. But it is not a skill that can easily be spotted in an interview, so why not hire and try?

On the side of the employees, there are also good reasons to test and try. Opportunities for jobs are plentiful, but good inside knowledge about companies is often limited. And in a culture where the loyal performers are the better rewarded employees, when remuneration is not as expected, the grass elsewhere quickly looks greener.

So, job hopping does not automatically mean a poor performer or a disloyal employee. Rather than simply discarding the resume of a job-hopping candidate, it is worthwhile to better understand specific circumstances since a lot of eager talent often hides behind the facts on paper.

Lack entrepreneurial talent? Ensure flawless execution!

We want to stress that not all employees are required to have entrepreneurial talent. Neither do all employees have to be highly qualified. Herein lies a significant upside: speed and quality of execution, another hallmark of successful entrepreneurial Chinese enterprises!

There is a notorious shortage of qualified and highly entrepreneurial people. Simultaneously, the labour force is large and the demand for jobs often insatiable. Combined with a Confucian belief of structure and hierarchy in which people are expected to observe values on rank and position and show humility and deference to their superiors, there is a natural demand for, and acceptance of roles and positions aimed at simply getting things done.

Traditional Chinese ideology endorses merit-based inequality. Historically, leaders in Chinese society were rewarded with various benefits and privileges based on how well they looked after their people such as providing goods and services to the public. That is, if the privileges enjoyed by the ruling class bring about desirable outcomes for others in society, unequal treatment is accepted and even encouraged in this Chinese meritocratic tradition.

Still today, many Chinese people may subscribe to the point of view that inequality is a necessary cost of economic development and that economic development requires some people to get rich sooner, the resulting inequality being a cost that must be paid. To some extent, the same applies to enterprises and their top-down organisations.

As we explained at the beginning of this chapter, management is centralized and has tight control. This central power determines the direction and provides the parameters in which the rest of the enterprise is able to operate. Beyond this core there is often a large need for affordable resources that simply focus on execution.

The quality to survive and add value in a top-down entrepreneurial environment, but without the required skills or connections to get to the top, is loyal and diligent execution. Ensure that what needs to be done, is done. No questions asked.

6.2.2 Relying on the inner circle

Family is one of the few places for trust in China and this extends into the business world. As explained in Section 6.1, China's business leaders are culturally predisposed to see the members of their organisations as family. They spend a lot of time caring for the personal welfare of their employees as a part of their job. But they expect trust and absolute loyalty in return.

Chinese business leadership is often referred to as a clan. A team that is often made up of direct family members of the founder or very trustworthy staffers that have been with the firm from very early on and have demonstrated their loyalty. Often such outsiders are former classmates.

Experience and capability are not necessarily the most important qualifications. Many founders are looking for harmony first and that means that they don't just need competent people. Especially when fast and loyal execution is key. Too much ego is not going to work anyway.

The head may have advisors who are family members or close friends. Such relationships are more important than what the organisational chart may imply. Often a lower-level staffer will go straight to the leader without going up through the chain of command.

People are evaluated informally, and personal reputation is more important than achievements. Decisions are made quickly, often based on personal recommendations.

With more and more Chinese entrepreneurs reaching an age when they need to hand over the reins, it remains to be seen how they manage to let go of control and to keep the inner circle together.

Since their founding days, most of China's family firms achieved competitive advantage through agile exploitation of opportunities and a low cost of operation. But emerging technologies and globalization are pushing innovation and internationalization to the forefront of such family firms' future development and key to success.

This means that they will need more talent and management resources. The familism-based social networks will no longer suffice. Hence, family firms must reorganize by changing the structure of their ownership and control rights to broaden participation. They must introduce professional and international talent to their boards of directors and top management teams.

The second generation has commonly received a good education, even higher education in the West, and entertain modern or Western ideas and values about business. As a result, some are unwilling (or unmotivated) or lack the ability to take over and grow the family business using their relationship network.

Some have values and business philosophies that conflict with those inherent to a more traditional approach. It is therefore not difficult to foresee that many successful family businesses, especially those that require the maintenance of multidimensional social relationships, may not have a family successor.[9]

Toward the end of this section, we will describe why, even with generational leadership changes on the horizon for many companies, the chance that existing leaders will automatically be succeeded by outsiders or so called 'professional' managers remains small.

But first, we will examine what the inner circle means to put that argumentation better into context.

When building their teams, Western company leaders will look for thinkers, people with proven intellectual capabilities, sanctioned by the right diplomas and will seek a range of qualifications suited for the available position.

In China, a feeling of belonging and the ability to contribute value is more critical. In Chinese companies, trust and loyalty need to be earned to gain access to the inner sanctum. And this can only be a long, multiyear process.

In 2007, James Zheng took a big leap from a successful and promising career in Adidas Group by moving to Anta Sports, now the 3rd largest sportswear group in the world but at the time a company that still had to prove long term success. In 2012, Holly Li followed a similar route by joining Xtep, a smaller competitor to Anta.

Both were hired for their expertise gained while working for a well-known and highly respected foreign company with proven success in China. Both were hired for senior positions close to the founder with the aim to help bring a higher level of category and management expertise into the organisation.

But both did not automatically get the power their role in a Western company would have yielded. As Holly described it,

> *When I joined, I had the title of CEO but all I had to prove for that was my secretary and my driver. Everyone continued working directly with the owner. But there was no point complaining about that. Had I done so, I would have remained an outsider. Instead, I was expected to first create value for the team and the company. Earn their respect and this can only be achieved gradually.*

> *For the first year or so, you can advise, but not make decisions. But once you're thinking and contribution lead to more and more wins, you earn acceptance. Once you gain the trust, you become part of the inner circle.*

Today, although both are not direct, blood related family, they are both very close to being just that.

The experience to make it into the inner circle, for people that came from outside the organisation, is not an easy one. And it is certainly an obstacle for bringing in more professional management, demonstrated by the personal experience from Sandrine at Dongxiang Group, a Hong Kong listed Chinese company in the sports sector, where she was CEO for a short while. She left after only ten months for lack of alignment with the founder. By then, she had not established any bond with her team and was frustrated about that.

But she recognizes today that, in a Chinese company, it takes a lot more than ten months to get accepted as the new boss — even more so when you are the only foreigner in the organisation — and to create the essential emotional bond without which the team is not engaged enough to fully support their leader's vision and projects.

Herein lies a valuable lesson for non-Chinese joining a Chinese firm. You will need to stick around long enough to gain trust.

No place for mercenaries.

The high demand for loyalty and the need for being immersed in the company culture makes it difficult to bring in professional senior managers. Simultaneously, or more as a result, the professional manager pool available is small and qualitatively not well developed.

Therefore, if a non-family member were to be hired as the manager of an enterprise, the risk is perceived to be high. Until they have a full understanding of the moral and professional qualities of a non-family member, family businesses will not easily give up control and hand over management rights to non-family members, making it near impossible for outsiders to be hired for important corporate positions.

While this more traditional aspect of the Chinese business family is likely to come under more pressure, and as markets become more global while founders do not have obvious family members to succeed them, there is not likely to be a surge of fresh outsider hires at the very top of such enterprises.

The inner circle is likely to change over time as business families are beginning to adopt business practices that are more consistent with other companies around the world, but it will be slow in coming.

In addition to personal character, managers are increasingly more likely to be valued for other attributes such as industry knowledge and digital capabilities. But despite these changes, the sense of the family and inner circle will remain strong.[10]

Even as founders pass on the reigns to the next generation, don't expect companies to act more like corporate organisations. Given the culture inside Chinese companies, new leadership will have been brought up from within, and will be highly skilled in all elements of Dragon Tactics. They are most likely a more modern version of their predecessors.

6.2.3 Real Incentives keep many happy

As mentioned in Section 3.2.3, there is quite some diversity among Chinese firms where benefit management is concerned. The distribution of staff perks, wages, and bonuses does not seem to have as many common threads among firms as do their methodologies to align the entire company behind a clear vision and goals.

In this section we provide insights in various schemes being used. However, even among the disparate methodologies, there is a common thread. Be it within a real 'family business' or in a 'business as a family', without fail, successful Chinese enterprises have created corporate cultures that are often described as very family like. This being a direct result of the role the founder or leader plays in creating such culture. Historically, the Emperor is expected to look after his people, and many take that role very seriously.

The manner in which they reward their teams is often closely related to this philosophy and our chapter about incentivizing would therefore not be complete if we were not to describe part of this *looking after your people* culture, as making and keeping staff happy in China goes far beyond simple financial incentive schemes such as year-end bonuses or share options.

This cultural aspect is where foreign businesses often underperform and thus put themselves at a disadvantage in attracting and keeping talent.

Being well looked after, a real incentive!

Haidilao again lends itself as being a good example since they pride themselves '*not to operate restaurants, but people*'. However, a lot of what Haidilao does, many other companies also do in some shape or form.

Haidilao's people motto is fully reflected in how they care for all their staff and how they leverage employee growth to drive corporate growth.

Zhang Yong's philosophy is simple: treat employees as family members. His business relies on a constant influx from relatively low-skilled workers that often travel away from their hometowns in search for work. If you want these employees to do such low-skilled jobs well, he believes the emphasis should not be on how to train them to do the job, but how to make them *eager* to do the job. And so, he literally gives them a home away from home.

In China the average waiter would live in a crammed basement. Not at Haidilao. Their employees live in formal residences with luxuries like air-conditioning, free internet, and tv. Hotel like room cleaning service is provided, too. Of course, this adds to staff cost (in 2017, Haidilao's per capita cost of employees was 1.68 times the average annual salary of the national catering service and hotel industry), but given the business performance, this investment pays itself back.[11]

Staff and managers are encouraged to look after the wellbeing of their employees. There are numerous examples of managers ensuring children of staff are being stimulated to study diligently, or who look after people in times of medical need. There are daily reward opportunities for employees with many choices of incentive, which may be food, daily necessities, fruits, movie tickets, or vouchers, and some can even earn a half-day leave on the spot. In Zhang Yong's vision, '*Things are not important, what is important is the attention and recognition of employees.*'

With managerial bench strength an ongoing challenge, Zhang deepens their commitment by offering generous additional incentives, such as trips outside China and education for their children.

Last but not least, he encourages them to build their own future. He offers aspiring entrepreneurs the opportunity to become a supplier with initial contracts that promise enough business to get started.[12] And so, his most entrepreneurial people become part of his ecosystem. True entrepreneurial talent, who are ultimately keener to build their own future with less concern for job stability, remain within his extended family.

Another notable example, though somewhat extreme, of how Chinese entrepreneurs go to lengths to look after their employees was given by Li Jinyuan, founder of Tiens Group, a health and household products provider. In 2014, the company flew 6,400 of its employees on a four-day trip to France.

Filling 84 planes to Paris, they packed into 4,000 rooms across 140 hotels. While in Paris they took over the Louvre for a visit and were given a private shopping session at luxury department store Galeries Lafayette. They then travelled to the French Riviera, where 'Team Tiens' gathered on Promenade des Anglais, on the waterfront, in blue and white colour-coordinated outfits, spelling out the phrase, *Tiens' Dream is Nice in the Côte d'Azure*, setting a Guinness World Record for building the largest human sentence in the process.

Elaborate performance schemes are well established.
Similar to companies based in the West, Chinese entrepreneurs provide performance-based incentives such as bonus schemes and it is also increasingly expected to offer employees an employee share plan in China.

A PwC survey of 337 public Chinese companies that listed in the US or Hong Kong from January 2016 to July 2019 showed that 52% of these companies have adopted equity incentive plans following an initial public offering (IPO).[13]

For domestically listed public companies in China, 337 companies announced share equity incentive plans in 2019, and the proportion of multi-phase equity incentive plan announcements has increased significantly. The equity incentive plan has become common and is considered an effective means for public companies to improve corporate governance and enhance their governance capabilities.

For private companies, more and more are gradually realising the importance of an equity incentive plan in improving their company's performance and their employees' loyalty. While this is especially true for start-up companies with limited capital in their early stages, companies that are private now also frequently use equity incentive plans to attract and retain talent. With ownership structures often more complex in these instances, it is common to provide 'phantom' shares, also called virtual stock.

As the market is transforming, even companies that have been around longer and have share-based incentive schemes in place are increasingly making adjustments to reflect changing realities. In our discussions we have come across examples of local companies admitting that their incentive schemes may no longer be good enough to really stimulate loyalty, especially among people more junior in the organisation.

Senior leaders, especially the ones in and close to the inner circle, historically are looked after very well. The earlier you became part of the inner sanctum, the better you will be rewarded. But this model does not work anymore.

Junior staff would normally get a standard bonus scheme, that is an objectives- and performance-driven program in which people can earn cash bonuses of several months' pay. Historically, owners would often support such schemes out of their own pockets. The boss and inner circle (family) members would make a concerted effort to look after the team and reward individuals, especially the people they think are important value contributors. But there are limitations to such generosity and as companies grow, the leadership cannot look after all of them.

In particular, there is now an increasing need to stimulate young leaders and talent. As we pointed out in the Wolf Culture chapter, there is less of a natural acceptance among the younger generations to consistently work so hard. To remain loyal and committed, they increasingly expect to be rewarded based on what they contribute.

Huawei and Alibaba are often seen as examples that look after their people; they take into account the ability and potential of individuals in the distribution of equity as we will point out in Section 6.2.4. A good return on the investment of their time and commitment still makes it worthwhile to keep pushing hard.

Before closing this section of the book, we need to point out that it is very common that top management is expected to invest toward ensuring loyalty and commitment. For example, when at Mengniu, a large diary company in Northern China, in 2016 a new CEO came in and the incentive schemes were adjusted, he insisted that each executive committee member invest several million RMB of personal funds into the company stock. Loyalty and commitment become stronger with real skin in the game.

Partnerships have gained popularity.
To ensure a broader sharing of created value, more companies are now organizing themselves around partnerships. For example, in 2010, Yonghui Superstores, one of the competitors of Carrefour, launched a partnership program, allowing store managers and even staff to act as partners.

As in the restaurant industry, a key challenge for supermarkets is that front-line employees are expected to do challenging and tiring work, but they have the lowest salaries. Staff turnover in the entire industry is therefore extremely high.[14]

Making just enough money each month only to afford basics like food and clothing poses serious problems with staff optimism and happiness, and by extension toward great customer service. A real challenge for physical retail in times when the internet is a serious threat.

Small salary increases don't have a significant effect on people's engagement and thus will not result in higher revenues. However, with margins so low in the industry, significant raises would have a materially improve the profitability of a supermarket.

To solve this dilemma, Zhang Xuansong, chairman of Yonghui, implemented a partner system for frontline employees, in essence a profit-sharing methodology, but one that gives employees a direct, almost entrepreneurial stake in the operation and productivity of the business, in areas where their own ability and commitment can make a difference. This can be a specific category, or a counter within the supermarket. Stakes can vary and are subject to performance and negotiation.

Seeing their income linked to their own area of influence ensures that they will provide significantly better customer service and show an increased willingness to avoid unnecessary waste. For example, loss of poor handling of fruit and vegetables at Yonghui is at only 4% to 5% compared to the 30% average for the sector.

Beyond profit share.

But the Yonghui partnership system is more than a revenue share. It is also a form of controlled decentralisation. For example, staff is given a direct role in the recruitment and dismissal of personnel within their span of control. Decisions are subject to the team being in agreement since not only all benefits, but also the cost impact, are shared.

Employees now feel much more a part of a group and as a result the turnover rate of Yonghui's frontline employees is significantly reduced. Efficiencies are higher and management cost has come down as well. Only one year after implementing the new measures, Yonghui's average employee pay had increased by 15%, and the employee turnover rate had decreased from 6.8 to 4.4%.

The company also adopted a performance competition system to complement its partnership plan. Based on evaluation results, the bottom 20% of employees were to be let go. The combination of the partnership plan and the performance competition drove strong growth and financial performance.

In the four years immediately after the changes, Yonghui opened numerous new stores and expanded from 249 stores in 2012 to 455 in 2016. After that time, beginning in 2017, and fuelled by the complete roll-out of the new motivational measures, the number of new stores grew exponentially. In 2017 alone, 128 new stores were opened. In 2018, more than 250 were added, bringing the supermarket chain to more than 70,000 employees and more than 600 stores in operation. Net profits outgrew operating revenue, which meant increased operational efficiency.[15]

Company co-ownership as the ultimate price!

Around the world, examples can be found where employees own significant stakes in the companies where they work, and China is no exception. Connecting long-term economic value creation to the highest contributing employees is a win-win model that many Chinese entrepreneurs have embraced, and often for a larger share of employees than their Western counterparts. Various co-ownership examples exist in the Middle Kingdom, but none is so extensive as the Huawei Employee Stock Ownership Program.

Huawei ESOP.

The Huawei Employee Stock Ownership Program (ESOP) has been in place since the very beginning of the company. In fact, it was launched to raise cash to fund the business when banks still deemed the company too risky. With Huawei still a privately held enterprise, no one can own a share without working at Huawei. There are now nearly 105,000 shareholding employees out of approximately 194,000 employees worldwide.

Huawei promotes itself as the only company of this size to be entirely owned by its employees. While this is technically not correct, as we explain below, the company has devised a structure that allows it to use shares to motivate a large number of employees while still remaining closely held.

Jorge Paolo, Warren Buffett business partner and founder of 3G Capital (a global investment firm), spoke highly of Huawei's ESOP, calling it '"a meritocracy plus partnership". But in China. And in tech. And at a huge scale', as quoted by Jeffrey Towson, a former professor of Investment at the Guanghua School of Management at Peking university.[16]

According to Chinese corporate records, Huawei Technologies is wholly owned by a holding company called Huawei Investment & Holding. This holding company has two shareholders. Mr. Ren Zhengfei, Huawei's founder and chief executive owns 1.01% of the shares. The rest is held by an entity called the Union of Huawei Investment & Holding. This is Huawei's labour union.

This union ownership exists purely in a legal perspective. Employees, as part of the ESOP, control — in the company's words — 'virtual shares' in this labour union entity. Shares of this virtual stock let employees share directly in the company's financial successes and losses. And they entitle their holders to elect members to the Huawei Representatives' Commission, which in turn elects the members of the board of directors.

Employees are invited to participate based on their assessed contribution to the value creation at the company. According to Huawei, seniority, age, years with the company, or connections do not matter in whether a person is eligible or not, but can have an influence on how many shares are allocated to someone. The shares are usually purchased with the employee's annual bonus. If a bonus is not enough for the number of shares distributed, the company will lend the money to the employee.

Huawei's virtual shares have both similarities to and differences from conventional shares. Huawei's employees buy into the stock plan using their own funds and bear all the usual risks and rewards of regular share ownership. But they cannot, for example, be transferred to others or owned by non-employees. If an employee leaves Huawei, the company buys the shares back, unless the employee has reached a certain level of seniority.

Shares are valued annually based on the company's net asset value as disclosed in its annual report; and owners of the shares receive annual dividends based on the number of shares they hold.

Huawei has credited their ESOP system with being instrumental to their rapid growth. The majority of value created by the company goes directly to current, high-contributing employees. This drives loyalty and helps attract talented people. With such a close relationship to company value, for truly committed long term-minded employees, the ESOP will create significant wealth.

6.3 INTERESTING BOARDROOM DEBATES AHEAD

People management in Chinese enterprises is very different from Western style human resource management.

We realize that whether or not a foreign enterprise can adopt any of the above-mentioned practices will depend on the type of company or development stage it is in or even in what political system and legal framework the company operates. But we believe there are lessons to be learned.

It is easy to reject the behaviour of the Emperor as paternalistic. And we recognize possible downsides as well to a clan-based business structure. An absolute leader often walks a fine line between keeping the clan happy at the potential risk of not making the best possible decisions for the company, for example, favouring loyalty over ability.

But perhaps companies in the West have gone too far in their drive to mostly see the need for efficiencies when looking at staffing solutions. Especially in larger enterprises, and increasingly in platform organisations, the emotional dimension seems increasingly overlooked.

Western companies often spend a lot of money and effort on increasing employee engagement, on having all share a common vision and mission usually spelled out on posters all over the office or in colourful PowerPoint presentations. But more often than not, this is perceived by employees as not truly meaningful because in spite of these tools and materials, they lack an emotional connection to their work or even to such a vision.

China leaders are much better at creating a real emotional bond inside their companies. Owners are more inclined to directly look after people and align them emotionally with their vision of the future. As we pointed out, Western managers are more inclined to focus on knowing and doing, but often forget or de-prioritize being.

When we speak with foreign business leaders in China, they eagerly describe the family-like atmosphere they have managed to create among their Chinese teams with a focus on mentoring, nurturing, and 'doing things together'. Yet, surprisingly, they are not able to explain why a similar culture does not exist in other subsidiaries around the globe. But as we have pointed out, such culture is driven from the top.

With global markets becoming more complex and unpredictable and the lure of creating a start-up on the rise among younger generations, participation models developed by China's entrepreneurs to identify and reward entrepreneurial talent could serve as examples for larger, more traditional companies in more mature markets. To become more agile, they will need to recruit and nurture more entrepreneurial talent and develop ways to keep their best employees happy and incentivized. It would certainly help them also to drop the over reliance on PowerPoint!

Create that family feel!

We see clear lessons to be learned for talent management at multinationals operating in China as well. To begin with, they need to ask themselves whether they are sending the right entrepreneurially minded people to China, and whether they are keeping them long enough in their position to create the necessary tight family atmosphere that will contribute to retaining much needed talent and ultimately drive company success.

This is all the more important as the foreign manager should act as the bridge to the parent company culture. He or she is the one who can infuse the key values of the global company — which is not only geographically far but culturally different — with a history and working style that does not easily resonate with Chinese employees.

The emotional bond created by the foreign leader therefore becomes a key success factor. It is very interesting to see that nearly 15 years after Sandrine left Adidas China, the company she built, she maintains strong enough ties with former colleagues in China to still count them among her friends. Occasional reunions with groups of people that since have all gone their separate ways are still a regular occurrence.

Rethink incentive schemes.

Another question multinational enterprises need to ask themselves is whether their incentive schemes are optimized for China realities. The lure of shares and participation models in a Chinese start-up or entrepreneurial endeavour far outweighs the offer of a salary and bonus from a global firm. As Chinese business leaders show, in order to win, you need to innovate your ownership and incentive systems.

Here we even have our own personal experience to share once again. We had to push hard for it, but in the end, the bonus and incentive scheme at Adidas China was redesigned in a way that was very different from the corporate scheme used globally. And it became a uniting force around the organisation to aim higher and try to outperform our targets on a yearly basis. And we consistently did, much to the delight not only of the China team but also the global management and the shareholders! A few years later, Adidas global decided to implement worldwide an incentive mechanism essentially similar to the Adidas China model.

Are participation models the way to close the increasing wealth gap in the West?

It is our belief that the participation models developed by Chinese entrepreneurs could be possible solutions in ongoing discussions about the increasing wealth gap in many Western countries, and inside companies between their leadership and staff.

Chinese founders and company leaders demonstrate that connecting a broad group of people — and not just a handful of senior VPs — more closely to the organisation through participation is a sustainable option. Aligning the objectives of many individuals much more with the objectives of the company seems a proven win-win.

There is a lot to say in favour of participation models at Yong Hui Superstores or incentive schemes at Haidilao and certainly also for the Huawei ownership system, particularly when compared to schemes common among global multinationals with guaranteed salaries, bonuses, and low-priced options. These often present a lot of upside and no downside and are often concentrated at the top.

Now compare this to the thousands of Huawei employees who could lose the bulk of their personal wealth if the firm decreases significantly in value. So, when Huawei talks about going into 'battle mode', you need to picture tens of thousands of employees all fighting together against big declines in their personal wealth.[17]

Or better still, they are all pushing in the same direction to increase its fortunes by finding entrepreneurial ways to grow the company and improve their own prosperity in the process.

The limitations when venturing outside China.
We also see lessons to be learned by Chinese companies that plan to expand abroad, especially when entering Western markets.

In such business environments, too much top-down control will have clear limitations among people used to being able to think and decide much more independently. In the short term, we see firms solving this problem by employing Chinese leaders in senior positions. But while we earlier quoted Chinese entrepreneurs such as Robin Li from JD.com who rightfully criticised multinationals for not doing enough to localize management, the same will be true for Chinese firms growing and developing in markets foreign to them.

Clan based people management and decisions not necessarily in the interest of the enterprise will prove to be obstacles when expanding abroad and bringing in much needed foreign talent. Running large enterprises with a few hand-picked, Western-educated Chinese nationals will turn out not to be sustainable in the long term.

Also, finding the right balance between capturing short term opportunities and following more structured planning models needed to provide the necessary strategic alignment will be another challenge for Chinese companies expanding outside their borders. Change is not a constant in more mature Western markets.

Trust (or rather the lack of it outside the inner circle) will also need to be addressed. A relatively small but telling example that really struck Sandrine when she sold her company, and which, when discussing with other Westerners who had sold their businesses in China, she found to be a common practice: at the very minute when she received payment for the transaction, she was asked to remit all bank codes and tokens, including for her Paris office. This is not something you would expect in the West, where it is assumed that a senior director will respect basic payment processes and that trust comes with the position.

There is still a long way to go for Chinese entrepreneurs to be comfortable managing responsible foreign managers in a culture that is deeply different from theirs.

The impact of technology.

On a closing note, another challenge, not just for family-led Chinese firms but also for multinationals doing business in China, is to navigate their companies in the current technological revolution — often called the Industrial Revolution 4.0 — in which a fusion of technologies is blurring the lines between physical, digital, and biological spheres.

This profound change is ripping through China, with hugely disruptive technologies leading China's effort to transition from a manufacturing-driven economy to a service-and consumer-oriented one.

Business models that worked well a few years ago may no longer function after the disruptions, and this is no exception to mainland family businesses. The quality of the succession of company leadership will decide the future of many Chinese enterprises over the next few decades.

As Chinese companies are well used to change, many are already well equipped to deal with the digital disruption. We will explore this digital revolution in more detail in the next chapter, It All Starts with Data.

数据为本

7

IT ALL STARTS
WITH DATA.

7. IT ALL STARTS WITH DATA.

'In stark contrast, China's startup culture is the yin to Silicon Valley's yang:
instead of being mission-driven, Chinese companies are first and foremost market-driven.'

Kai-Fu Lee

President, Sinovation Ventures Artificial Intelligence Institute

7.1 DATA DISRUPTION

For millennia, the abacus (算盘, pinyin: Suànpán literally 'calculating tray') was the main form of calculator in China. A simple device both in shape and operation, it was widely used for anything that required numeric computations.

A wooden frame, split into an upper and lower section, with a horizontal beam separating the two parts, the abacus is fitted with up to thirteen vertical rods containing beads. Two beads on each rod in the upper area and five beads each in the bottom.

The value of each bead in the upper section of the first vertical column is 5, and in the bottom section, 1 per bead. Values then move up by a factor of 10, from right to left or left to right, depending on user preference. Counting takes place by moving the beads up or down toward the beam; beads moved against the beam are counted, while those moved away from it are not. A quick shake and the beads can be reset to their starting position.

Even after China opened up to the outside world in the late 80s, the abacus continued its presence in the daily lives of most Chinese. When we arrived in China, it was still commonly and persistently used everywhere. For example, the lady that managed the first Adidas warehouse would recalculate everything on her abacus that she had previously tallied with a calculator, just to be sure the numbers were correct!

Only when the digital revolution started in earnest did the abacus dwindle in popularity, or to be more precise, when the mobile revolution began around 2010. While most of the world was using PCs and initially developed a PC-based digital economy, in China mobile computing took hold much faster, with a large majority of users skipping PCs altogether. As early as January 2012, Chinese users accessing the Internet via a mobile device surpassed the percentage of users with a PC.[1]

China now has the world's largest number of internet users. About one billion people — a penetration rate of over 70%[2] — are online, active on social media,[3] and are smartphone users.[4] In 2018, smartphone ownership in China reached 96% of mobile users, 6% higher than the global average ownership at that time.[5]

While the mobile user and penetration numbers by themselves are impressive, they do not immediately explain why in China the internet has mostly been a mobile internet.

Unlike many Western economies, China's market was not yet mature when the digital revolution started. In many of the industries most affected by digital technologies, offline offerings were limited, physical infrastructure was lacking, and other essential market components, such as suitable payment systems, did not exist. Thus, digital technologies offered a solution to fundamental bottlenecks in consumption rather than a disruptive alternative to existing solutions as was the case in Western societies. China's digital market developed in an exceptionally rapid and dynamic manner, based on need rather than preference.[6]

And, with limited personal budgets, most people gravitated to a mobile device, which in turn accelerated a mobile computing landscape that is the basis of the data economy that has developed since. Nothing was more instrumental in driving this fast mobile internet adoption than mobile payment solutions, most notably Alipay and WeChat Pay.

In Section 4.1 we described that when we both arrived in China in the early 90s, the only way to pay was with cash, often with very old and crumpled notes, and yet today, China has the highest rate of digital payments via mobile applications globally, exceeding 80% of all transactions!

As we also explained in Chapter 4 Adapt to Change or Die, Chinese users are enthusiastic early adopters, very open towards technology, and are very keen on the latest new New. And with less personal concern about privacy, they adopted mobile payment solutions extremely quickly, transforming Chinese society from cash to mobile payments. Even in the remotest parts of the country, a visitor will come across signs indicating mobile payment is accepted.

This enthusiasm about technology also comes from the significant and visible quality improvement it has brought to large parts of the population. For example, e-commerce has brought unlimited access — both for buying and selling products — to many rural areas that otherwise would not have been able to participate so broadly in the modern retail economy. Access to quality healthcare in low tier cities or in the countryside would not have been possible so fast if it had only relied on traditional hospitals. Telemedicine and AI has been a life changer for many people.

Top-down technological revolution.

In the previous chapters, we have looked to the past to explain what has made Chinese entrepreneurs successful and have described methodologies that are rooted in Chinese history and culture. For the remainder of the book, however, it is important to understand where the future is headed based on what is happening today.

China is increasingly leading a digital revolution which is changing the way business is done and go-to-market strategies are implemented. How entrepreneurs and business leaders around the world adapt to this digital disruption will be a decisive factor between success and failure for many enterprises.

To better understand what the future may look like, lets first examine what has been behind the unfolding digital revolution and the rapid rise of technological progress in China.

Although most internet companies are private, China's government has been instrumental in ensuring the right environment for investment. From its early days around 2010, it created the right conditions to support the Chinese tech revolution. In 2015, as part of its 13th Five-Year Plan, the China State Council formalized and structured its initiatives and set the country on the road toward the fourth industrial revolution. They devised a policy aimed at turning the Middle Kingdom from a global sweatshop into an all-around high-tech superpower that excels in many fields, from space and deep-sea mining to the development of nanomaterials, from biomedicine to new energy vehicles.[7]

In other words, after having taken advantage of its surplus of low-cost labour to become the world's second largest economy, China now wants to make innovation in general and information technology and artificial intelligence in particular a key growth lever.

Part of this vision is 'Internet Plus', the application of internet and other digital technologies in conventional industries, similar to what is often referred to as industry 4.0. Artificial intelligence is stimulated through the 'New Generation of Artificial Intelligence Development Plan'.

Facing an aging population and a consequent shrinking work force in their immense country, with its great diversity and increasingly striking inequalities, Chinese leadership is taking a holistic view and see AI as an essential tool for reducing the gap between rural and urban areas, accelerating productivity gains, and ensuring more harmonious growth.

Both initiatives aim to boost digital innovations by leveraging the Internet of Things, 5G mobile, big data, cloud computing, and AI technologies to construct a 'Digital China'.

Both the Chinese Government and private businesses have taken a very pragmatic joint approach toward the acceleration of the development and implementation of technology. In official and unofficial alliances between government and private companies, investments are encouraged and protected (as long as they serve the government vision, as recent developments have made clear).

For example, Alipay could never have been rolled out so extensively if it had not been tolerated by the authorities, as Ant Financial was not a bank. As the predicament of Jack Ma and his fintech company — described in Upstream rearrangements in Section 4.1 of Chapter 4 Adapt to Change or Die — indicates, this pragmatism has its limitations. In the end, the Emperor decides whether specific activities fit his long-term vision. But the incentive is large for the entrepreneurs that stay within clear parameters.

This win-win tactic has enabled the Chinese government to rapidly achieve its goals and private businesses to develop into global tech giants. This joint approach, combined with the high level of AI acceptance in the population, has led the whole nation to treat technology and AI as a strategic priority.

This uniquely Chinese approach is very well described in a recent article by François Candelon from the BCG Henderson Institute and his co-authors:[8]

> In keeping with its past practice of picking national champions, the Chinese government chose Tencent to lead A.I. innovation in computer vision for medical imaging; Baidu for autonomous driving; Alibaba for smart cities; Sense Time for facial recognition; and iFlytek for voice intelligence.

Another telling example is the tender by the Ministry of Science and Technology issued In October 2017, for 13 'transformative' technology projects that would receive preferential government funding for projects to be completed within 2021.

One of these projects is the development of AI chips that are expected to be more powerful than any product from leading U.S. semi-conductor players. Although at the time of writing the development of such semi-conductors has not yet succeeded, China — backed by strong government mandates, incentive plans, and billions of dollars in both private and public investment — has made significant progress in building a solid digital foundation to cement itself as a leader in the global innovation arena.

Based on latest data, China spends roughly $530B per annum on R&D, which represents an 11-fold increase over the past two decades.[9] To put this scale in perspective, the current annual R&D spent by China is more than that of Japan, Germany, France, the UK, and South Korea combined and only slightly shy of the US, which is around $ 600B.

This sustained investment over the past few years has pivoted China as a serious contender in the technology race with AI, digitalization, space exploration, and high-end manufacturing being some of the primary sectors focused on.

China is also leading the world in the development of AI enabled digital infrastructure, possesses a state-backed digital currency, and even leads the US on the number of patents filed for AI related topics.

It now ranks among the top three nations for venture capital investment in key areas such as virtual reality, autonomous vehicles, 3D printing, and robotics.[10] China is also the world's largest e-commerce market and is a major force — increasingly internationally as well — in mobile payments.

The consumer internet is mobile.

For most Chinese people, especially in areas that are commerce related, a lot of this technological investment ultimately finds its way to their mobile device.

China was an early adopter of 4G technology, starting their roll-out in 2014. With the digital infrastructure in place, commercial players focused on creating mobile-focused solutions.

An interesting example to illustrate this is Pingduoduo (PDD). Founded in 2015, PDD is currently the fastest growing e-commerce company and is disrupting the status quo.

Imagine a five-year-old US or European e-commerce company growing so fast that it would be threatening Amazon's long-established leadership. Unthinkable. And yet, Pingduoduo is doing just that. Not to Amazon, since they are no longer a player in the China market, but it is a real challenger to Alibaba and is already larger than JD.com.

In just over five years, PDD's Monthly Active Users (MAU) grew to 643 million, which took Alibaba 15 years to achieve, while PDD's Gross Merchandise Volume (GMV) reached half of Amazon's global GMV in 2020.[11]

And yet, Pingduoduo is 100% mobile and does not have a PC based internet presence! For more on the phenomenal success of Pingduoduo [see Section 7.2.2].

5G, bandwidth for innovation by experimentation.

Mobile internet innovation will take another leap in the years ahead given China's lead in 5G technology. The build-out of this high-speed network will strengthen China's emerging role as a global innovator.

China's 5G leadership is in fact Huawei's 5G leadership. As early as 2009, Huawei started investing in the research and development of 5G technology and today is recognized as the global leader of this latest generation of mobile equipment.

5G enables transmission speeds that surpass any previous generation of wireless communications and the experience and value that 5G will bring to individuals, families, and industries will surpass any previous digital era. With 5G, people will be able to enjoy immersive AR and VR experiences, enabling previously impossible expressions of thought and feelings within a digital world. 5G is also likely to have a great impact on the development of many industries and will create new business opportunities in IoT, the cloud, AI, and social digital transformation.

5G is just a network, but its success will be driven by application services. Therefore, innovation around 5G applications is the focus of the next 5G development stage. New possibilities and experiences will create unprecedented new value. As 5G mobile broadband matures, high-definition video services will drive large-scale growth of 5G B2C services. Future industry-to-industry cooperation will also be completely different from before and we are likely to see the build-up of a new cross-industry 5G ecosystem.

This will further accelerate the commercial application of 5G technology in areas such as smart manufacturing, multimedia, energy, and transportation. Elsewhere, in areas including smart cities, health care, and autonomous driving cars, China can serve as the testing ground for trial-and-error innovation.

For example, in the recent fight against Covid-19, 5G telemedicine has played an important role. The 5G remote consultation platform supported by Huawei and China Telecom was battle tested by various hospitals when traveling was not an option due to Covid restrictions.

China's leading position in 5G deployment means that China's entrepreneurs will be able to experiment with user applications at scale before anyone else and it is not hard to imagine that successful applications tested in China — be it augmented reality, new gaming experiences, or 'consumer-to-maker' business models — will later be introduced to other countries.[12]

What works, what doesn't, and how 5G can best facilitate these long-term revolutions will only be answered through real-life experiments. And innovation by experimentation is a capability well established within the entrepreneurial community in China as we described in detail in Chapter 4 Adapt to Change or Die.

Mobile payment triggered the data explosion.
With data seen as a new currency, China has the massive advantage of enjoying more data value than any other market, due to the size of its population, the

relative homogeneity [See comment on page 41] of its internal market, and the pace of its digitization.

Just to give a simple example to put this in better context: take Didi Chuxing, the largest ride-sharing company in the world today. According to its CEO Liu Qing, each day, Didi processes more than 70TB of data, with 9 billion routes being planned a day and 1,000 car requests each second.[13]

A service such as Didi would not have been able to operate at such a scale without a seamless connection with a remote payment system. As mobile payment solutions were instrumental in the acceptance and rapid scaling of mobile commerce, the technology is also the driver of the Chinese data explosion. More than any other app or technology, mobile payment enables myriad services, and its payment data is the holy grail of user knowledge, as it is the closest one gets to understanding actual behaviour.

Not only is a mobile device more intertwined with a person's life, as it is always on and around, but mobile payment data captures the core of what is needed to understand a person's habits, movements, preferences, and actions. And with mobile payment now more widely spread in China than anywhere else in the world, it comes as no surprise that there is not only a rapid increase in data quantities, but also in the use of it.

What has also given China an advantage is the concentration of users within large ecosystems that are, through shared systems, well connected.

And beyond the large data pools of the main ecosystems, a lot of data aggregators have sprung up over the last few years, helping companies to better integrate various data sources. These are local solutions, developed by companies such as EZR, link CRM, and social media platforms. They stitch together systems with data derived from WeChat mini programs and offline sales channels.

With the growth of private traffic [see Section 4.2.1 in Chapter 4 Adapt to Change or Die] and tagging users across ecosystems while combining offline data sources, the sheer size of data generated and turned into intelligence is still exploding. China has rapidly developed a data culture that not only could become an inspiration for many Western companies but should also become their guiding principle.

Data generation and usage goes far beyond consumer data.
Driven by the objectives of Internet Plus, China is also a pioneer in ideas for the smart and connected city, with a metropolis like Shenzhen being a benchmark for the world on digital infrastructure, including facial recognition-enabled services.

Online education is a priority as well and, for example, software and game developer NetDragon is developing an AI teaching assistant, Qiqi, that can check for absenteeism through facial recognition and help with customized learning solutions for individual students.

Moreover, with the Chinese population rapidly becoming older, the data revolution is also seen as the only solution to ensure adequate health care to such a large and scattered population, and so start-ups developing AI driven medical solutions are mushrooming.

For example, during the fight against Covid-19, medical diagnosing benefitted from AI development. Artificial intelligence start-ups supported medical workers on the frontline to deal with the novel coronavirus outbreak, using medical imaging devices embedded with AI for more rapid clinical diagnosis of the disease.

When suspected cases piled up in early 2020 in Hubei province, the initial epicentre of the global pandemic, medical AI was able to help doctors provide faster and more accurate clinical diagnosis while reducing their workload.

Deepwise Healthcare, a medical artificial intelligence start-up, quickly employed AI-powered imaging systems in more than 30 hospitals and upgraded AI imaging systems in more than 400 others across the country. Their AI solutions can identify patients' CT scan features associated with the novel coronavirus very quickly, deliver detailed and quantitative evaluation reports on the infection, including the size and location of the infected areas and the impact on lung function, as well as provide treatment advice.

Yitu Healthcare, the health arm of Shanghai-based AI start-up Yitu Technology Co Ltd, also launched an updated version of an AI imaging evaluation system for the virus. Their system can diagnose and classify viral pneumonias according to the shape, extent, and density of lesions found by a CT scan and can precisely calculate the disease burden on the lungs.

According to the company, traditional manual methods for such a quantitative assessment generally require five to six hours, while the new AI system can perform the analysis in two to three seconds.[14]

The potential use of AI in healthcare goes far beyond diagnosing tools and holds promise to fundamentally change the medical world, from how medication is developed, to how the doctor-patient relationship evolves, and to how medical insurance is approached. No wonder that the Chinese government is supporting data and has made AI in healthcare a priority.

China in the data and AI adoption lead.
The rapid 'datafication' of Chinese society is a culmination of various factors that together have given China an invaluable advantage in the innovation race. The combination of ravenous demand of leapfrogging consumers with a fo-

cused and top-down driven government approach, which ensured the right political framework and needed incentives, has encouraged the private sector to invest and innovate.

The unique scale of China and its consumers who are open to, and fast adopting, new technologies, have done the rest to create data pools that are larger and more diverse than anywhere. China, more than any other country in the world, is embracing technological innovation as the driver of progress, and becoming a world-leading tech player is a stated government objective.

Meanwhile, at the company level or where consumer expectations are concerned, there are already clear signs that China is leading the way and thus companies around the world should be looking to China to understand what their own future could look like.

For a century, the world's consumer businesses have looked to America to spot new trends, from scannable barcodes on Wrigley's gum in the 1970s to keeping up with the Kardashians' consumption habits in the 2010s.[15]

Yet, when it comes to digital commerce, China is now setting the trends. Online-shopping platforms in the Middle Kingdom blend digital payments, group deals, social media, gaming, instant messaging, short-form videos, and live-streaming celebrities into a social shopping experience. The process completely transforms market strategies and purchase processes.

This multi-dimensional approach is also gaining steam in other parts of the world, where Western digital companies are not yet as established as they are in their home markets, most notably among leading platforms in South-East Asia, India, and Latin America.

Multinationals with a large presence in China, and so by default were dragged into the digital revolution early (L'Oréal, KFC, and Adidas, for example) are already looking East to stay in tune with the latest in digital marketing, branding, and logistics and use these insights to transform their global business.

7.2 WHAT THE USE OF DATA IS TELLING US

Before proceeding, a word of clarification. Neither of us are tech experts. At heart, we are brand and consumer business specialists, whose professional lives have been deeply transformed by the profound changes brought by technology to the point that e-commerce became the core business of the company founded by Sandrine in the beginning of the 2010s. We have therefore purposefully concentrated our examples and case studies in the consumer industry and the B2C sector at large.

It must be noted however that the Chinese tech revolution has also affected the B2B sector and much of what we conclude is equally applicable for sectors beyond B2C.

With data increasingly available in vast quantities and in very sophisticated formats, China's commercial environment is increasingly data driven and data dominated. Embracing digital commerce in all its facets and the use of data to transform business models may not be directly grounded in China's culture or history but are clear derivatives of what Dragon Tactics are about: pragmatism, speed, and adapting to new realities.

We see three trends that will have an overwhelming effect on how businesses will be managed in a digital business world and where Chinese entrepreneurs are leading the way.

1. Intelligence is increasingly very artificial;
2. Data and AI enable ultra-consumer-centricity;
3. Consumers become users.

7.2.1 Intelligence is increasingly very artificial

In artificial intelligence, China has gone from a fringe player to a global leader in fundamental research in less than two decades. Various Chinese tech giants, encouraged and supported by the State, and powered by the AI ecosystems they have developed, are ahead in the global AI race.

According to Harvard Business Review, in 2019 China had more than 1,150 companies specializing in AI and ranked second only behind the United States, which had over 2,000 active AI firms.[16]

But it is likely only a matter of time that China will catch up or even surpass the US since China has a focused development plan centred on the creation of the next generation of artificial intelligence. And this plan is not just theoretical. Formalized in July 2017 by the State Council, it covers a three-step vision for the AI sector:

— 2017–2020: maintain pace of technological and application progress in line with other nations;
— 2020–2025: produce major breakthroughs in AI, enabling China to reach the highest level globally;
— 2025–2030: become the world's leading innovation centre for AI, with innovations eventually turning China into the decision-making country on the matter.

In effect, the first implementation measures were taken six months after the presentation of the AI development plan and included a detailed action plan published by the Ministry of Industry and Information Technology in December 2017.

And the results of this AI drive are not going unnoticed. Since 2010, MIT Technology Review,[17] a wholly owned yet editorially independent magazine of the Massachusetts Institute of Technology, has been creating an annual list of the 50 most intelligent innovative companies worldwide. Titled '50 Smartest Companies', or 'TR50', this annual list has become one of the most authoritative overviews of companies involved in AI.

As early as 2017, seven Chinese companies were selected to appear on the global TR50 list, including Tencent, face recognition specialist Face++, iFlytek (the leader in speech recognition), and fintech Ant Financial. Then, in 2019, the magazine created a special China focused edition to underscore the progress made in China.

The 2019 and the subsequent 2020 lists contain a few international players active inside China, such as NVIDIA and Tesla. But for the rest, beyond the better-known traditional internet giants, the list covers a broad array of disciplines, such as biotech companies Fosun Kite and Wuxi Apptec, insurance company Ping An, industrial AI solution provider AInnovation, and Pinduoduo, the disruptive e-commerce player, to name a few.

The needed conditions for very smart machines.

A 2020 report on AI by BCG and MIT[18] states that Chinese companies are leading in AI adoption compared to Western firms due to their access to large digital ecosystems from internet giants such as Alibaba and Tencent [for more, see next section] and their participation in relevant local platforms.

For example, by developing mini programs for established systems like WeChat and Alipay and leveraging existing popular streaming platforms such as Meipai, Momo, YY.com or apps like ByTheDance or Xiaohongshu, etc. a wide variety of local companies can plug into existing digital infrastructure for rapid market access and capital efficient scalability.

Mobile phones, used every day, also provide enormous amounts of training data for machine learning, further providing tailwinds to China becoming a superpower in data applications.

While China's large population and installed mobile base provide real scale in generating and utilizing big data, another clear advantage is China's decades-long effort in promoting technology and engineering, which now ensures a rich supply of high-quality computer scientists and engineers.

These advantages are further amplified by large open-source communities and vast user demand. And with mobile phones an ideal vehicle for AI-based applications on the customer side, there is no surprise behind the rapid growth of AI-powered mobile apps.

With all these technological developments, it is certainly not unexpected that the Chinese public has a high AI awareness, with a majority expressing support for comprehensive AI development in a study published by the Tsinghua University-based China Institute for Science and Technology Policy (CISTP).[19] A further indication of the acceptance of AI driven technologies is a survey from Deloitte[20] that shows that Chinese users utilize mobile phone-based AI-powered apps far more than global users, as is illustrated in the below graph.

Fugure 7: Comparison of AI-based apps in Chinese and global mobile phones

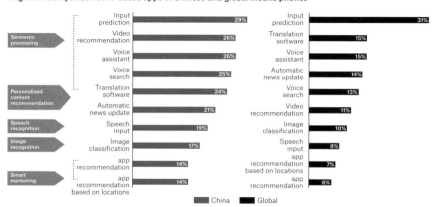

Where AI adds, not scares.

Among the Chinese public there seems to be less concern about the use of AI than is being expressed elsewhere. According to the 2020 MIT-BCG survey we referenced in the previous section, 86% of users in China trust AI-made decisions, while only 39% of Americans and 45% of Europeans do. According to the CISTP report we also quoted above, worries include the replacement of workers and social crises that might arise if AI runs out of control. Overall, the Chinese public seems to be neither overly optimistic or overly pessimistic and appears quite rational about AI.

Needless to say, one would not expect to read possible concerns about the growing reach of China's surveillance state in such a report, but while there are aspects of the Chinese government's approach to AI that are concerning, such as a wide use of face recognition, and are, rightly so, being challenged around the world, it is critical that such concerns are not dominating the overall AI debate and evaluation.

The China AI landscape is much more diverse and offers many promising advances in useful AI applications. While it is easy to just focus on facial recognition, or social governance systems, a lot is being developed that is user focused and will help humanity, as our examples about the use of AI in healthcare and in combating Covid-19 shows. And there are many applications that are highly relevant and value adding in the business arena as well.

That is because a lot of the AI in China is actually very user friendly. For this it is important to understand the current state of AI development. According to AI expert Diatian Li[21], the majority of AI developed in China currently is 'weak AI' — AI that solves narrowly defined problems — and requires domain-specific knowledge and user-generated data to improve.

For example, AI often needs to be customized to specific business scenarios. You first make a product (e.g., voice recognition). Then, you attract many users and these users generate data. Finally, you use machine learning to improve products with data. Enhancements occur through this virtuous cycle.

Given the solution-driven and user-driven mindset of many Chinese entrepreneurs, they have created a vibrant market that is receptive to these new AI-based products, and Chinese firms are relatively fast in bringing useful AI products and services to the market. With Chinese consumers fast in adopting such products and services, the environment supports rapid uptake and subsequent refinement of AI technologies and AI-powered products.

In his fascinating book, AI Superpowers,[22] computer scientist and AI expert Kai Fu Lee could not agree more. He argues,

China's start-up culture is the yin to Silicon Valley's yang: instead of being mission-driven, Chinese companies are first and foremost market-driven. Their ultimate goal is to make money, and they're willing to create any product, adopt any model, or go into any business that will accomplish that objective.

As we enter the age of AI implementation, the cutthroat entrepreneurial environment China is known for will be one of China's core assets in building a machine-learning-driven economy. The dramatic transformation that deep learning promises to bring to the global economy won't be delivered by isolated researchers producing novel academic results in the elite computer science labs of MIT or Stanford. Instead, it will be delivered by down-to-earth, profit-hungry entrepreneurs teaming up with

AI experts to bring the transformative power of deep learning to bear on real-world industries.

Over the coming decade, China's entrepreneurs will fan out across hundreds of industries, applying deep learning to any problem that shows the potential for profit. If artificial intelligence is the new electricity, Chinese entrepreneurs will be the tycoons and tinkerers who electrify everything from household appliances to homeowners' insurance.

Their knack for endlessly tweaking business models and sniffing out profits will yield an incredible array of practical — maybe even life-changing — applications. These will be deployed in their home country and then pushed abroad, potentially taking over most developing markets around the globe.

To put this in better context, we have listed some of the interesting applications of AI that are likely to fundamentally change how business will be done. This list is far from exhaustive; we have concentrated on areas that are focused more on consumer business and are outside the better known or somewhat mainstream AI areas, such as smart speakers, drones, and robotics.

Anti-fraud – Maxent:
Maxent has developed AI-powered, automatic, intelligent, anti-fraud technologies and systems that help enterprises build user behaviour tracking and analysis and automatic anomaly detection capabilities to achieve controlled real-time identification of new fraud patterns. This system effectively combats increasing cybercrime and fraud-based forgery and impersonation that cause massive losses to consumers and financial institutions.

Smart homes: Personalized services – Xiaomi, Midea, and Haier:
Speech recognition and natural language processing technologies enable users to control home devices, such as window curtains, lights, and TV sets by talking to them and telling them what to do; smart devices can learn about the user and through subscriptions can order shopping or recommend media content accordingly.

Facial recognition in Retail – SENSETIME & Suning:
Suning, one of China's leading retail companies, is cooperating with Sense-Time, a leader in facial and body recognition, to jointly explore the applica-

tion of identification in automated shopping, membership management, and payment verification, as well as the role of artificial intelligence in enhancing personalized shopping experiences.

Smarter decisions – 6ESTATES:
6ESTATES is a major player in AI in the field of consumer and finance focused technologies, and a specialist in digital ethnography and social and societal listening. Originating within universities in Singapore (NUS) and China (Tsinghua), 6ESTATES helps companies gain knowledge and improve their efficiency by better knowing their customer in terms of fashion, attitude, and social context.

Speech synthesis – Panda Reader and Baidu:
Panda Reader is an application that reads books and articles to its users. Using a text-to-speech technique based on Baidu's AI, the system can not only turn text into speech, but also do so with the right pauses and intonations, which provides a much more immersive and expressive experience. The AI can also respond to user requests.

Art creation – Meitu:
Meitu is a popular photo editing and sharing app that claims to have launched the world's first drawing Artbot called Andy. Unlike traditional photo filters that add effects to images, Andy deconstructs a photo and can reassemble it into a new form to make an original image or work of art. It took Andy six months to go from producing ridiculous images to producing portraits in a believable 'handmade' style. A wide range of options are now provided, and the resulting images can be delivered on physical objects such as phone cases or t-shirts.

What these examples above have in common is a clear end-user benefit that fits perfectly with the intense consumer focus, which successful Chinese entrepreneurs have made their hallmark to become and remain competitive.

7.2.2 Data and AI enable ultra-consumer-centricity
Often not hindered by legacy IT architecture, Chinese firms aggressively invest in building the systems that collect, bring together, and interpret various streams of information.

When speed and tenacity as well as trying and learning are favoured over sticking to a long-term plan, good data becomes even more meaningful and effective: each trial is proven right or wrong with data. If wrong, a decision to move on to the next trial can be made even faster. If right, the power of data enables a level of amplification that one could not reach before.

Chinese entrepreneurs have always been very close to the market and extremely reactive to consumers. In many cases their speed of new product launches is incomparably higher than in Western markets.

With the wealth of data now available in China, the ability to understand consumers' reaction and act on it has increased massively and seems to further prove Chinese entrepreneurs' approach right.

This ultra-consumer-centricity makes them better at this than most of their Western rivals. Additionally, they have access to far more data through the massive ecosystems that combine social media and e-commerce and that result from the exceptional speed of adoption of new technologies by Chinese consumers.

Databanks.

Giant digital platforms such as Tencent, Alibaba, and Baidu have amassed huge data stocks to train their machine learning algorithms. This abundance of data is all the more advantageous because the use of it is enabled by relatively flexible Chinese data privacy regulation. Although with new legislation introduced in the summer of 2021 that strengthen privacy rules, the available data sets are likely to remain most comprehensive and multi-dimensional.

Alibaba leading the way.

As early as 2017, Alibaba Group officially released its Brand Databank, a consumer data asset management centre and service for brands. This data source enables brands to fully manage their consumer data assets.

The Alibaba Brand Databank can absorb and store every online and offline interaction between brands and their consumers, and track the status of the consumer journey throughout the awareness-interest-purchase-loyalty (AIPL) process.

The Brand Databank allows individual brands to match their own data with the proprietary 'Uni-Identity' within the Alibaba Group ecosystem. The database integrates customer relationship management (CRM), e-commerce data, advertising data, media data, social media attribute data such as from Weibo and Momo and product comments in the Alibaba ecosystem, turning aggregated consumer data into a real brand asset in real time.

In this way, the Brand Databank helps brands to continuously accumulate and aggregate consumer data assets and augment their relationship with consumers. Moreover, Brand Databank provides a platform for brands to independently operate consumer data, helping them optimize customer lifecycle management.

Based on massive quantities of accumulated consumer data in the Alibaba ecosystem, brands can study consumers in the Brand Databank in a more comprehensive and panoramic way so that consumer profiles can be enriched. This allows the brands to analyse and understand their consumers in different contexts and develop specific products and market strategies.

This wealth of data and the increasing ability of companies in China to use them bring science to the Chinese trial-and-error approach and enable ultra-consumer-centricity as the following examples show.

Mars China: the databank invented the spicy Snickers.
A prominent case is the cooperation between the Alibaba Tmall Innovation Center (TMIC) and the China subsidiary of Mars, Inc that led to the development of a new variant of the Snickers chocolate bar: the Spicy Snickers, in China, for China.

Mars capitalized on the growing popularity of 麻辣 (pinyin: málà, literally: numbing spicy) and created a chili-infused Snickers bar.

The collaboration involved the integration of analytics from Mars' consumer research, the 500 million-plus users of Alibaba's online marketplaces, and a customer survey aimed at finding a new flavour to bring to the market. The result showed that not only did Chinese consumers love spicy food, but that they were also willing to try chocolate with an extra kick to it.

Spicy Snickers was a big hit immediately and is a perfect illustration of the reversed manufacturing process enabled by data and analytics — a customer-to-business (C2B) approach that taps customer preferences and feedback to develop and design products, rather than the traditional top-down approach.[23] And indeed, beyond the creation of new products based on data and AI, what we are seeing in China is that data and AI ultimately lead to disruption of traditional processes and business models.

Another example is how Xtep, a sportswear company, created a product line for a new target audience.

Xtep: the databank revealed untapped opportunities.
Xtep partnered with the Alibaba databank to better understand targets beyond their existing main customer base, which is rooted in a more working-class male audience in lower tier cities.

Alibaba Databank category data revealed a target group with a passion for fashionable products and hip hop-inspired street wear. This target was, for Xtep, surprisingly female, younger, and living in higher tier markets with a higher spending power.

The analysis created a new business opportunity as well as a change to extend the brand beyond its existing core.

An ad-hoc team was set up to develop products for this new segment and to create an online driven distribution and a new marketing approach by partnering with the interactive TV reality show 'This Is Street Dance'.

Their hip hop- and celebrity-inspired new product line was a big hit. Manga inspired graphic designs were a new territory for Xtep but brought in a large number of young, trendy female consumers into the brand.

With such a clearly defined target group, and deep insights into their needs and preferences, the product creation cycle was entirely revisited and optimized, leading to a much shorter lead time of going to market for this trendy and more fickle audience.

Xtep received an award from Alibaba for this initiative.

Perfect Diary – perfect AI driven consumer centricity.
In Section 4.2.1 we wrote about Perfect Diary and we highlighted the phenomenal rise of this online cosmetics sensation. In a brief summary, we described its core success factors.

A key element of Perfect Diary's innovative approach is its smart use of artificial intelligence — particularly grouping likeminded people together in mini online user groups — to create very targeted platforms of similar young women who interact about their user needs.

Perfect Diary has created a digital account matrix that enables a very customized service. Through a variety of methodologies (such as a QR card inside a delivery box, a promise of 'lucky money', or via KOL recommendations), the brand encourages consumers to connect with its WeChat channel.

Once they have entered its WeChat channel, a fictional, artificial intelligence-driven avatar called Xiao Wanzi, a girl modelled after its target audience, gives customers access to their lucky money and invites the user to post about herself on Xiao Wanzi's WeChat moments.

This enables Perfect Diary to tag users and assign specific values. Perfect Diary is then able to better match each user with others that have similar characteristics, such as the same hobbies, and will subsequently send a personal invitation to the user to join a specific likeminded group. Now they can optimise purchase offers and communication for each of these myriad groups with a specific user profile.

This is an almost perfect way to be user centric. Consumers feel they are being understood and appreciated as Xiao Wanzi acts as a reliable friend, is their beauty consultant, and provides exclusive services for the consumers in the group. This personal approach and product optimization significantly increase users' desire to purchase.

Without AI and an automated digital approach, Perfect Diary would not be able to interact so personally, constantly, with such a large number of users.

PingDuoDuo – AI created consumer needs create hyper growth.

PingDuoDuo is another interesting example of an AI-driven user focus creating real business success. In fact, the business model of the company is so successful that the firm, within only a five-year period, has surpassed JD.com to become the second largest e-commerce player in China, just behind Alibaba.[24]

How did Pingduoduo achieve such am incredible feat? By pushing product recommendations based on user interest.

E-commerce marketplaces like Amazon allow buyers to search for what they need out of 'unlimited' selections as they want products that fit their individual needs. This creates 'long tail' demand, meaning demand for low volume niche products wanted by many different people.

Companies like Amazon can capture the long tail demand and realize significant profit by selling obscure hard-to-find items held on stock by others, rather than selling popular best sellers. E-commerce marketplaces therefore provide niche products to attract different consumers with diverse interest.

PingDuoDuo does the opposite. Rather than trying to monetize many consumers by maximizing product selection to satisfy their long-tail demand, PDD consolidates similar needs among people into a limited variety of products through team purchases. When demand is consolidated, products can be made available at lower cost to consumers through economies of scale in production. To optimize this model, PDD has pioneered the so-called Consumer to Manufacturer (C2M) model.

Pioneering C2M.

From day one, PDD devoted itself to the mission of 'Benefiting All'. In the C2M model, consumers save money as the consolidated purchase orders go directly to manufacturers, bypassing all the middle layers (distributors, retail outlets, and supermarkets).

Manufacturers increase their income while still giving discounts because (1) Their production cost is lower due to economies of scale from a team purchase; (2) Directly selling to end-consumers allows them to charge the retail price instead of the wholesale price (3) There is less waste by producing to demand, backed by consumer data.

The C2M model thus becomes a virtuous cycle for both manufacturers and consumers. Production efficiency leads to lower prices for consumers, which stimulates more team purchases for manufacturers.

No C2M without AI.

Pingduoduo developed a sophisticated approach to ensure a leading user understanding: an AI data-driven mobile consumer platform that is 80% e-commerce and 20% social media and gaming.

PDD uses an AI recommendation feed to push products to consumers instead of having them search for products. They push relevant product recommendations to different consumers based on their interest, or better yet, pushing different products to the same consumer to satisfy his or her different needs. This AI recommendation feed has been proven to increase sales dramatically.

Gaming is the secret to knowing.

While competitors like Alibaba are now copying the same AI recommendation feed, PDD's viral growth secret remains in the social element of team purchases and its tie with WeChat.[25]

PDD compares itself to Disney and thinks that shopping should be fun. Users are rewarded with deeper discounts or even free products by sharing their shopping experience with friends on WeChat.

As team purchase was first launched in low-value everyday goods like fruits, discounts incentivized users to frequently share the products with friends. Through this user sharing on WeChat, PDD gains further insight into the users' and their friends' shopping preferences, which further improves their AI recommendations.

PDD also pioneered the gamification of shopping. 'Duo Duo Orchard' is a game in PDD's app designed to incentivize consumers to browse, share, and purchase every day. Users need virtual water and fertilizer to grow their virtual tree, and those items can only be collected through daily log-in, product sharing, spending time in-app, and product purchases.

When the virtual tree is fully grown, PDD will deliver a box of real fruit for free to the user as a reward. Over 60 million users log on to play Duo Duo Orchard every day. As a result, PDD orders tons of fruit from struggling farmers, helping them to improve their livelihood while avoiding their harvest going to rot.

The addictive gamification design is another 'Benefitting All' example: users have fun, PDD gets users' attention, and farmers are helped.

Shein demonstrates that the model can be exported beyond China.

Unless you are a teenaged girl or the parent of one, the chance is high you have never heard of Shein. And yet this Chinese company is giving Zara and other established fast fashion players a serious run for their money and is redefining the fast in fast fashion.

Shein is also demonstrating that with the right digital approach it is possible to develop a brand in China with worldwide appeal and reach. The company is disrupting the fashion industry globally by using slick social media campaigns and aggressive promotions on TikTok, Facebook, and Instagram to sell ultra-low-cost clothing to teens and college-aged consumers around the world. And it's doing it primarily through online clicks. It seems hard to believe, but the brand is simultaneously the world's most highly tracked website in the lifestyle, fashion, and apparel category. Shein now ranks first, ahead of global brands like Nike, Zara, H&M, Uniqlo, and Gap, according to the web analytics firm Similarweb.[26]

A recent report by investment bank Piper Sandler, which tracks fashion trends, says Shein is now the most popular fashion brand among teenage shoppers in the United States. One measure of its online popularity is its social media metrics: it has 19 million followers on Instagram and nearly 2 million on TikTok. It succeeds by purchasing ads on Facebook and hiring micro-influencers — people paid in gifts of free clothing or cash — to promote its brand online.

The company has managed to create a brand and product offer that appeals to a world-wide audience, has mastered the art of trendspotting globally, and developed a sourcing model that enables an ultra-fast and flexible consumer experience.

The brand introduces up to 1,000 algorithm determined new items daily, and yet the company doesn't own a single factory. Instead, it simply spots online trends, sources from a network of supplier factories, and then ships directly around the world, at prices that are virtually impossible to beat.

Changing attitudes toward sustainability have not yet slowed Shein down. For now, many of their global young consumers seem unconcerned about the waste and environmental degradation that are the inevitable by-products of producing mass quantities of cheap clothing. For now, they are more than happy to post themselves modelling their latest purchases, further feeding the algorithms that make Shein such an ultra-consumer-focused consumer darling.

YUM CHINA DIGITAL - AI-POWERED SUPER APPS THAT INSPIRE THE GLOBE.

March 2020: Fast Company names Yum China one of the world's most innovative companies.

WHAT IS SO INNOVATIVE?

- A powerful digital ecosystem, integrating online platforms with offline stores, enhances the customer experience and engagement throughout the customer journey.
- Data and artificial intelligence capabilities enable more informed and improved decisions throughout the entire business, including menu innovation, delivery, marketing, store operations, and supply chain management.

POWERFUL DIGITAL ECOSYSTEM FOR AN IMMERSIVE CUSTOMER EXPERIENCE.

- At the heart of Yum China's digital ecosystem are the *KFC and Pizza Hut Super Apps.*
- They enable engagement with customers wherever they are, and extend beyond food to music, games, sports, and entertainment, giving Yum enormous insight to what buyers like.
- Integrated are individual digital features such as coupons and vouchers, privilege memberships, e-commerce, payment options, and corporate social responsibility activities.
- In addition to the widely used Alipay and WeChat Pay platforms, *YUMC Pay,* a payment option in partnership with Union Pay, offers another convenient option for customers. Up to 97% of all payments are digital.

CREATING VALUABLE AND INSIGHTFUL USER DATA.

- **300 million-plus digital members** at KFC and Pizza Hut provide a wealth of valuable customer feedback and knowledge across different cities.
- This data helps determine the most effective and preferred store formats, store locations, and menu items.
- It also significantly increases the effectiveness of marketing campaigns while building awareness and loyalty quickly.
- Additionally, exciting offers within the Privilege Program drive frequency, value perception, and customer loyalty.

A DISRUPTIVE DIGITAL 'NEW RETAIL' EXPERIENCE.

- Self-ordering kiosks with Alipay's 'Smile-to-Pay' facial recognition payment technology can be found at over one thousand KFC stores and fully automated dessert stations are available in selected stores.
- Delivery 3.0 is Yum China's intelligent trade zone-focused platform that optimizes delivery services and improves efficiency. The platform's AI-driven

dispatching system and logistics overflow support is transforming the relationship between customers, riders, and stores.

DATA AND AI DRIVE SALES AND OPERATIONAL EFFICIENCY.
— Data enables a flexible yet targeted approach to marketing based on consumer preferences.
— Yum China rolled out AI enabled menus and recommendations for all mobile pre-orders, providing personalized customer interaction and trade-up opportunities.
— Using AI-based technology, Yum China significantly improved sales forecasting, leading to better inventory management and store labor scheduling.
— Yum China has developed tailormade algorithms that help evaluate changing data patterns at the store level, such as location, sales performance, weather, promotions, and holidays.
— The company is also rolling out smart watches that enable managers to closely monitor the ordering and serving status of their restaurants and quickly identify and rectify any issue.

AND THE GLOBAL OPERATION BENEFITS.
— In 2019, inspired by what Yum China had created, Yum Brands launched a global digital innovation lab to dig deeper into and react faster to customer preferences.
— A year later, both KFC and Pizza Hut were able to adjust worldwide to the pandemic when in-dining was suspended in many markets.

Source: Yum China

7.2.3 Consumers become Users

In 'The Social Dilemma', the fascinating 2020 Netflix documentary about the addictive nature of social media, Edward Tufte, computer scientist and professor emeritus of computer science, political science, and statistics at Yale University, makes a telling statement. 'There are only two industries that call their customers "user": illegal drugs and software.'

Pony Ma, the founder of Tencent, recognized this very early when he started calling his customers users as far back as 2012. And he is correct; digital ecosystems, mobile applications, and data-driven consumer knowledge are turning the customer relationship from a purchase occasion into an 'always on' connection.

Unlike illegal drugs, however, this user relationship is much more a two-way street. Brands are actively looking for ongoing consumer input to optimize their offer and AI systems will increasingly be able to determine when a customer is ready for a purchase in specific conditions.

China, with its lead in mobile technology, its abundance of data, and a population open for digital transformation, is the country that is leading the trend where consumers are turning into, or have already become, users. Five developments are behind this generational and fundamental change:

— HIGH SHARE OF ONLINE RETAIL: The highest portion of total retail consumption is done online, even estimated to exceed 50% within 2021 by emarketer;[27]
— HIGH PLATFORM CONCENTRATION: main data is found within a handful of connected ecosystems. The largest three (Tmall, JD, and PDD) cover more than 90% of B2C transactions;
— DIVERSE ECOSYSTEMS: Platforms are not specialized — lines are fully blurred between communication, social media, social commerce, and e-commerce and are tied to mobile payment;
— THE CHINESE CONSUMER IS YOUNG: Unlike in the West, purchasing power is with the youth supported by their families (13% of family spending is dedicated to the kids compared to 4% in France);
— A HIGHLY CONSUMER-CENTRIC MARKET: Everything the consumer wants is created (as opposed to a more top-down brand approach), which makes data essential.

Creating Users: still early days.
We believe this development toward users is only in its early stages. Digital innovation will enable a variety of new business models, and China will lead the way. Just imagine a cosmetics company that — with the advances in gene-based therapies — is able to send the recipe of your skin cream daily to your home-based Haier machine, which automatically mixes and excretes your daily dose of tailor-made moisturizer. It may not even be too farfetched to see Haier, or start-ups within their ecosystem, branch out into the cosmetics or medication business.

Or imagine a sports company that tailor-makes your daily exercise program and projects these on your home screen to ensure the fastest route back to beating an injury. A service, free of charge, of course, for users within the top-tier of their loyalty program.

When you come to think of it, the more digital our environment becomes, and the more this environment is driven by AI and optimized for individual users, the more digital business models are bonding people much tighter to a company than was possible before. The cost to the user for switching to an alternate service company will go up.

A plethora of brands in China has meanwhile understood the changing status of consumers and has created digital strategies to benefit from it already. Beyond the large internet platforms whose ecosystems are built to keep users loyal, fast food and beverages chains have jumped on it early.

We already mentioned that Luckin coffee created a seamless online to offline user-driven experience [see Section 3.2.2]. Heytea, the tea-based competitor of Luckin coffee, is another company that has a well-known digital user strategy. Another good example is Perfect Diary with their always on customer relationship.

It is, however, equally interesting to shine a light on the endeavours of foreign players operating in China who realized this new trend very early and acted on it with vigour: Starbucks and KFC.

In Section 1.2 Success in China is possible, provided you create the right circumstances, we highlighted Starbucks as a company that managed to find success with a clear China for China-focused strategy. A central part of this approach has been their digital vision and the near flawless execution of it.

Starbucks – full integration of systems with the user at its core.
Starting from zero in 2015, with no existing model to learn from, the Starbucks China digital capability has evolved into a market leading approach, which has become the standard within Starbucks globally and has meanwhile successfully been rolled out in the US and other markets. It certainly can serve as an example for many other businesses, both within China and in foreign markets.

Ordering, delivery, e-commerce, or gift-related, Starbucks China realized the full integration of its membership services and their online business in its own apps and third-party platforms, now enabling a seamless multi-channel business. The management system, customer service system, store operating system, invoice system, and the ability of various business centres are all digitally combined.

This integration enabled a high degree of agility, and the expansion of digital channels accelerated the growth of its online business, which was the basis for a fast recovery in the aftermath of the 2020 Covid pandemic lockdowns.

Starbucks China's drive toward digitization initially gained speed due to the Luckin Coffee threat [see Section 3.2.2] and then further accelerated when stores were forced to close due to Covid-19. The global pandemic was also the reason behind expanding the pioneering work done in China around the globe. For example, coffee delivery was at first in China only and then, during Covid-19, extended to many other markets.

The Starbucks China digital approach is fully multi-channel from collaboration with Tencent (APP) and Alibaba (delivery, Tmall store, participation in big sales festivals such as 11.11) to O2O (online/offline) integration so that a coffee can be ordered online and delivered or collected in store. Mobile payment is fully integrated (via WeChat and Alipay). And what made the digital development even more outstanding is that it is supplemented with a rich membership program that is seen by many as one of the best in China at present.

The secret: Bring an emotional connection to the digital user experience.

When it comes to digital innovation, you may first think of channels, traffic, user operations, technology, small programs, and big data. These are the basic capabilities that an enterprise must possess in the process of digital expansion.

But, in the eyes of Belinda Wong, Starbucks China's CEO, these basic skills are only the part of the iceberg hidden underwater. Whether a brand can organically integrate its products, culture, and values with these basic skills is the key to making the iceberg emerge, jump into view, and impress users.

In addition to accumulating basic capabilities, Starbucks focuses on what customers need most when connecting with the brand at different touchpoints and takes these needs into consideration when cultivating various positions, such as apps and stores. Starbucks digitally records the preferences of high-frequency users and creates different personalized experiences based on the characteristics of different platforms.

Users can either go to the app's fastest place for a cup of 'My Daily Standard' when they go out in the morning or go to the Tmall flagship store to fight for a limited-edition cup. Or they can make orders on the WeChat applet and share afternoon tea with friends. Also possible: determine your route on a digital map to your destination Starbucks while ordering a cup of coffee, a service welcomed by highly mobile people.

Social gifting.

Adding to the emotional connection, in 2017, Starbucks pioneered the concept of social gift cards, otherwise called 'Speaking with Stars', which refers to the use of the value of collected 'starpoints' to be donated to friends instead of used for a personal discount or service. This social gifting allows customers to easily send out a coffee voucher or gift card online, adding another dimension to the user relationship.

In August 2020, a new feature was launched called Heart Delivery. Through Speaking with Stars, you can order a drink for a beloved person online and combine the drink with something to say. The message will be posted on the cup, so that the recipient can be surprised when receiving the brew.[28]

It's the data that makes the difference!

Aside from the increase in revenue associated with the app, the real value lies in the innovative potential uses for the large amounts of user data collected, which forms the base of Starbucks' digital strategy.

Starbucks has begun experimenting with AI-driven digital menu boards in their physical locations to allow for a dynamic menu based on customer demand (varying with regional preferences and times of day) that would ideally continue to boost same-store sales. The decision of where to place new stores and how to expand has also been driven by user data.

The ways in which this user knowledge can be utilized in the future are important in the ever more personalized retail world, where users want less of being talked at and more of being included in a conversation.

As Starbucks gains access to more customer data, its ability to continue to create more meaningful, personal relationships with customers increasingly turns them into real and regular users.

It seems that for a product with a very regular user frequency, their implementation strategy has appeared more urgent, or perhaps simply easier, given that so many players in fast food and beverages have meanwhile developed user-focused digital strategies. But in our view, this is perhaps merely the tip of the iceberg.

Brands like Nike have also built strong user-focused digital strategies. And, as highlighted earlier, companies such as L'Oréal are certainly at the forefront of implementing such a strategy with a user-driven approach inspired by the digital environment in which they operate in China. These are strategies that go beyond existing models but are built for a digital user economy.

The digital luxury consumer journey.

A sector that has understood this fundamental change as well is the global luxury industry. Initially very sceptical about digital platforms and the use of online selling as part of their target market mix — luxury brands were probably the last to give in to the obvious trend of sales via platforms such as Alibaba and JD.com — several luxury brands have become leaders in digital user connection within a few short years.

Realizing that consumers under 30 years of age are responsible for 47% of all luxury spending in China[29] and are native to the digital world, luxury players rushed online to appeal to this demographic. Now, 33% of all luxury sales are made online. Moreover, luxury brands have entered an age when they are vying to achieve digital firsts. Burberry became one of the first brands to engage in luxury livestreaming and in 2020 became the first to open a social retail concept store [see separate box] which seamlessly blends a user's online social life with offline user engagement.

BURBERRY'S SOCIAL RETAIL STORE - A USER JOURNEY IN A BOX.

Burberry has always been a brand of firsts. We test new ideas and push the boundaries of what's possible. When it came to innovating around social media and retail, China was the obvious place to go as home to some of the most digitally savvy luxury customers. Together with Tencent, we pioneered a new concept that will redefine expectations of luxury retail. Burberry's social retail store in Shenzhen is a place of discovery that connects and rewards customers as they explore online and in store. It marks a shift in how we engage with our customers.

Marco Gobbetti
CEO Burberry

Luxury's first social retail store blends the physical and social worlds in a digitally immersive retail experience. It is a space of exploration, designed to inspire and entertain luxury customers, where they can interact with the brand and product in new and exciting ways, in person and on social media. The concept takes interactions from social media and brings them into a physical retail environment. Through a dedicated WeChat mini program, customers can unlock exclusive content and personalised experiences and share them with their communities. The 539m² store is made up of a series of spaces for customers to explore. Each of the ten rooms has its own concept and personality and offers a unique interactive experience. The mini program brings the store to life through exclusive content and personalised experiences that can be unlocked on WeChat, whether customers are in the store physically or virtually. The app gives access to features such as a store tour and product information. It also provides a platform for dedicated client services, in-store appointment bookings, events, and table reservations in Thomas's Cafe, the in-store café and community space.

SOCIAL CURRENCY, EXCLUSIVE CONTENT, AND PERSONALIZED EXPERIENCES.
The more the customer engages with Burberry, the richer their experience becomes.
— Each customer is given a playful animal character that evolves as they engage in-store and socially, with new characters and outfits to discover.
— A customer's journey is guided by a digital point system called 'Burberry Social Currency', which accumulates a customer's in-store activity and social engagements with the brand.
— With the social currency, customers collect rewards and unlock exclusive content and personalized experiences.
— Rewards range from exclusive café menu items to mini program content.
— Each fitting room has a dedicated library of playlists to listen to. Customers can pre-book their preferred room through the mini program.
— The Trench Experience is an exclusive space that customers can unlock as they build their social currency. An homage to Burberry's iconic breathable weatherproof trench coat, the room is designed as a digitally immersive journey through nature, bringing Burberry's heritage of exploration to life and creating unique and personal content for the customer to share on social media.

INTERACTIVITY AND QR CODES.
Upon entering the store, customers discover the first digital experience. Scannable QR codes on product tags throughout the store add a digital layer of discovery.
— An interactive window at the entrance reflects the viewer's shape in a living sculpture that responds to body movement, creating a unique moment that can be captured and shared with friends.
— The window evolves through the seasons to reflect the latest collections.
— All products throughout the store are labelled with QR codes that connect to digital screens, further enhancing the in-store experience.
— Customers can find Burberry's latest collections and seasonal products and discover exclusive pieces only available to buy in the Shenzhen store.
— Scanning the QR code unlocks additional content and product storytelling within the mini program and contributes toward building social currency.

SOCIAL SPACE.
— Thomas's Cafe, named after the fashion house's founder, Thomas Burberry, is a dedicated space for the Burberry community to connect.
— The café is designed to be a dynamic area, which can be converted into a

community space for activities including talks, workshops, exhibitions and live performances, with bookings made through the mini program.
— The café menu can also evolve as customers engage with the WeChat mini program and their social currency advances, unlocking new menu items.

Personalized customer engagement was always at the forefront of the sales and marketing approach for luxury brands, but technology is helping to take this individualized experience a step further.

Leading luxury players such as LVMH, Prada, and Burberry now have a fully integrated online/offline consumer journey that enables a high degree of personalisation through in-depth user understanding.

Tagging individuals at various touchpoints of the omni-channel shopping experience, an OTO (One-to-One) sales approach and full integration with CRM systems enable full personalized user interaction that boosts loyalty and repeat purchasing. Social media such as WeChat, Weibo, and Xiaohongshu serve as platforms to spread a brand's social influence, increase its visibility, attract new consumers, and drive conversion rates.

As we have seen in previous cases in the book, most notably Perfect Diary, WeChat plays a crucial role in the personalization of the user interaction. It enables a digital, always-on connection between the user and the brand, such as enabling a personal and direct one-on-one relationship with a favourite sales assistant in an offline store, the sharing of a personal experience on WeChat moments, and direct purchase access via WeChat mini programs.

An ongoing relationship with highly brand loyal individuals is often the secret behind the success of luxury brands, for which ongoing commercial achievement and growth depends on repeat purchases of a relatively small high net-worth audience. The digital possibilities that are created in China help the luxury brands to make this user journey even more personal. A tight ongoing digital relationship is — also in the luxury category — turning consumers into users.

Digital development is the starting point for a new era of user-centric innovations. Through connecting social and retail environments, innovative digital services and exciting new experiences for users are being created, helping brands build deep emotional connections and support the laying of strong foundations for long-term growth.

7.3 INTELLIGENT LESSONS

More than with any other country in the world, in China the Government, its population, and its entrepreneurs are embracing technological innovation as the driver of progress and commerce and consider it a strategic priority.

While many of the base technologies that enable the digital revolution in China are similar to or even the same as what is available around the world, what sets China increasingly on a leading path toward a digital and AI driven society and even global leadership, is China's (long term) government vision, ambition and top-down action combined with the Dragon Tactics of its entrepreneurs, most notably their user centricity, their penchant to experiment and innovate forward, their perceived need for speed, and their constant adaptability.

Also, Chinese society with its relative homogeneity [See comment on page 41], its willingness to try new things, and its openness to a digital lifestyle facilitates a digital roll-out within a shorter time compared to other parts of the world.

Moreover, the early roll-out of 5G and the diverse and integrated ecosystems with their vast and multi-dimensional quantities of data will make it easier to experiment with new and innovative business models. It is precisely the diverse and rich data sets that will prove to be a game changer. As the examples we highlighted in this chapter demonstrate, the broader a view one has of a persons' social context, the more robust a data set becomes.

With China's ecosystems broadly integrated, covering a wide spectrum of user behaviours and combining commerce and entertainment, the foundations are in place for rich, multi-layered data sets needed to optimize machine learning and artificial intelligence solutions.

While large Western internet players, mostly based in the US, are also amassing user data on their platforms, that data concentrates heavily around online behaviour, such as searches made, photos uploaded, YouTube videos watched, and posts liked. Chinese companies, however, are gathering data from the real world as well. Enabled mostly by mobile payments, China's ecosystems are gathering and understanding the what, when, and where of physical purchases, meals, social activities, and transportation.

Deep learning can only optimize what it can 'see' by way of data, and China's technology ecosystems give these algorithms many more eyes into the content of our daily lives. In the words of Kai Fu Lee, 'As AI begins to "electrify" new industries, China's embrace of the details of the real world will give it an edge on Silicon Valley'.[31]

China's digital models will have an international market.
Chinese innovation is not easily and automatically accepted in the West. Rath-

er, it is often initially ignored or at best dismissed as copying and only at a later stage reluctantly acknowledged and embraced around the world.

The same is happening with digital development. The first internet players were merely laughed at and derided as copycats. Increasingly, however, the Chinese market is being seen as the centre stage for (mobile) business model innovation and AI development where solutions with global appeal are being created.

Meanwhile, Chinese consumers' tastes and habits are now crossing borders too. At the same time, China is championing globalization, with a strong focus on growth in developing countries. By offering an alternative vision of progress and support, China will increasingly be able to persuade (parts of) the world to embrace its initiatives as well as its technology.

It is made more so since Chinese entrepreneurs, when venturing abroad, tend to focus on investing in local solutions with an aim to improve their capabilities through applying their expertise and technology, rather than trying to make their existing products fit local conditions. For example, this is exactly the approach adopted by Alibaba when they bought a controlling stake in Lazada in 2016, the biggest South-East Asia e-commerce platform. They let it operate with their existing processes and only after a few years of observation did Alibaba start to leverage its technology to improve specific Lazada capabilities, yet without changing its brand name nor its specific features. This is in stark contrast to many, predominantly, US based digital players that adhere to a much more one size fits all roll-out approach.

It therefore seems only a matter of time for a wider outreach and acceptance of Chinese digital solutions, and this should be a wake-up call for political leaders and entrepreneurs around the world who want to stay competitive in the digital society of tomorrow.

More than any development, the rise of artificial intelligence poses the real threat that a limited number of winners take all and many laggards will indefinitely fall behind.

The risk of such falling behind in the West, in Europe in particular, is very real and the cost of that is growing exponentially. Kai Fu Lee ominously predicts in his book AI Superpowers:

> *In the past, the dominance of physical goods and limits of geography helped rein in consumer monopolies. (Antitrust laws didn't hurt either.) But going forward, digital goods and services will continue eating up larger shares of the consumer pie, and autonomous trucks and drones will dramatically slash the cost of shipping physical goods.*

Instead of a dispersion of industry profits across different companies and regions, we will begin to see greater and greater concentration of these astronomical sums in the hands of a few, all while unemployment lines grow longer.

Will data privacy remain a stumbling block for Western competitiveness?
Not all the technological advances in China will immediately be transferable across borders due to privacy and data governance regulations elsewhere, but the digital privacy gap is closing rapidly.

The European Union released its first-ever European Data Strategy in February 2020. Under the motto of searching for a single framework for the design, management, access, use, and sharing of data, the EU has ambitions to build up a European data common market with reused, interoperable, and replicable data (pooling and sharing) across all strategic sectors. A more integrated data approach 'would certainly improve both the EU's internal as well as external competitiveness', according to the Royal Elcano Institute, a Brussels based think-tank for international and strategic studies.[32]

At the same time, the Chinese government is heeding public calls to better protect consumers. In August 2021, the latest data privacy law, one of the world's strictest, was passed and together with existing provisions, such as those included in the 2017 Cybersecurity Law and 2018 e-commerce Law, will form comprehensive protections for individual data rights, much of it being modelled after the European Union's 2018 General Data Protection Regulation (GDPR).

While in the US consumer concerns over data privacy are also growing, leading data collectors there are not waiting and are innovating toward models that will still leverage personal data but will avoid overt personalisation of specific data sets.

A better understanding about the need for staying in the race toward AI leadership combined with innovations such as Google's FLOC — which stands for Federated Learning of Cohorts, a technology aimed at grouping people together (cohorts) based on their browsing behaviour but without actually sharing the actual data beyond someone's own device — could potentially convince enough people to worry less about perceived individual loss of privacy.

It seems that where digital protection regulation and technological workarounds are concerned, the three continents are growing closer, and on a midterm basis, differences in privacy environments should play less of a defining role, making it easier also for Chinese data-driven business models and products to become more relevant globally.

Young consumers, the likely game changers.

Privacy models in the West are very much driven by the establishment and led by organisations and individuals that did not grow up as digital natives. Regulations are dominated by solutions fitting new media and digitalisation into the world they know.

In China, the development of digital solutions is often driven by a younger audience. Not because the overall population is younger, but in China's commercial reality, it is the young who have the power and certainly the purchasing power. These younger audience-focused models already have spilled over into the West and are eagerly accepted by its young users. They are less concerned about personal privacy and will adopt the models directly if they cannot get the same models from their own providers, as the global TikTok hype and the success of fast fashion player Shein [see Section 7.2.2] demonstrate.

With a likely increasing convergence of what young people around the world like and consume digitally, and with Chinese solutions and platforms having access to more robust and comprehensive data sets than their competitors in the West, the Chinese applications seem to have a natural advantage in understanding what consumers want, putting Chinese entrepreneurs in a very good position to take their business models and products international.

So, what is a non-Chinese business to do to remain competitive?

Ultimately, concerns about data privacy, governmental facilitation, and investment in AI and a digital society remain to be resolved at a macro level and is up to the relevant governments to decide. Such decisions go beyond the realm of this book, which focuses on what businesses can learn today from a successful Chinese approach.

Build ecosystems and alliances.

A decisive factor toward competitiveness in AI is multi-layer, diverse data. In his book, Kai Fu Lee only half-jokingly states that there is no better data than more data.

Later in his book he concludes that the invention of deep learning means that we are moving from the age of expertise to the age of data. Training successful deep-learning algorithms requires computing power, technical talent, and lots of data. But of those three, it is the volume of data that will be the most important going forward. That's because once technical talent reaches a certain threshold, it begins to show diminishing returns. Beyond that point, data makes all the difference.

The more examples of a given phenomenon a network is exposed to, the more accurately it can pick out patterns and identify things in the real world.

Algorithms tuned by an average engineer can outperform those built by the world's leading experts if the average engineer has access to far more data.[33]

And herein lies the secret for anyone who wants to make progress in AI enabled solutions. As is clear from the Chinese market, in a truly digital world, relationships are no longer linear, but fully connected. A business cannot just rely on its own assets anymore. Creating an ecosystem around one's business or tapping into an existing structure will bring the needed multi-dimensional environment. Starbucks and KFC would not have been able to become digital so quickly without deep partnerships with Alibaba or Tencent or by including music and other cultural elements in their apps.

Despite data privacy restrictions, partnerships toward multi-layer data integration are being created in the West as well, with the alliance between LVMH and Google announced in June 2021 being a high-profile example. Aimed at maintaining the ultra-personalisation of their customer offer within a digital environment, the partnership between LVMH and Google should enable the luxury giant to improve its performance in custom-tailored online shopping experiences.

Develop a relationship mindset.
For two reasons a great place to start is consumer loyalty models. Not only are they a great platform on which to build multi-dimensional partnerships and alliances, but equally importantly they must evolve to better fit changing realities. Too many schemes in the West are still too focused on transactions and are often discount driven. In a world where buyers become users, loyalty will increasingly revolve around customer experience, which is made up of every touchpoint and will need to include moments when a business does not focus on sales.

Firms should develop a relationship mindset, not a transactional one. A relationship mindset will enable you to put your brand in a broader cultural context, which will — even within the limitations of data privacy — give you a richer understanding of the people you target and the environment in which your brand interacts. More importantly, it will increase the trust in your brand of a user who will likely become more open to giving consent for the use of their data.

Connect, but do not centralize your data.
An important lesson is also how data is managed within an organisation. Because companies in the West scramble to aggregate data and are trying to connect various data sources from various legacy systems that poorly or not at all connect with each other, the more obvious solution seems to be to centralize data management.

Such central data organisation, however, could increase lead times and pose a real risk of losing connection with the business. It can lead to decisions being made that are potentially a distortion of reality or even biased. On the other hand, decentralised data management (for example within business units) could mean inconsistencies and reduced overall view or knowledge of the entire business and will affect IT infrastructure.

Chinese entrepreneurs don't seem to mind the possible downsides of decentralised data solutions. While Chinese enterprises are often top-down, in the previous chapters we have outlined that they have created organisations that are more like networks and operate with multiple connections between nodes within the network. They treat their use of data in the same way.

Their adaptive and user-focused approach, by default, takes them away from being overly organised and from filtering data centrally. Data is collected, analysed, and used in a more organic way. Data is connected but made available where it is collected and used.

Are you experimenting enough?

Chinese enterprises have built very innovative digital business models, but this has often been a string of incremental user-focused improvements rather than sudden, massive, and disruptive breakthroughs. Very often, they pragmatically repurpose what has already been figured out and apply it to a different context. Chinese innovation is mostly not about fundamental research, but about experimentation and fast implementation.

Throughout the book we have written extensively about the trial-and-error nature of Chinese enterprises and the use of collective thinking from within the organisation, such as bottom-up alignment with a high-level vision and regular brainstorm huddles to find solutions for everyday problems.

We see such an approach as highly beneficial in the development of a user-focused digital business strategy and for innovation. The changes that a digital society brings may be disruptive but, as experience in China shows, cannot be achieved overnight. Instead, a very practical step by step approach involving a broad section of the company and building on existing infrastructure and processes seems highly appropriate.

Process innovations often come from lower levels in the organisation where people are much closer to day-to-day realities. Regular brainstorm sessions involving a broad spectrum of employees will yield considerable insights into where or how to start with digitizing processes or machine learning experiments. Gen Z will drive the digitalisation revolution in the years to come; so empowering young people in the organisation will be game changing.

There are countless ways to start experimenting with the buildout of multi-layer data lakes and data-driven machine learning. For businesses with a China presence, the Middle Kingdom would be the logical choice for testing novel approaches, as pioneering companies such as Starbucks, Burberry, and KFC have. Another example is carmaker BMW: it opened access for start-ups in China to their incubator Garage so that it can be exposed to new innovative technologies that are gaining traction in China so much faster than in the West.[34]

What can Chinese companies do?

While China's leadership in 5G develops and the country is becoming an AI superpower, the (Western) world will likely grow increasingly critical of its technologies, foremost among them likely to be the solutions that have an easy association with possible oppression such as facial recognition and other security related applications.

This is often an oversimplification. Even facial recognition technology can have upside, as a team at the University of Hong Kong in early 2020 has proven. They launched an app that is able to identify illegally harvested Napoleon fish, increasing the pressure for Hong Kong restaurants to stock only legally caught and imported specimens of this endangered fish.[35]

Yet, in such a critical macro environment, Chinese digital companies venturing abroad will have to make extra efforts to gain trust both from governments and consumers.

This will not be easy in a climate where foreign governments worry about cybersecurity, consumers worry about data protection, and Western companies worry about Chinese competition.

But let's also be realistic; while surveillance tech is clearly a delicate topic in the West, the fear that Beijing can simply impose authoritarianism through the sale of its equipment is a dark fantasy and not to be taken seriously.

For China and its companies, the key will be to show sincerity toward creating a win-win situation through strategic partnerships that drive mutual economic benefits within and outside of China. Meanwhile the rest of the world should relax a bit. Having dual, or even multiple, engines of innovation is not a bad thing.

Address branding issues and win hearts and minds.

In addition to trade friction and security-related rhetoric, which has created headwinds against the acceptance of Chinese technology, the Made in China label may still have legacy branding and perception challenges that must be addressed.

While we are experiencing a change in the image of China where manufacturing quality is concerned, we believe it is not yet common knowledge that China is developing from a low-cost and low-quality country to a higher quality, higher price, and especially higher technology value-added nation. Companies marketing high-tech solutions will need to address this.

A possible solution here lies in partnerships. As the example of the joint venture with 3Com that Huawei established when entering the US market demonstrated [see Section 3.2.2, Chapter 3 Wolf Culture], a trustworthy local partner can really make a difference and help overcome preconceptions.

While finding common ground at a political level in the short term, or even mid-term, will not be easy [see also our final chapter], proactive communication and enhanced commercial integration can help bridge the gap and Chinese companies can play a leading role in winning back hearts and minds and ultimately expand to global markets.

Stay organic and extend ecosystems.
Europe, in particular, needs to scale up innovation in AI and is trying to do so by encouraging the formation of start-ups and SMEs. Here lies another clear opportunity. Rather than imposing its own products, Chinese enterprises can help bring innovation to Europe. It can extend its ecosystems by providing funding and expertise to budding entrepreneurs.

And with European and Chinese data regulations growing more similar, it may also prove an interesting win-win proposition to test Chinese solutions within a more restricted environment and thus optimize future products for the Chinese market while developing products suitable for the European market.

Understand possible limitations of Dragon Tactics.
It seems inevitable that the future for many Chinese digital players venturing abroad will lie in cooperation, creating partnerships and alliances, and extending ecosystems to gain trust and market access. This means more interaction with a broader set of cultural values and realities. And herein looms a challenge that is bigger than the digital world alone, but one which Chinese firms need to address to become successful in the long term outside their borders: Chinese entrepreneurs will need to realise that not all their Dragon Tactics will be transferable. Parts of what has made them successful in their home markets may not be the optimum approach for gaining similar levels of success on foreign soil.

Aspects of Wolf Culture such as a 996 mentality or different ideas about strategy or staffing are concerns that will quickly come to the fore when investing in companies abroad. Chinese entrepreneurs will need to learn how to deal with possible limitations of their existing approach, however successful that may be within China, and learn how to overcome cultural barriers getting in their way toward becoming successful in foreign countries.

In our last chapter, we will address this in more detail.

PART 3

EMPLOYING DRAGON TACTICS

别有玄奥

8

IMPLICATIONS.

8. IMPLICATIONS.

8.1 DEMONS AND DRAGONS

Over the course of writing our book, we have witnessed a deteriorating global relationship between China and large parts of the world. The geopolitical tug of war for global leadership ignited by the Trump administration in the USA seems to be continuing under the Biden administration. Simultaneously, the China–EU relationship has turned sour and reached depths not seen since 1989, culminating in tit-for-tat sanctions and an abrupt freezing of the EU–China investment treaty, which, as recent as early 2021, was hailed as a welcome achievement by both parties.

With values and visions that are dissimilar, disputes may not be so easy to solve or to bridge at a political level. What seems even more disconcerting is a deteriorating opinion of China in many parts of the world as an October 2020 Pew Research Center survey showed.

Views of China have grown more negative in recent years across many advanced economies, especially over the past year. In various countries included in the survey, negative views have reached their highest points since the institute began polling on this topic more than a decade ago.[1]

While we are concerned about the speed at which things are unfolding, we also have to remain realistic. China's increasingly important global role is growing at the expense of other countries' influence, which may not be easy to accept for them.

While there is no point in making exact predictions, there is plenty of consensus among economists worldwide that, by the end of this decade, the Chinese economy, as measured by GDP, will be the largest in the world. China's increasing influence is not limited to its growing economic power. With initiatives such as the 'Road and Belt Initiative', the '4th Industrial Revolution', and even a plan to rival the Bordeaux wine region, Beijing is actively pursuing a greater role in the world of tomorrow.

So, it is certainly not surprising that China is steering a more assertive course. Or as the central Chinese leadership prefers to put it, China is once again occupying its rightful place in the world order.

But being number one comes with responsibilities.
While Beijing finds that it has more power to defend its growing interests, for-

eign concerns about the way it applies that power continue to grow as is made clear from the PEW study.

As a result of being strong, China is now being scrutinized, and that leads to discomfort among Chinese leaders who get annoyed with critics abroad. For the moment it seems the Chinese reaction is one of attrition, closing up, not making an effort to be a responsible global leader. China increasingly seems to think only for China.

We are hopeful this can and will not last indefinitely. Chinese leaders should not dream of a world where other countries butter them up, like ancient Chinese emperors once enjoyed. It would be wise for them to start to learn to live with international critics.[2]

China has changed rapidly and dramatically in recent decades. However, sometimes it seems that Beijing does not have a clear idea of its influence and potential threat to others, and thus does not adjust to its new global leadership role fast enough.

It seems that China behaves like an ostrich burying its head in the sand, rfusing to fix its unpractical view and foreign policy and to recognize the important ongoing divergence. But unfortunately, these divergences will not vanish by themselves. Instead, they will accumulate and eventually lead to greater troubles.

A global PR drive will never fix such issues. Even if it could help, it takes skill and time, perhaps decades, to have an effect. An improved image may well diminish, but will not eliminate, critics. Only real action will.

So ultimately, a more inclusive, or at least less obviously self-centred, policy will also be in China's interest. It's in their self-interest to be a China that takes on a more responsible role befitting its position as global leader; that realizes that despite having become the largest economy according to GDP numbers, there is still a lot to learn from other parts of the world; that recognizes that finding a win-win approach will ultimately go farther than being a self-righteous bully. This evolution perhaps may be wishful thinking on our part, but China and the world will become more intertwined regardless.

Decoupling. Unreal.

To us, as long-term China veterans who understand the country well, a deteriorating relationship between China and the rest of the world seems both inevitable and unnecessary.

As we have pointed out previously in the book, we are not blind China fans. While the Middle Kingdom has given us much and we feel there is a lot to learn from it, we are also concerned about China flexing its muscle within and beyond its borders and its insistence on its unique economic system, which still too often hampers foreign companies from developing within its domestic market.

Yet rather than blindly focusing on geopolitical pain-points and what makes us different, businesspeople around the world should take a second, or rather closer, look.

To begin with, we are hesitant to believe in a seriously decoupled world in which 'the West' will operate separately from China. China's position in the global economy, both as its largest supplier of manufactured goods and its second-largest market for imports ($2 trillion in 2020), makes it undesirable and extremely difficult to fully separate from economically.

Decoupling thinking, even in light of increasing trade barriers erected by the US and Europe, also ignores a growing overlap in interests and the resulting need for interaction in other parts of the world, most notably Asia, Africa, and increasingly South America.

In the end, it is also not in China's interest to decouple. Although China can increasingly rely on a growing domestic market to win its own internal race toward prosperity for its entire society, before its inevitable increase of an aging population and reduction of its working age population, it needs to maintain a high level of growth. Reduced demand from Europe and the United States will affect its growth rate, which the country can ill afford.

Moreover, contrary to popular belief, China actually ranks in the World Bank's latest report on the Top 10 economies showing improvement across multiple metrics for ease of doing business. Coupled with China's clearly outlined vision for achieving high-quality growth in the latest (fourteenth) five-year plan, the country still promises to be an exciting growth destination for multinationals that figure out how to do business in China.[3]

Yes, the Covid pandemic has accelerated the development of shortening supply chains with companies planning to bring production closer to their home markets, but China will continue to be utilized as a manufacturing hub for companies around the world.

At the same time, despite current geopolitical tensions, companies should continue to find ways to enter and grow their presence in China. Ultimately, the Middle Kingdom is simply too big and important in terms of its consumer base for companies around the world to ignore.

At the same time, Chinese entrepreneurs are eying global expansion. With a large home market, they are building vast resources to take on the world. With a risk-taking attitude, the ability to adapt, and the resources that a China-sized scale allows them, venturing beyond China's borders is their next logical endeavour. It is clear that over the next decade and beyond many more interactions between companies from China and around the world will take place.

Both China and the West will benefit from a better understanding.
Such interaction has been our reality over the past two or three decades, and we are well aware of how important it is to understand China, its culture, its companies, and their capabilities., especially in light of the tremendous changes underway in the structure of China's economy, and by extension, the world's.

China is at a crossroads, and its success will have global repercussions for generations to come. Businesses leaders in the West would be better taking notice because it presents ample opportunity to tap into Chinese enterprises for innovation and to draw inspiration for innovative business models. But it will require an open mind and an eagerness to learn.

Meanwhile, it may seem to the outside world that China often speaks with one voice, but there is more division in the country than its imposed consensus seems to suggest, and many interesting companies are open for international trade expansion. Increasingly aware of the challenges they will face, Chinese firms will be looking for the right partner to achieve their goals.

Understanding the modus operandi of such enterprises is therefore crucial, not just to succeeding in China, but also in countries such as India and Indonesia. Equally important is to learn how to work with Chinese firms in developed economies since this will provide valuable insight into how China's digital giants and the start-ups following in their footsteps might compete as they go global.

Because, as Kai Fu Lee so eloquently summed it up in his book,[4]

> *As remarkable as the accomplishments of many Chinese entrepreneurs have been up till today, these achievements will pale in comparison to what they will do with the power of artificial intelligence.*
>
> *The dawn of the internet in China functioned like the invention of the telegraph, shrinking distances, speeding information flows, and facilitating commerce. The dawn of AI in China will be like the harnessing of electricity: a game-changer that supercharges industries across the board.*
>
> *If artificial intelligence is the new electricity, big data is the oil that powers the generators. And as China's vibrant and unique mobile internet ecosystem took off after 2012, it turned into the world's top producer of this petroleum for the age of artificial intelligence.*

The artificial intelligence age will disrupt and create uncertainty everywhere.

Working with disruption requires flexibility and managers who can act independently. Chinese companies have only ever known disruption and fast-changing, uncertain operating circumstances. They have developed the skills to survive and prosper.

With rapid digitization reducing market stability in the West, these abilities are increasingly critical in the Western business arena as well, and nothing is better suited to ensure survival in uncertain times and environments than mastering Dragon Tactics.

8.2 CORE ATTRIBUTES OF DRAGON TACTICS

The following 16 alphabetically ranked elements are the key components of the Dragon Tactics we have described throughout the book. The list includes references to where in the book examples or more details on the topic can be found.

Adaptability/Flexibility

The expectation that the world is constantly changing is elemental in Chinese culture. Since China created its market economy just over 30 years ago, the development in all aspects of this market has been breath-taking. Moreover, market expectations toward innovation are uniquely high. Only with an unrelenting mentality and ability to adapt is a business able to survive.

→ Part 1, Chapter 1,

→ Part 2, Chapter 4, Section 5.2.4, Section 5.3, Section 7.3.

Agility/Speed

No market in the world changes as fast as that in China, at least no other market of comparable size. Not many markets have such high levels of global competition. Only businesses that move faster than the market have a future. And with a culture skewed toward hard work, an 80/20 approach to innovation and quality, plus a survival-driven fear of not being first, Chinese entrepreneurs are masters at getting things done fast.

→ Part 1, Chapter 1

→ Part 2, Section 3.2.2, Chapter 4, Section 5.2.1, Section 5.2.3, Section 5.2.4, Section 5.3, Section 7.2.2

Building Alliances

Cash strapped and operating in markets that lacked many basics, early-stage entrepreneurs looked for ways to minimize risk and increase resources and capabilities to accommodate fast growth. Alliances became and still are the norm. Disruptive digitalisation further accelerates the need to become faster and to cooperate. Organisations are now becoming ecosystems with lines between internal and external blurring.

→ Part 2, Section 5.2.4, Section 5.2.5, Section 7.2.2, Section 7.3

Collective/Family
Throughout history, Chinese philosophers have placed the collective over the individual. Even in today's society, the collective is still highly valued. And there is no tighter collective than family, one of the few places for trust. China's business leaders are culturally predisposed to see the members of their organisations as family but, in return, demand a lot from them.

→ Part 2, Section 3.2.3, Section 6.1, Section 6.2.2, Section 6.3

Consumer Focus
While in Western philosophy the important thing is to think well, for the Chinese the important thing is to observe well. If you combine this with a faddish and fickle, hyper-competitive business environment in which staying ahead is requisite for survival, then a true consumer understanding is of vital importance. Only products that are highly relevant to a target audience are acceptable. Getting it wrong means that you will fall behind. Or worse, you are out of the game. Chinese businesses often built competitive advantages through an organisation-wide consumer-first mentality. With the wealth of digital data available in China, the ability to understand consumer reaction and act on it has increased substantially and seems to further improve a laser sharp consumer focus.

→ Part 2, Section 3.2.1, Section 4.2.1, Section 7.2.2, Section 7.2.3

Data Reliance
China has the immense advantage of possessing more data than any other market, due to the size of its population, the relative homogeneity [See comment on page 41] of its internal market, and the pace of its digitization. Often not hindered by legacy architecture, Chinese entrepreneurs aggressively invest in building systems that collect, bring together, and interpret various streams of information. Chinese entrepreneurs have always been very close to the market and extremely reactive to consumers. With the wealth of digital data available in China, the ability to understand consumer reaction and act on it has increased substantially and seems to further improve a laser sharp consumer focus.

→ Part 2, Section 4.2.1, Section 5.2.3, Section 5.2.4, Section 7

Devotion to Learning

Respect for learning is intrinsic to Chinese society. Knowledge as a competitive edge is ingrained in Chinese history and culture. Chinese entrepreneurs and their people continuously look for ways to educate themselves, be it through formal education or continuous internal and external data sharing. Digitalisation is further accelerating information distribution and data mining possibilities.

→ Part 2, Section 3.2.2, Section 4.1, Section 4.3

Loyalty

In Chinese history and culture, absolute loyalty to absolute leadership has been the accepted norm, but under the condition that the leader looks after his underlings in return for their loyalty. Loyalty to the cause is the prerequisite for gaining the trust of leaders and colleagues. Loyalty is often more important than ability.

→ Part 2, Section 3.2.4, Section 5.1, Section 5.3, Section 6.2.2

Opportunistic/Aggressive

Survival mentality has shaped the business culture in many Chinese companies. The need to survive creates high levels of opportunism, both good and bad. Risks are judged differently when survival is at stake. Assumptions about what is right or wrong can also be affected by the belief that you can win against all odds and the belief that your rules can differ from the rules others may follow. Chinese entrepreneurs do what it takes to survive.

→ Part 2, Section 3.2.1, Section 3.2.2, Section 4.2.4

Pragmatism

The fast-moving Chinese society and business world bring with them consistent change and uncertainty. The emphasis on long-term planning, without a detailed and inflexible strategy, provides opportunity and a need to act based on the actual situation in the here and now. Each action therefore must have practical application and requires rapid result feedback. Practical experience comes first. Theory and fundamental research are secondary. Survival-focused pragmatism shows itself in the ability to adjust fast, brainstorm day to day problems, and waste no time in solving problems in one go. It leads to experimenting as a method, and to a preference for incremental innovation.

→ Part 2, Section 4.2.3, Section 7.1, Section 7.3

Risk taking/Managing

Chinese entrepreneurs are well known for taking risks, often very big risks. But, in a business world that is moving so fast and where hyper-competition is more rule than exception, not taking a risk, or being prudent, is often seen as the far more dangerous option. With overall levels of optimism toward success and the belief in a positive outcome high, risks are evaluated in a very different context.

→ Part 2, Section 3.2.1, Section 4.2.2, Section 5.2.4

Survival Skills

Most entrepreneurs grew up in times of unprecedented hardship. The Chinese market moves at breakneck speed and hyper-competition is rampant. Survival of the fittest is an accepted norm. Survival skills are constantly honed and are ingrained in company culture.

→ Part 2, Section 3.1, Section 4.2.2, Section 5.2.3

Tenacity

Survival depends on how many problems you solve and how you get yourself back up again after failures. Chinese entrepreneurs possess incredible capabilities for not giving up. Try. Fail. Try again. Fail again. Keep trying until you succeed. In an environment where you need to adapt or die, only a desperate need to succeed and a never-say-die attitude will keep you going. A persistent mindset, a powerful work ethic, and the ability to make sure things happen are essential weapons in the arsenal of Chinese entrepreneurs.

→ Part 2, Section 3.1, Section 4.1, Section 4.2.2

Think Big

Covering approximately 9,600,000 square kilometres, with a population of over 1.4 billion, the scale of China is unique. For a business operating in China, this scale is both a challenge as well as a great opportunity. Hyper-competition often means bigger is stronger, so the race to outsize the competition is always on. Scale also means larger profits. And with a vast home market and an openness toward alliances and ecosystems, Chinese entrepreneurs can build scale quickly. With a risk-taking attitude, the ability to adapt and the resources that scale allows them, venturing beyond China is the next logical frontier.

→ Part 1, Section 1.2

→ Part 2, Section 3.2.2, Section 4.2.2, Section 5.2.4, Section 7.1

Top-down Authority

Throughout most of its history China has been ruled by demi-god sovereign.

The Heavenly Mandate gave legitimacy to central rulers and Chinese philosophers such as Confucius have mostly adhered and supported absolute leadership. Most Chinese private companies still show a Confucian preference for top-down organisational structures. But in an unstable business world, where speed of decision making and improvisation are crucial success factors, the absolute bosses have managed to keep their organisations surprisingly agile.

→ Part 2, Section 3.2.4, Section 5.1, Section 5.2.1, Section 6.2.2, Section 7.1

80/20

Hyper competition drives the need for innovation and for being the first to market. Chinese entrepreneurs are masters at valuing timing over perfection by applying the 80/20 principle, internally by favouring initial thinking rather than detailed plans, and externally by preferring speed to market over product readiness. Perfection is never reached. But there is no need for it. Products that are still in an early stage of development are launched anyway to learn from and improve upon.

→ Part 2, Section 4.2.3

As we have personally experienced, Dragon Tactics behaviour is not easily understood outside the borders of China, even considering the growing respect for and interest in the success of Chinese enterprises. Some elements are simply misunderstood due to a lack of cultural understanding, something we hope this book will have contributed to solving.

Other characteristics are seen as dishonest or overtly aggressive. This of course often applies to parts of Wolf Culture. What is also clear is that some components will simply not be transferable, or even desirable.

To ensure an unbiased view, in the next section we will therefore summarize the possible downsides of Dragon Tactics and highlight what their consequences could be going forward, both inside China and abroad, as well as our thoughts on possible remedies.

Finally, we will conclude the book with clear recommendations on how Dragon Tactics can help make a difference in your business, here and now.

8.3 NOT ALL DRAGON TACTICS ARE SUSTAINABLE, ESPECIALLY OUTSIDE CHINA

As we explained early in the book, survival skills have enabled a lot of success in China over the last few decades. But survival means there can be losers too. Also, in a (changing) environment that depends less on survival, others may not look so kindly upon uncompromising survival behaviour. It can also breed too much of an us against them mentality that will inevitably lead to unwanted side effects.

The Billibilli generation and Wolf Culture.

Wolf Culture has led to a few of such consequences as we have detailed in Section 3.3. Inside China, the Millennial and even more so the Gen Z generations are particularly affected as we highlighted using the limitations of the 996 work culture as an example.

Having grown up in relative prosperity, especially compared to their parents' generation, today's youth in China are both literally and figuratively less hungry and have faced no real hardship. Often raised as 'little emperors', they are also more individualistic and think less collectively. They will fight more for themselves rather than for their communities. It is too early to fully see the effects this will have on work and company culture but surely Chinese companies, over time, will have to adapt to this changing reality.

What is more worrisome, ultimately both for China as well as the rest of the world, is that, as a result of a more prosperous and assertive China, this generation has become more nationalistic. Some would say, irrationally nationalistic. With more self-confidence has come the risk of becoming arrogant.

If this next generation becomes the ambassadors of their companies abroad over time, this will make it harder for enterprises to work together and find common ground.

When diplomats become warriors.

An area where this is sadly already on display is in diplomacy. For example, the recent deterioration in the China–EU relationship seems a victim of a more assertive, more nationalistic style of foreign outreach. Chinese leaders are encouraging their people to be more confident in their country and urge diplomats to show more of a fighting spirit. This does not leave much room for listening, let alone compromising.

Hostile talk could easily lead to unwanted consequences and really seems out of place when China has so much to gain from a strong relationship with Europe. With the EU playing such an important role in resolving global problems such as climate change and infectious diseases, and with global trade on the line, we can only hope warrior diplomacy will not become the new standard. The world and China will both benefit greatly from finding solutions for various politically sensitive hot-button dilemmas around the world.

We would also urge Chinese company representatives not to follow the lead of their foreign service. Many successful Chinese entrepreneurs are known for their humility. Using this quality to help their young future business leaders avoid the negative consequences of hubris resulting from over-self-confidence could separate the winners from the losers in an overseas business environment.

The China business community has built up an important relationship with its counterparts globally over recent decades and has enjoyed plenty of advantages from strong international relationships, even while at home this openness and market access was not equally replicated. Enterprises that manage to find the right tone and manner in conducting business abroad will be rewarded for it.

There is opportunity in efficiency, too.

A very interesting element of Wolf Culture has been seeking opportunity over efficiency. While, in general, we are advocates of such an approach in a fast-moving market like China, we are mindful that it can also lead to a waste of resources.

Top-down mandates to expand investment and production can send the pendulum of public and private investment swinging too far in the wrong direction, leading to companies pursuing goals that are out of reach. In recent years, this has led to a massive glut of supply and unsustainable debt loads in various Chinese industries as boom-and-bust categories such as solar panels and the bike-sharing craze have painfully demonstrated.

The increasing cost of operations in China begs the question, how long can pursuing all opportunities be all important? While we believe that such behaviour is ingrained in many entrepreneurial companies — and we will continue to see evidence of it both within China and among Chinese companies venturing abroad — inside the Middle Kingdom, when growth rates inevitably come down, we will see an increasing balance toward a more efficient use of capital. Especially among listed companies, the need for efficiencies will increase to protect their bottom-line.

While this may also affect their overseas expansion strategies — for as long as the China operations produce sufficient cash flow and growing abroad is determined to be an important objective — efficiencies will matter less when international opportunities come calling.

When the Emperor rules but does not let true innovation happen.

A top-down Emperor culture can ultimately also have its limitations, especially when combined with a more assertive, aggressive stance in the international community. Nowhere is this risk greater than when innovation needs to keep up with market needs.

China is expert at incremental innovation, the step-by-step improvement of what exists. It is also expert at experimenting forward.

But, often as a result of its rote-learning type of education that favours reproducing knowledge over the application of it, China and its firms often lack the raw form of creativity needed for breakthrough, highly ingenious innovation. A top-down culture, where adherence to an agreed direction is the norm and non-conformation is discouraged, can breed herd mentality and will produce more of the same, rather than breed disruption.

Yet, truly disruptive innovation needs confrontation, behaviour and actions that go against the grain. New ideas will only blossom in an environment where individuals can pursue dreams and hunches that others may disagree with.

Real leaders set trends. But that is often only possible based on disruptive innovation. Many of the recent innovators and a large number of the founders and leaders of innovative enterprises lived, studied, and worked abroad. Not only has this helped expose them to a broader set of stimuli and a different way of applying knowledge, but it has also helped them better understand how to get the most out of their people.

To become a true global leader, beyond simply a GDP total, Chinese companies must acquire and develop more talent for innovation. Countries in the West, for decades, have welcomed large numbers of Chinese nationals studying at their best schools. There still is much China can learn about educational methodologies that exist abroad and that can help it improve its own ways of teaching — another reason why an aggressive and nationalistic approach will ultimately prove to be counterproductive.

A trust culture is not easy to export.
Low trust culture creates a reliance on people who are often blood related. The family makes up an inner circle which can be trusted on all matters related to business, especially in an environment with hyper competition and where laws are vague and enforcement of them is irregular or unpredictable.

What will be interesting to see unfold is how entrepreneurs handle trust and reliance when going outside this culture. Trading favours will be harder in environments that are more focused on formal business relationships. Also, total loyalty and unflinching acceptance of what the leader decrees will be a lot less easy to obtain in societies where individualism and independence are treasured privileges.

Multi-cultural staffing versus building Chinese enclaves.

Historically, to overcome this challenge, creating a Chinese office away from home has often been the norm. Largely staffed with Chinese nationals, sent directly from China or hired locally after they finished their studies in the territory, many companies have tried to export or replicate their existing culture. This is not a sustainable method.

Many multinational firms failed in China because they did not adjust fast and sufficiently enough to local conditions. Many neglected to hire the right local talent who understood the market much better. Chinese firms pursuing a similar inward-looking methodology abroad can expect nothing but the same inevitable result. Moreover, in an environment where China needs to win hearts and minds, such an overtly culturally insensitive approach could make it harder for enterprises to gain market acceptance and will also make it harder to understand local consumers.

It will be challenging, but Chinese companies venturing abroad will need to create a multi-cultural approach, as is increasingly the norm in business circles in the West. This undoubtedly — beyond solving trust problems — will mean dealing with other cultural differences and the downsides of key components of Dragon Tactics.

Compromising to adapt successfully.

High on that list will be learning how to work with people, especially in lower parts of the organisation, who can and want to think for themselves. That means granting local managers sufficient autonomy to make local decisions and accepting a culture of empowerment without a strict process of supervision and top-down decision making.

Working without a clear and linear strategy will also prove to be a challenge in this new cultural environment. It is possible, but it will require adaptation on both sides. Repeatedly updating objectives and testing them against an overall long-term vision will require new employees unfamiliar with such a way of working to adjust. To avoid excessive short-term fluctuations in planning, however, expectations toward changing course often will have to be scaled back. But that should be possible in an environment that moves slower to begin with.

This brings us to another challenge. The (perceived) lack of the need for speed. Having worked so long in China, we are constantly surprised and often dismayed by the leisurely work pace, especially in Europe. This is often a frustrating experience for us, but will be a real challenge to accept for a Chinese entrepreneur who expects things to be addressed and improved overnight. Adjusting expectations will be more than necessary.

One of the most interesting developments to watch will be the use of 'quick and dirty' in various aspects of the business — an approach that works so well within an ever-changing Chinese environment, even when it comes to launching products.

We are optimistic, though, that with the right level of compromise and adaptation, a more rapid-fire and trail-and-error market approach can work. Consumer expectations in particular will have to be dealt with but, in a digital environment, improvements can be made quickly. And by managing expectations, communicating clearly, and creating the needed incentives to increase risk acceptance, we see no reason why testing a way forward won't work in the West as well.

8.4 FACING REALITY

The world around us is changing in two fundamental ways, which, combined, provide the fertile breeding ground for the application of the discoveries in this book. On a global scale, an ever-faster developing rate of technological and digital possibilities will profoundly change the way we live, consume, and do business. Meanwhile, climate change will force us to abandon polluting oil-and-plastic habits and reinvent how we generate energy, how we interact, and how we construct our supply chains, just to name a few.

Simultaneously, what is already the world's most populous nation and will soon be the world's largest economy will pivot from being the world's supplier of goods to a nation that is increasingly competing for technological dominance. And with it will come a shaking up of the global order.

This seismic shift will not just have repercussions outside of China. Within the Middle Kingdom it will require a significant retooling of the internal structures and will lead to job losses and a re-evaluation of the cost required to create wealth.

Chinese policymakers have already laid out how they will deal with these challenges and have set priorities toward the improvement of air, soil, and water quality, better education, and green energy.

China is also very intent on developing new markets. The Belt and Road Initiative, ASEAN, and the African continent are all areas that will in the future be new markets and, in worst case scenarios, could replace lost opportunities in the US and Europe.

The changes on the horizon will bring unprecedented levels of uncertainty to many businesses around the world. Although change may have been a constant historically, the seismic shift that lies in front of us will be larger, more fundamental, and have more impact globally than ever seen before by many businesses in existence today. And it will more than likely have a drastic influence over how they relate and interact with China and its enterprises.

Are you the Priest or the Merchant in the new global reality?

In an environment where China on the one hand and the US and Europe on the other are drifting apart, leaders both in government and commerce may need to ask themselves a fundamental question.

Do we focus on the negatives we see in each other's societies, wag our finger disapprovingly and proclaim what is wrong about it all and what must change? Or are we the merchant that happily trades his wares in an environment he knows is not all up to his own standards?

Having lived in China for many years and having immersed ourselves in its culture, its companies and its people, we know there is no need for such an either-or outcome or for such a black and white equation. The country is just too complex and diverse and has many more voices than what is heard from outside. Even while acknowledging the various political hot-buttons, there is simply too much at stake for all parties to drive a wedge and pursue the road toward decoupling.

The reason businesses falter — even leading companies with smart leaders — is that they fail to recognize the chaos principle of innovation, globalization, technology, and forces of entrepreneurship that characterise the modern marketplace.

The size of a business no longer is a guarantee for longevity: it is now possible for anyone anywhere to design an app and, with the right digital marketing approach, reach a global scale and a mass following. Reigning business leaders cannot afford to remain complacent.

Our simple conclusion is that the old ways of working and working together will no longer be sufficient. Amidst so much disruption, business models and the way companies are being run and organized must inevitably evolve.

Chinese entrepreneurs have already proven they can thrive in a hyper competitive fast-changing world without certainties. They have built the capabilities and the companies suitable for such an environment and they understand how to deal with chaos. For the short term it will therefore be many companies in the West that will need to adapt to survive. Companies will have to upgrade their engine while running it at full speed.

But China needs to adapt as well, if only to realize the risk of nationalism or that of an overtly aggressive approach to how it presents itself on the global stage. China and its companies are facing profound challenges they cannot solve alone. There is plenty of opportunity for win-win outcomes. When it comes to education, climate change, and improving the environment there is a lot to learn from both the US and Europe.

Mind the knowledge gap.
Americans and Europeans still see the US as the centre of the universe and have a limited understanding of what's happening in China. We hope this book has helped your exploration of the Middle Kingdom a step further. But there is a lot more to learn and we encourage you to do so, knowing that many (young) Chinese readily follow and absorb international trends and news and we dare say that many of them in China have a better understanding of the US and Europe than their counter parts in the West about China.

Meanwhile, outbound Chinese investment will continue to rise and with it Chinese management practices will be exported. Many Chinese entrepreneurs are discovering they are better equipped to compete abroad than they themselves expected, which will embolden them to increase speed and risks and thus competitive pressure for incumbents.

Moreover, with such large numbers of Chinese studying abroad, many earning PhDs, the 'knowledge lead' the West had over the past decades is closing as well.

Attitudes, the will to win, and the ability to adapt will increasingly make a difference globally. In all this lies the opportunity to apply Dragon Tactics, to combine our strength with their strength.

Scale up your China existence.
We believe that too many companies may have given up on China as they think they cannot be successful there.

That is not necessarily true, even in today's environment in which China is often in the news for reasons that may not always be business friendly. Not only have we demonstrated in this book that success is possible, but also a study[5] from management consultancy BAIN is showing that more companies are finding a way to achieve positive results:

> *The year 2019 marked a turning point in the intense competition between foreign brands and domestic brands in China. For the first time, foreign companies outpaced their domestic counterparts in value growth. Foreign fast-moving consumer goods company sales grew by 9.5% in value in 2019 vs. Chinese company growth of 7%. Some of the gains have been quite dramatic; for example, L'Oréal grew sales by 35% in 2019.*

An important success factor doing business in different countries, and especially in China, is to adapt to local norms and practices.

One way foreign companies can do that is using the 'Engine 1 and Engine 2' approach, which we described in Section 1.2. Develop your business in China separately from your international set-up, based on 'China for China' principles, and import Chinese capabilities into your global set-up.

Ultimately, true global scale can only be achieved by leveraging the scale that China offers. And that can only be achieved by becoming successful in China. And that can only be achieved by acquiring and implementing Dragon Tactics skills.

The latter can be sped up by bringing Chinese leaders and their thinking into the top of your global management and building an infrastructure in China that works independently from your worldwide organisation. Create an entity in China that is built and empowered to operate like a Chinese entrepreneurial company.

8.5 FOLLOWING THE DRAGON'S PATH

Carrefour was a very successful company in China, until it was outcompeted in only a few years.

In less than ten years, Chinese smartphone manufacturer Xiaomi became the third largest smartphone manufacturer in the world and already outsold Apple in China within four years after being founded.

Pingduoduo, barely five years old, is rivalling Alibaba and could do so to Amazon. Luckin coffee built 3000 stores in less than three years, giving Starbucks a real scare and forcing it to dramatically upgrade its digital strategy to remain relevant.

Shein and TikTok have captured the hearts and wallets of teenage girls globally, almost completely under the radar of mainstream media.

Perfect Diary came out of nowhere but has built a business model to rival well-established global cosmetic giants.

All of these success stories were created within the last ten years, and indeed most in just the last five years! Chinese business success is developing exponentially.

Even if you don't see a future for your company in the domestic Chinese market, you should still apply Dragon Tactics to steel yourself for the uncertain and competitive times ahead. If it were up to us, we would do the following:

1. *Really* stimulate entrepreneurship.

At most multinationals we have worked for and with, the global leadership always talked about people needing to be entrepreneurial. Sadly, this mostly remained talk and we have seen too many staffers with a strong entrepreneurial spirit leave in frustration.

One of the key barriers to entrepreneurship within a multinational is the reluctance to break with global processes and standards and a tendency to pursue global efficiencies over local opportunities. This is in stark contrast to Chinese entrepreneurs who mostly see risk in *not* making such a move.

The phenomenal rise of Starbucks in China after 2010 is one of the best proofs that entrepreneurial environments require the right people who need to be fully empowered. They must also be rewarded so that they have real skin in the game. Make them hungry and they will deliver. As Huawei's Ren Zhengfei would say, just make sure there is enough meat and your people will become wolfs.

2. Think in vision, not in strategic planning.

Uncertain times and environments cannot be planned. Speed, agility, and adaptability will make all the difference. Create an inspiring long-term vision but remain as fluid as water to get there. In uncertain environments, it simply can't always be about satisfying shareholder value on a quarterly basis.

Chinese entrepreneurs see inflexibility as stupidity but have shaped the processes to ensure the organisation stays in sync with changing realities.

3. Think BIG.

In a borderless, digital business world, scale will determine your ability to learn about your diverse users and will define the amount and quality of your data to feed and train algorithms.

Resulting from the mere size of their home market, Chinese entrepreneurs have a natural advantage: being a leader in any industry in China places a company at least in the top five globally.

To keep up will require serious efforts from business owners and leaders in other parts of the world. You must think scale. To succeed, you will need to review your risk profile and acceptance. Can you afford to lose? Are you taking survival into consideration?

4. Become (part of) an ecosystem.

Platform organisations and alliances are the organisational and economic models of the future and enable scale at a limited cost.

After years of not believing in the need for partners, even the world's premium luxury brands so used to sell only via their own bricks-and-mortar stores are now tapping into the online platforms in China. Among them LVMH, well-known for their obsession with a total control over their business, caved in and created a partnership with JD.com to attract customers and grow.

When it comes to organisational models, even large enterprises, and emerging global leaders, like Huawei, Haier, and Xiaomi are proving it is possible to operate very successfully with very agile organisations and a project focused business methodology.

Outside China, where similar ecosystems do not yet exist, adopt a much more proactive approach toward developing vital alliances. Find likeminded partners outside your direct sector and leverage each-other's (consumer) insights. Leverage these collaborations digitally.

5. Be consumer centric. Let data make you ultra-user-focused.

Winning in the uncertain digital world will require companies to respond quickly by adopting a savvy, consumer-first mentality and to be always on, everywhere.

Xiaomi, Tencent, Perfect Diary, Pingduoduo, and many others have created processes and business models that have placed consumer centricity at the heart of their organisations. Consumers can voice their opinions, loyal consumers are recognized and rewarded for their contributions, and products can be optimized based on those who are in the market for them.

Only when you truly know your consumer can you transform them into users and can you ensure your offer meets their true needs. Understand what your user needs to make a purchase, and make sure you provide all that you can to make it happen. This will require you to truly embrace multi-layered data. Without adopting machine learning and AI you will never be as knowledgeable as you will need to be.

6. Learn to deal with chaos.

We hear a lot of advice about developing the power of focus and concentration to 'filter out the noise'. The idea being to focus on what is essential and needed while at the same time not being swayed by the rush of chaotic trends and events that demand creative and well thought out solutions and responses. We disagree with such advice.

Uncertainty and disruption are here to stay for the next decade and probably beyond. Winners will be fully equipped to deal with chaos and able to successfully adapt to constant change. Chaos is not a problem, if you don't let it surprise you. If everyone is aware that their circumstance is fluid but are given the right tools to deal with it, sanity can be maintained even within presumed insanity.

7. Speed up your development in non-established markets.

China's giants are late movers in global expansion, but they are beginning to explore international opportunities more aggressively. For example, Alibaba aims to generate 50% of its revenue from overseas business by 2025.

Chinese entrepreneurs have developed the skills to grow rapidly in immature economic sectors and markets, and they invest in infrastructure and are willing to build ecosystems with local players.

They will likely adopt collaborative overseas expansion models — making strategic investments and using alliances to adapt quickly to local market conditions. You should do the same. Dragon Tactics skills are ultimately suited for scaling up in emerging markets.

8. Create more effective participation models.

There is wide consensus that in Western countries the wealth gap is growing beyond reasonable levels. In Europe in particular, there is much debate about top-executive remuneration, especially when compared to people lower in the organisation. Taxing is not an option since it fights the symptoms but does not address the underlying issues.

Chinese entrepreneurs with their participation models have shown the way forward. Their models bring people closer into the organisation and the majority of value created by the company goes directly to current, high-contributing employees. This drives loyalty and helps attract talented people.

More importantly, it gives people a chance to better participate in the global economy, and it incentivises them to look beyond their own borders.

9. Stimulate a more active role of your government in developing AI leadership.

The idea that governments should only act when private markets fail completely seems out of place when so much is at stake. Many disruptive innovations are the result of public investments in, for example, the military or space travel. The internet and GPS would most likely not have been created without government funding support.

As the Chinese approach makes abundantly clear, public rallying of resources and investment precedes private investment.

Artificial intelligence will create winners and losers. The stakes are too high and the need to act too urgent for market forces to play out.

10. Be Tenacious and remain flexible.

From Jack Ma who, starting out as an English teacher, revolutionized consumption in China with Alibaba in less than 20 years, to Ren Zhengfei, the founder of Huawei who became a world leader in 5G technology, or Zhang Ruimin who made Haier a global powerhouse of appliances, or more recently Lei Jun from Xiaomi who managed to rival a success story such as Apple's in a handful of years, entrepreneurship in China is full of examples of remarkable tenacity along with exceptional flexibility to seize opportunities.

These are the big names many in the West have heard of, but there are millions of others in China building their companies with the same idea that the future is malleable and who possess a never-give-up attitude to deliver that future, no matter the difficulties they come across.

Their stories remind us of when entrepreneurship is at its best: an adapt-or-die mentality, stubborn resilience, unbridled optimism even when the going gets tough, and a vision of the future that not many people can see, yet with the ability to turn opportunities into reality and make things happen.

Many of our corporations have grown too large, often through mergers and acquisitions, and have lost their entrepreneurial soul. If only they would make a real effort to recapture some of the entrepreneurial magic of their founders. They will need it in the digital and uncertain times to come.

The world around us is changing at an unprecedented pace and the business world in the next decade will look very different. Companies will have to change with it or risk fading into obscurity. They must build capabilities that make them more flexible, allow for more risk taking, and make them more innovative.

Thrive in uncertainty. It's the difference between Adapt and Die!

Let Dragon Tactics be your guide!

ACKNOWLEDGEMENTS

The basis for this book is our own extensive experience in China, each of us spanning a period of 30 years working in international firms with their many local partners, with and for local Chinese private enterprises, and in our own created venture in China.

With many of the brands and companies we describe in this book, we have had some form of involvement or a working relationship with the founders, owners, or other most senior leaders. In addition, we have conducted various interviews to further develop our knowledge. We learned a lot from all of these entrepreneurs. And we hope, they from us. We would like to thank them for their education. Their day-to-day habits, actions, and knowledge are the foundation on which we built our thinking.

In particular we would like to thank 丁世忠 (Ding Shizhong) and 郑捷 (James Zheng) from Anta Sports, 仇文彬 (Vincent Qiu Wenbin) of Baozun, 盛百椒 (Sheng Baijiao) of Belle International, 陈义红 (Chen Yi Hong) of Dong Xiang, 郭广昌 (Guo Guangchang), 汪群斌 (Wang Junbin) and 程云 (Joann Chen Yun) of Fosun International, 赵迎光 (Zhao Yingguang) of Handu Yishe, 李琳 (Li Lin) of JNBY, 雷军 (Lei Jun) and 洪峰 (Hong Feng) of Xiaomi, 丁水波 (Ding Shuibo) and 李冠仪 (Holly Li) of Xtep, and all the owners of the Adidas China, Lacoste China, and Kappa China franchisees and manufacturers.

Besides the business leaders who inspired us to write this book, we are also indebted to various other contributors. Without their input, their critical comments, suggestions, and encouragement, we would not have been able to create this book. In particular we would like to thank Anders Kristiansen, Angel Yu, David Baverez, Frans Greidanus, Gert-Jan van Eck, Grace Gu, Jonathan Seliger, Mark Schaub, Pierre-Alain Ceralli, Richard Spaans, Rina Joosten-Rabou, Stéphane Wilmet, and Thierry Garnier.

A special thanks goes to Simon Wang, husband of Sandrine. Simon has been especially important to the development of the book as a great source of information, but most vitally, by making sure that the cultural context of the book is correct and historically accurate.

Additional words of thanks go to Annette Nijs and François Candelon whose constructive criticisms have enabled us to sharpen the ideas and content of our book.

Dragon Tactics uniquely brings together many aspects of Chinese business management. Yet, prior to our book, others have published their thinking on some of the topics we cover. Our manuscript would not have been complete without utilizing some of this existing material such as books, videos, reports, scientific research, and published articles. A full list of these sources is listed below in either *References* (which are numbered throughout the book) or *Sources*.

We have included extensive Chinese material, some of which are blogs or social media posts, that reflect the current mindset in China on the topics covered in our book.

A final note is dedicated to the representation of Chinese names. Out of courtesy to the entrepreneurs we thanked in the section above, we have used their Chinese names complemented with a pinyin-based or — for those who use this regularly — a Western-style name representation. However, throughout the rest of the book for the purpose of simplicity, we have only reflected names, both for people and companies, using the commonly accepted pinyin conversion or Western-style name.

ABOUT THE AUTHORS

ALDO P.H.M. SPAANJAARS

Since 1992, Aldo Spaanjaars has been involved in business in China, building bridges between Chinese and Western cultures. His vast China understanding and experiences range from creating award-winning advertising to managing retail chains and investment management.

During his nearly 25-year career in China, Aldo has had extensive exposure to business practices in both global and local companies, enabling him to compare the effectiveness of various methodologies and realizing that not all he had learned in business school would automatically lead to success in China.

Working for Fosun International, China's premier private equity company, Aldo worked directly with some of China's leading entrepreneurs and witnessed first-hand what enables their success.

Previously, Aldo was CEO of Lacoste Greater China and COO at Adidas Greater China, and he is one of the co-founders of J.Walter Thompson Beijing (an advertising agency). Throughout these stages of his career, Aldo worked extensively with local customers and manufacturers and learned early in his career that success in China, and increasingly abroad, requires the acceptance of new ways of thinking.

SANDRINE ZERBIB

Sandrine Zerbib has over 25 years of experience in the consumer business in China.

Back in the mid-90s, as the President of Adidas Greater China, she created and developed the China business of Adidas from its nascent stage to its present market-leading position.

She later became the CEO and Executive Director of Chinese group Dongxiang, which gave her a perfect observation post to understand Chinese entrepreneurial management from within and compare it with her experience in a Western multinational.

Today she runs the business she founded in the e-commerce operation industry, (www.fulljet.com.cn), in competition with mostly Chinese private enterprises. In early 2021, this company was acquired by China's leading e-commerce service provider, Baozun, which gives her additional insight on successful Chinese enterprises.

Thanks to her many years leading both Western, Chinese, and ultimately mixed businesses in China, she was able to observe the changes in the Chinese market and the rapid evolution of Chinese private companies. It gave her a chance to truly challenge what she used to take for granted, to analyse the pros and cons of Western and Chinese approaches to business, and to learn from the latter and adopt the relevant ones.

REFERENCES

PROLOGUE

1 & 2 **Harvard Business Review**, Thomas Hout and David Michael, September 2014 – A Chinese Approach to Management – https://hbr.org/2014/09/a-chinese-approach-to-management

PART 1, CHAPTER 1, WHY IN CHINA, DO SOME FAIL AND OTHERS SUCCEED?

1 **Alizila**, March 2015, Amazon Opens Flagship Tmall.com Store – https://www.alizila.com/amazon-opens-flagship-tmall-store/
2 & 3 **CNBC**, Arjun Kharpal, April 2019, Amazon is shutting down its China marketplace business. Here's why it has struggled – https://www.cnbc.com/2019/04/18/amazon-china-marketplace-closing-down-heres-why.html
4 **iQiYi**, 2015 Interview with Pony Ma at the University of Hong Kong – https://www.iqiyi.com/w_19ruvuq6s1.html#curid=10578008509_086d184672028cfaeee214cf9c61101f
5 **China Business Journal**, Li Huiling, April 2019, Amazon abandons China's self-operated market and initiates layoffs – http://www.cb.com.cn/index/show/zj/cv/cv13446721262
6 **Harvard Business Review**, Feng Li, August, 2018, Why Western Digital Firms Have Failed in China – https://hbr.org/2018/08/why-western-digital-firms-have-failed-in-china
7 **Harvard Business Review**, David Bell and Mary L. Shelman, November 2011, KFC's Radical Approach to China – https://hbr.org/2011/11/kfcs-radical-approach-to-china
8 **Bain & Company**, Foundersmentality Blog, James Allen, June 2018 – https://www.bain.com/insights/the-changing-question-of-china-fm-blog/

PART 2, CHAPTER 3, WOLF CULTURE. HUNGER TEACHES LIFE LESSONS.

1, 3 & 11 **MBA Think Tank Forum**, https://wiki.mbalib.com/wiki/华为企业文化
2 **Huawei website** – https://www.huawei.com/en/corporate-information
4 **London Business School**, Julian Birkinshaw, Enrique de Diego and Dickie Liang Hongke, September 2018 – Seven lessons from Tencent's Pony Ma – https://www.london.edu/think/seven-lessons-from-tencents-pony-ma
5 **Un succès nommé Huawei: S'inspirer du champion mondial du numérique pour réussir**, Vincent Ducrey (Hub Institute), Eyrolles, November 2019
6 **Worldcoffeeportal**, 29 October 2019, How Luckin Coffee is racing ahead in China – https://www.worldcoffeeportal.com/Latest/InsightAnalysis/2019/October/Racing-Ahead-The-Remarkable-Rise-of-China-s-Lucki
7 & 8 **Wired**, James Crabtree, February 2018, Didi Chuxing took on Uber and won. Now it's taking on the world – https://www.wired.co.uk/article/didi-chuxing-china-startups-uber
9 **Old Dominion University**, Ying Liu, 2006, Teamwork in Chinese Organisations: A New Concept and Framework
10 **Management and Organisations in the Chinese Context**, pp 269–282, Xiangming Chen, James W. Bishop and K. Dow Scott, 2000 – Teamwork in China: Where Reality Challenges Theory and Practice
12 **Management and Organisation Review**, Xiao-Ping Chen, Xiaofei Xie, and Shiqing Chang, Cooperative and Competitive Orientation among Chinese People: Scale Development and Validation – https://www.researchgate.net/publication/228253102_Cooperative_and_Competitive_Orientation_Among_Chinese_People_Scale_Development_and_Validation
13 & 16 **Nanfang Metropolis Daily**, Feng Jia An, Apr 2014 – "Wolf culture" in the workplace, good use is positive energy, otherwise it will be counterproductive – http://news.sina.com.cn/c/2014-04-05/054029869989.shtml
14 **Line Today**, Abacus, Dipublikasikan, Mar 2020, Experience the damaging reality of China's 996 work culture in a new game – https://today.line.me/id/v2/article/Experience+the+damaging+reality+of+China+s+996+work+culture+in+a+new+game-y9J7gz
15 **NYT**, Raymond Zhong, Dec. 18, 2018, Huawei's 'Wolf Culture' Helped It Grow, and Got It Into Trouble – https://www.nytimes.com/2018/12/18/technology/huawei-workers-iran-sanctions.html

PART 2, CHAPTER 4, ADAPT TO CHANGE OR DIE.

1 & 21 **Le paradoxe du poisson rouge: Une voie Chinoise pour réussir**, Hesna Cailliau, Editions Saint Simon, 2016
2 **Sina.com**, 2021-01-20, – https://finance.sina.com.cn/jjxw/2021-01-20/doc-ikftssan8788538.shtml
3 & 16 & 20 **Harvard Business Review**, Thomas Hout and David Michael, September 2014 – A Chinese Approach to Management – https://hbr.org/2014/09/a-chinese-approach-to-management
4 **Roland Berger**, Henrik Bork, August 2019, The rise and fall of Chinese bike-sharing startups – https://www.rolandberger.com/en/Insights/Publications/The-rise-and-fall-of-Chinese-bike-sharing-startups.html
5 **1421 consulting**, Allison Iapehn, January 2020, Bike Sharing in China: What happened to the craze? – https://www.1421.consulting/2020/01/bike-sharing-in-china
6 **BCG** & **Tencent**, September 2020, Digital luxury report
7 **ChinaDaily**, Chen Yingqun and Liu Ce, May 2015, Internet-Plus_Motto for the Internet age/ adapt or die – http://europe.chinadaily.com.cn/epaper/2015-05/08/content_20654030.htm
8 **Strategy+Business**, Art Kleiner, November 2014, China's Philosopher-CEO Zhang Ruimin – https://www.strategy-business.com/article/00296
9 **Beijing Review**, Zhang Shasha, February 2021, The rise of China's cosmetic brands – https://www.bjreview.com/Business/202102/t20210203_800234721.html
10 & 11 **Reuters**, Sophie Yu, Scott Murdoch, August 2020, 'All girls, buy it!' In China, Perfect Diary gives cosmetics world a makeover with live streams, low prices – https://www.reuters.com/article/us-china-cosmetics-perfectdiary-idUSKBN25M0BP
12 **Daxue Consulting**, Allison, February 2020, How Perfect Diary got to the top of China's cosmetics market – https://daxueconsulting.com/perfect-diary-case-study-how-this-chinese-makeup-brand-got-to-the-top/
13 **Business of Fashion**, Casey Hall, February 2021, Chinese Brands Can Teach Victoria's Secret How to Sell Lingerie Today – https://www.businessoffashion.com/briefings/china/chinese-brands-can-teach-victorias-secret-how-to-sell-lingerie
14 **China's Next Strategic Advantage, From Imitation to Innovation**, George S. Yip, Bruce McKern, MIT Press, 2016

15 **Xiaomi**, August 2017, De Liu About the Products of Tomorrow – https://xiaomi-mi.com/news-and-actions/de-liu-about-the-products-of-tomorrow/

17 **IDEO website** – https://www.ideo.com

18 **Payback, reaping the rewards of Innovation**, James P. Andrew and Harold L. Sirkin, Harvard Business Review Press, 2007

19 **Bain & Company**, Foundersmentality Blog, James Allen, June 2018 – https://www.bain.com/insights/the-changing-question-of-china-fm-blog/

22 **London Business School**, Julian Birkinshaw, Enrique de Diego and Dickie Liang hongke, September 2018 – Seven lessons from Tencent's Pony Ma – https://www.london.edu/think/seven-lessons-from-tencents-pony-ma

23 **Adizilla**, Christine Chou, April 2019, Taobao Helping Farmers Reap Gains in Livestream Boom – https://www.alizila.com/taobao-helping-farmers-reap-gains-in-livestream-boom/

24 **Harvard Business Review**, Martin Reeves, Ming Zeng, and Amin Venjara, June 2015, The Self-Tuning Enterprise – https://hbr.org/2015/06/the-self-tuning-enterprise

PART 2, CHAPTER 5, THE EMPEROR DECIDES. BUT AGILITY RULES.

1 **Confucius**, Book The Analects, Lau [13:13]

2 **Korean Educational Development Institute (KEDI)**, Jeong-Kyu Lee, Ph.D., 2001, Confucian Thought Affecting Leadership and Organisational Culture of Korean Higher Education – https://files.eric.ed.gov/fulltext/ED504451.pdf

3 **Un succès nommé Huawei: S'inspirer du champion mondial du numérique pour réussir,** Vincent Ducrey (Hub Institute), Eyrolles, November 2019

4 **Walk the chat**, May 2019, WeChat Management Culture: compare to Google and Netflix – https://walkthechat.com/wechat-management-culture-a-sneak-peek/

5 **IDC** – Xiaomi market share: https://www.idc.com/promo/smartphone-market-share.

6 **London Business School**, Julian Birkinshaw, Enrique de Diego and Dickie Liang hongke, September 2018 – Seven lessons from Tencent's Pony Ma – https://www.london.edu/think/seven-lessons-from-tencents-pony-ma

7 **MIT Sloan Review**, 2012, Amoeba Management: Lessons From Japan's Kyocera – https://sloanreview.mit.edu/article/amoeba-management-lessons-from-japans-kyocera/

8 **University of North Texas Department of History**, Tanner, 2014, Lin Biao's Principles of Tactics vs. the Human Wave: A Disagreement with Edward C. O'Dowd – https://www.academia.edu/22996048/Lin_Biao_s_Principles_of_Tactics_vs_the_Human_Wave_A_Disagreement_with_Edward_C_O_Dowd

9 **Bain & Company**, Foundersmentality Blog, James Allen, June 2018 – https://www.bain.com/insights/the-changing-question-of-china-fm-blog/

10 **Time Inc**, Charlie Campbell, November 2020, China's Cainiao Is Revolutionizing How Goods Get Delivered. Will the Rest of the World Follow Its Rules? – https://time.com/5914173/cainiao-logisitics-alibaba-china-trade/

11 **Medium**, Cainiao network, September 2020, A Closer Look at Alibaba's Logistics Arm, Cainiao's Globalization Journey – https://cainiao.medium.com/a-closer-look-at-cainiaos-globalization-journey-197ffcecf3f

12 & 15 **Dialogue Review**, Greeven & Nieto-Rodriguez, January 2019, Agility Chinese Style – https://dialoguereview.com/agility-chinese-style/

13 & 14 **Fosun 2019 Annual Report** – https://en.fosun.com/Upload/File/202104/20210401180431_5926.pdf

16 **Corporate rebels**, Joost Minnaar, December 2019, 4 Future-Proof Organisational Models Beyond Hierarchy And Bureaucracy – https://corporate-rebels.com/4-future-proof-organisational-models-beyond-hierarchy-and-bureaucracy/

17 **Strategy+Business**, Art Kleiner, November 10, 2014, China's Philosopher-CEO Zhang Ruimin – https://www.strategy-business.com/article/00296

18 **MI Translations**, October 2015, Chinese Culture Vs the U.S.: 3 Main Differences in Management Culture – https://mitranslations.com/chinese-culture-vs-the-u-s/

PART 2, CHAPTER 6, PEOPLE COME AND GO. THOSE WHO FIT STAY LONGER.

1 & 3 **International Journal of Humanities and Social Science**, Grace Hui-Chen Huang & Mary Gove, February 2012, Confucianism and Chinese Families: Values and Practices in Education –

2 **Global Market Information Herald**, Li Jia Rui & Fu Bi, August 2012, Talking about the Characteristics and Development Causes of Chinese Family Enterprises – https://wenku.baidu.com/view/eca179154531b90d6c85ec3a87c24028915f8591.html

4 **School of Economics, Central University of Finance and Economics, Beijing**, Chuanchuan Zhang, October 2017, Culture and the Economy: Clan, Entrepreneurship, and Development of the Private Sector in China

5 **CEIBS Business Review**, Zhi wei Yong, July 2011, Every Chinese company needs an emperor – https://www.163.com/money/article/7986M79B00253G87.html

6 & 7 **Peking University Press,** Xiao Bei, September 2020, Why is Haidilao's "business path" so wild? – https://baijiahao.baidu.com/s?id=1677062247819110496&wfr=spider&for=pc

8 & 12 **Harvard Business Review**, Thomas Hout and David Michael, September 2014 – A Chinese Approach to Management – https://hbr.org/2014/09/a-chinese-approach-to-management

9 **Management and Organisation Review**, Xin Chun Li et all, December 2015, Research on Chinese Family Businesses: Perspectives – https://www.cambridge.org/core/journals/management-and-organisation-review/article/research-on-chinese-family-businesses-perspectives/1F333F7E584BB5FAC5B-8CEF335A978EC

10 **Inside Chinese Business: A Guide for Managers Worldwide,** Author Ming-Jer Chen, July 2003

11 **Sohu.com**, Shi Yong Hong, September 2019, Haidilao employee incentive system – https://www.sohu.com/a/338835730_798937

13 **Thompson Reuters Law**, Gordon (Minghao) Feng et all, May 2020, Employee share plans in China: regulatory overview – https://content.next.westlaw.com/9-507-4557?__lrTS=20210615153300276&transitionType=Default&contextData=(sc.Default)&firstPage=true

14 **Sohu.com**, Qiao Mu, Mar 2019, Detailed explanation of Yonghui Supermarket's partner system – https://www.sohu.com/a/299264466_100010274

15 **Tsinghua School of Economics and Management and Ivey Business School Foundation**, Xiaoming Zheng and

Ziqian Zhao, 2019, Yonghui superstores: profit-sharing and partnership reform – https://store.hbr.org/product/yonghui-superstores-profit-sharing-and-partnership-reform/W19100

16 & 17 Jeffrey Towson, Digital China and Asia's Latest Tech Trends, October 2019

PART 2, CHAPTER 7, IT ALL STARTS WITH DATA.

1 China Internet Network Information Center (CNNIC), July 2014, https://www.cnnic.net.cn

2 CIW, China Internet Users 2008–2020, December 2020 – https://www.chinainternetwatch.com/statistics/china-internet-users/

3 Hootsuite, Data Portal, January 2021 – https://datareportal.com/reports/digital-2021-china

4 Statista.com – https://www.statista.com/statistics/467160/forecast-of-smartphone-users-in-china/

5 & 20 Deloitte, China Mobile Consumer Survey 2018, Chinese consumers at the forefront of digital technologies – https://www2.deloitte.com/cn/en/pages/about-deloitte/articles/pr-deloitte-2018-mobile-consumer-survey.html

6 MITSloan Management Review, 2018, Shu Li, François Candelon, Martin Reeves, Lessons From China's Digital Battleground – https://sloanreview.mit.edu/article/lessons-from-chinas-digital-battleground/

7 The China Factor, Annette Nijs, The China Agenda, 2019

8 Fortune, François Candelon, Michael G. Jacobides, Stefano Brusoni and Matthieu Gombeaud, July 2021, China's business 'ecosystems' are helping it win the global A.I. race – https://fortune.com/2021/07/02/china-artificial-intelligence-ai-business-ecosystems-tencent-baidu-alibaba/

9 & 18 & 34 Fortune, François Candelon, Akhil Puri and Shameen Prashantha, January 2021, Your company needs a new China strategy in the 'decoupling' era – https://fortune.com/2021/01/28/china-strategy-multinationals-chinese-decoupling-market-consumers-trade-manufacturing/

10 Daxue Consulting, Jeffrey Craig, April 2019, Open Innovation: Transforming your Business in China – https://daxueconsulting.com/open-innovation-in-china/

11 & 24 & 25 CIGP, David Ho, December 2020, Focus: The Rise of Chinese Tech and Why it Matters – https://cigp.com/insights/focus-the-rise-of-chinese-tech-and-why-it-matters

12 Nikkei Asia, Nina Xiang, September 2020, How China winning the race to install 5G will be good for the world – https://asia.nikkei.com/Opinion/How-China-winning-the-race-to-install-5G-will-be-good-for-the-world

13 & 16 & 21 Harvard Business Review, Daitian Li, Tony W. Tong, and Yangao Xiao, February 2021, Is China Emerging as the Global Leader in AI? – https://hbr.org/2021/02/is-china-emerging-as-the-global-leader-in-ai

14 China Daily, Liu Zhihua, April 2020, Tech-powered imaging devices offer faster and more accurate diagnosis – https://global.chinadaily.com.cn/a/202003/04/WS5e5f0bf2a31012821727c28f.html

15 The Economist, Jan 2021, Why retailers everywhere should look to China – https://www.economist.com/leaders/2021/01/02/why-retailers-everywhere-should-look-to-china

17 MIT – https://www.technologyreview.com/lists-tr50/what-are-the-50-smartest-companies/

19 CISTP, 2018, China AI development report – http://www.sppm.tsinghua.edu.cn/eWebEditor/UploadFile/China_AI_development_report_2018.pdf

22 & 31 & 33 AI Superpowers, China, Silicon Valley and the new world order, Kai-Fu Lee, Houghton Mifflin Harcourt, 2018

23 Alizila, April 2018, Alibaba Now Product Designer, as Well as Seller, for Brands – https://www.alizila.com/alibaba-tmall-innovation-center-brands/

26 The Wire China, Lily Meier, June 2021, Fast fashion, Faster Profits - https://www.thewirechina.com/2021/06/06/fast-fashion-faster-profits/

27 eMarketer, Ethan Cramer-Flood, February 2021, In global historic first, ecommerce in China will account for more than 50% of retail sales - https://www.emarketer.com/content/global-historic-first-ecommerce-china-will-account-more-than-50-of-retail-sales

28 Weixinqq.com, January 2021, Starbucks ushered in a digital explosion – https://mp.weixin.qq.com/s?_biz=MzU3MDA0NzE5MA==&mid=2247530364&idx=1&sn=fb6cc936e8098afc93f72888eafaf559&chksm=fcf758c5cb80d1d3e-831c8efb8f5789f5cbca5c4e12ee7dd78f30d36a9519664f08b0f70b157&mps

29 BCG & **Tencent**, September 2020, Digital luxury report.

30 Burberry Website – https://www.burberryplc.com/en/company/social-retail.html

32 Royal Elcano Institute, Raquel Jorge-Ricart, November 2020, Data governance: EU–China competition approaches – https://blog.realinstitutoelcano.org/en/data-governance-eu-china-competition-approaches/

35 National Geographic, Danielle Beurteaux, March 2020, This fish is 'king of the reef.' But high-end diners may change that. – https://www.nationalgeographic.com/animals/article/facial-recognition-humphead-wrasse-disappearing

PART 3, CHAPTER 8, IMPLICATIONS.

1 Pew research.org, Laura Silver, Kat Devlin and Christine Huang, October 6, 2020, Unfavourable Views of China Reach Historic Highs in Many Countries – https://www.pewresearch.org/global/2020/10/06/unfavorable-views-of-china-reach-historic-highs-in-many-countries/

2 The Diplomat, Xue Qing, May 25, 2021, How China Is Losing Europe – https://thediplomat.com/2021/05/how-china-is-losing-europe/

3 Fortune, François Candelon, Akhil Puri and Shameen Prashantha, January 2021, Your company needs a new China strategy in the 'decoupling' era – https://fortune.com/2021/01/28/china-strategy-multinationals-chinese-decoupling-market-consumers-trade-manufacturing/

4 AI Superpowers, China, Silicon Valley and the new world order, Kai-Fu Lee, Houghton Mifflin Harcourt, 2018

5 Bain, Bruno Lannes and Derek Deng, August 2020, In 2019, Foreign Brands Outgrew Chinese Brands in China – https://www.bain.com/insights/in-2019-foreign-brands-outgrew-chinese-brands-in-china-snap-chart/

SOURCES

NOTES OF THE AUTHORS

Ny.zdline.cn, Bo Ji Tian Juan, July 2017, There are many differences between Eastern dragon and Western dragon, you don't know 《东方龙与西方龙的区别，你不知道的还有很多》– http://ny.zdline.cn/h5/article/detail.do?artId=2872

Sohu.com, Zhang Wen Ping, July 2017, There is a big difference between the Chinese dragon and the Western dragon. Foreign netizens: China's is the real dragon 《中国龙和西方龙差别大，外国网友：中国的才是真龙》– https://www.sohu.com/a/155725397_716280

Zhihu.com, Jin Gui Zi, July 2018, The dragons in Western mythology are very different from the Chinese dragons, so why are they also translated as "dragons"? 《西方神话中的龙与中国龙造型差异很大，为什么也译作「龙」？》– https://www.zhihu.com/question/282137226/answer/425318300

PART 1 – THE NEED FOR UNDERSTANDING DRAGON TACTICS
Chapter 1, Section 1.1 Failure to adapt, the basis for failure
Academy of Management Insights, January 2017, Thirteen Reasons Why Western Internet Companies Fail in China – https://journals.aom.org/doi/10.5465/amd.2017.0102.summary

CNBC, Benjamin Carlson, September 2013, Why big American businesses fail in China – https://www.cnbc.com/2013/09/26/why-big-american-businesses-fail-in-china.html

CompuFocus UK, September 2020, Why Big Companies failed in China? – http://compufocus.co.uk/blog/14-why-big-companies-failed-in-china

On Amazon
DW, April 2019, Why Amazon struggled to beat Alibaba online in China – https://www.dw.com/en/why-amazon-struggled-to-beat-alibaba-online-in-china-a-48403733

Ittime.com.cn, Li Hai Gang, June 2014, What is destined for Amazon to lose out to China? Is it policy restrictions, the absence of localization, the siege of local companies, or a user experience that is just talking? 《什么原因注定亚马逊将败走中国？是政策限制、本土化缺位、本土企业的围追堵截、还是光说不练的用户体验？》– http://www.ittime.com.cn/news/news_1002.shtml

Medium.com, Ren & Heinrich, April 2019, Why Amazon failed in China – https://medium.com/@Ren_and_Heinrich/why-amazon-failed-in-china-37dc2cceadc5

New York Times, Karen Weise, April 2019, Amazon Gives Up on Chinese Domestic Shopping Business – https://www.nytimes.com/2019/04/18/technology/amazon-china.html

SCMP, Josh Ye, April 2019, Consumers say Amazon failed in China because it didn't adapt – https://www.scmp.com/abacus/tech/article/3029294/consumers-say-amazon-failed-china-because-it-didnt-adapt

Zhihu.com, About Amazon China, May 2018, A consumer's perception of the boom to bust of Amazon operations in China 《一个消费者对中国亚马逊经营从兴旺到没落的感受》– https://www.zhihu.com/question/269847525/answer/351421288

Chapter 1, Section 1.2 Success in China is possible, provided you create the right circumstances
On KFC
China Daily, Wang Zhuoqiong, October 2019, McDonald's eyes faster expansion in lower-tier cities – https://global.chinadaily.com.cn/a/201910/23/WS5dafab2ea310cf3e35572041.html

Insead Knowledge, 2009, KFC's recipe for success – https://knowledge.insead.edu/leadership-management/strategy/kfc-chinas-recipe-for-success-1706

MarcoPolo, Neil Thomas, August 2018, How KFC Changed China and How China Changed KFC – https://macropolo.org/analysis/how-kfc-changed-china-and-how-china-changed-kfc/

YUM China, Fiscal 2019, Annual Report

On Carrefour
ChinaTechBlog, Makha Varunpaijit, January 2019, Hema – Jack Ma's Innovative New Retail Business At the intersection of online retail and traditional brick and mortar – https://www.chinatech-blog.org/blog/hema-jack-ma-s-innovative-new-retail-business

Daxue Consulting, Matthieu David, June 2020, Carrefour in China: 25 years of success ends with slow market exit – https://daxueconsulting.com/carrefour-in-china/

Daxue Consulting, Allison, December 2019, Walmart in China: Market entry case study – https://daxueconsulting.com/wal-mart-in-china/

Huxiu.com, Chen Jing, June 2019, Carrefour's defeat to China can only be blamed on itself 《家乐福败走中国，只能怪自己》– https://www.huxiu.com/article/305992.html

The World Financial Review, Lisa Qixun Siebers, August 2019, Carrefour's History and Exit from China – https://worldfinancialreview.com/carrefours-history-and-exit-from-china/

PART 2 – MASTERING DRAGON TACTICS
Chapter 3, Wolf Culture. Hunger Teaches Life Lessons.
The Economist, September 2019, A transcript of Ren Zhengfei's interview – https://www.economist.com/business/2019/09/12/a-transcript-of-ren-zhengfeis-interview

The Interpreter by The Lowy Institute, Elliott Zaagman, June 2019, The Huawei Way – https://www.lowyinstitute.org/the-interpreter/huawei-way

Voices of Huawei, June 2019, Ren Zhengfei's Interview with UK Documentary Producer – https://www.huawei.com/en/facts/voices-of-huawei/ren-zhengfeis-interview-with-uk-documentary-producer

Sohu.com, Potom, September 2018, Behind the success of wolf culture is only high salary system? Ren Zhengfei: The bird that never burns is a phoenix 《狼性文化成功的背后只是高薪酬制？任正非：烧不死的鸟是凤凰》– https://www.sohu.com/a/253670841_100245552

Zhihu.com, Ying Jia Wei Ye, October 2019, Why do many start-ups advocate wolf culture? 《为什么很多创业公司都提倡狼性文化？》– https://zhuanlan.zhihu.com/p/86240399

Zhihu.com, on social media, May 2020, Discussion on company wolf culture 《关于企业狼性文化的讨论》– https://www.zhihu.com/question/397713838

On Danone & Wahaha
Baidu Forum, 2010, Danone Forced Purchase of Wahaha Incident – https://baike.baidu.com/

item/%E8%BE%BE%E8%83%BD%E5%BC%BA%E8%B4
%AD%E5%A8%83%E5%93%88%E5%93%88%E4%BA%8B
%E4%BB%B6/7975445?fr=aladdin

China Business Review, Jingzhou Tao and Edward Hillier, May/June 2008, A Tale of Two Companies – https://www.jonesday.com/files/publication/6027415e-bc9d-44b2-9e90-f8ef4870150d/presentation/publicationattachment/a602d7dc-b34c-4f3a-8041-fdde482927ac/a_tale_of_two_companies.pdf

European Journal of Law Reform, 13 (3–4). pp. 614–628, Quingxui Bu, 2011, Danone v. Wahaha: Who Laughs Last? – http://sro.sussex.ac.uk/id/eprint/45622/

Sina.com.cn, Wang Ran, April 2007, Wahaha and Danone: Can unequal contracts be torn up? –http://blog.sina.com.cn/s/blog_47665bc1010008cb.html

On WeChat

IMD, Howard H. Yu, December 2016, In mobile social networks China's WeChat shows the way forward for Facebook – https://www.imd.org/research-knowledge/articles/in-mobile-social-networks-chinas-wechat-shows-the-way-forward-for-facebook/

Wechat.com, March 2019, What is WeChat's dream? WeChat founder Allen Zhang explains – https://blog.wechat.com/2019/03/18/what-is-wechats-dream-wechat-founder-allen-zhang-explains/

On Huawei vs Cisco

The New York Times, Laurie J. Flynn, October 2003, Cisco Agrees To Suspend Patent Suit For 6 Months – https://www.nytimes.com/2003/10/02/business/technology-cisco-agrees-to-suspend-patent-suit-for-6-months.html

On Luckin Coffee

Bloomberg, Quint, Selina Wang & Matthew Campbell, July 2020, Luckin Scandal Is Bad Timing for U.S.-Listed Chinese Companies – https://www.bloombergquint.com/businessweek/luckin-coffee-fraud-behind-starbucks-competitor-s-scandal

Technode.com, Michael Norris, March 2019, From jail to java: How Luckin's CMO is hacking China's coffee market – https://technode.com/2019/03/25/from-jail-to-java-how-luckins-cmo-is-hacking-chinas-coffee-market/

On 996 culture

Forbes, Rebecca Fannin, May 2019, Why China's 996 Work Culture Makes Sense Right Now – https://www.forbes.com/sites/rebeccafannin/2019/05/05/why-chinas-996-work-culture-makes-sense-right-now/#6ec1279d7802

OneZero, James Starnier, May 2019, The Rebellion Against China's 996 Culture, https://onezero.medium.com/the-rebellion-against-chinas-996-culture-b5b21b6a92c0

Chapter 4, Adapt to Change or Die.

China Britain Business Council, Hugh Peyman, September 2018, What can be learned from China? Long-term thinking and the ability to adapt is the answer – https://focus.cbbc.org/what-can-be-learned-from-china/

China Daily, Chen Yingqun and Liu Ce, May 2015, Motto for the Internet age: adapt or die – http://www.chinadaily.com.cn/a/201505/01/WS5a2b5383a310eefe3e99fc5d.html

Conseillers du Commerce Extérieur de la France Chine, Rapport du Groupe de Travail Innovation Chine, April 2020, COVID-19, Veille Technologique sur les Innovations en Chine (translated as COVID-19, A Catalyst for Innovation)

French Foreign Trade Advisors (CCE), April 2020, Covid_19 a catalyst for Innovation

Nexxworks, Ken Hughes, March 2021, Why business needs chaos to thrive – https://nexxworks.com/blog/why-business-needs-chaos-to-thrive

The New York Times, Raymond Zhong, November 2020, In Halting Ant's I.P.O., China Sends a Warning to Business – https://www.nytimes.com/2020/11/06/technology/china-ant-group-ipo.html

Sohu.com, Zhu Mingqi, December 2019, The decision-making mechanism of Tencent, Huawei, and Alibaba 《腾讯、华为、阿里的决策机制》 - https://www.sohu.com/a/238936542_283333

Sohu.com, Liu Xiao Yue, January 2021, Three predictions of the fate of "ants" in 2021 《2021年,"蚂蚁们"命运的三大预测》– https://www.sohu.com/a/441985441_532789

The Wall Street Journal, Paul Clifford and Larry Alberts, January 2000, After WTO, Chinese Firms Will Adapt or Die – https://www.wsj.com/articles/SB948318290586562977

Yale Insights, Deborah S. Davis, August 2013, What's the business landscape in China today – https://insights.som.yale.edu/insights/what-s-the-business-landscape-in-china-today

On Perfect Diary, Neiwai and Livestreaming

Daxue Consulting, March 2021, Perfect Diary case study: How this Chinese makeup brand got to the top – https://daxueconsulting.com/perfect-diary-case-study-how-this-chinese-makeup-brand-got-to-the-top/

Forbes, Lauren Hallanan, June 2020, The Greatest Threat To Global Cosmetics' China Success: An Interview With D2C Unicorn Perfect Diary – https://www.forbes.com/sites/lauren-hallanan/2020/06/24/the-greatest-threat-to-global-cosmetics-china-success-an-interview-with-d2c-unicorn-perfect-diary/

JingDaily, Yaling Zhang, March 2020, How Lingerie Brand NEIWAI Connects with Chinese Women – https://jingdaily.com/lingerie-neiwai-chinese-women-body-diversity/

JingDaily, Wenzhuo Wu, July 2020, NEIWAI Founder Reimagines Female Empowerment Through Lingerie – https://jingdaily.com/neiwai-founder-reimagines-female-empowerment-through-lingerie/

First Financial, November 2020, Perfect Diary tops the list again on "Double 11", and its parent company Yixian E-commerce goes public in the United States 《完美日记"双11"再登榜首,母公司逸仙电商赴美上市》– https://finance.sina.com.cn/tech/2020-11-12-doc-iiznezxs1559059.shtml

LinkedIn, Sandrine Zerbib, March 2021, How to become a market leader in China in 4 years – https://www.linkedin.com/pulse/how-become-market-leader-china-4-years-sandrine-zerbib/

SupChina, Zishu Sherry Qin, February 2021, How China's livestream industry is revolutionizing ecommerce – https://supchina.com/2021/02/03/how-chinas-livestream-industry-is-revolutionizing-ecommerce/

De Volkskrant, Leen Vervaeke, October 2020, Made for China: livestreamen voor een sterke natie – https://www.volkskrant.nl/kijkverder/v/2020/chinese-verkooprevolutie-eindeloos-livestreamen-tot-je-een-rage-ontketent-v402959/

Chapter 5, The Emperor Decides. But Agility Rules.

163.com, by China-Europe International Business Review, July 2011, Every Chinese company needs an emperor 《每个中国企业都需要一个皇帝》- https://www.163.com/money/article/7986M79B00253G87.html

infzm.com, Wang Shi, February 2008, When did Chinese entrepreneurs lose the idea of emperor? 《中国企业家何时丢掉帝王思想?》– http://www.infzm.com/contents/475

On Decentralisation

Asian case research journal, vol. 20, issue 2, 401-427, Xiaoming Yang, Sunny Li Sun, Ruby P. Lee, December 2016, The Case of WeChat – https://www.researchgate.net/publication/312488740_Micro-Innovation_Strategy_The_Case_of_WeChat

ixueshu.com, Zhang Hui, November 2011, Changes in the relationship between central and local governments and decentralization, Competing with local government —Thinking about the motivation of China's economic growth 《央地关系变迁、分权 与地方政府竞争—对中国经济增长动因的思考》– https://www.ixueshu.com/document/0c25ea62490640e5e345de584ff-9f011318947a18e7f9386.html

London Business School, Julian Birkinshaw, November 2019 - WeChat: behind the scenes at China's most successful app – https://www.london.edu/think/we-chat-behind-the-scenes-at-chinas-most-successful-app

TechInAsia, Apoorva Dutt, August 2018, How Tencent used 'micro-innovation' to make WeChat a success – https://www.techinasia.com/tencent-set-wechat-success-microinnovation

On Projects and Flat organisations

163.com, Liu Zhi Ze, January 2019, Zhang Xiaolong: How I invented WeChat 《张小龙: 我是如何发明微信的》– https://www.163.com/dy/article/E6OPTAE50518PKBU.html

Baijiahao.baidu.com, Guan Li De Chang Shi, February 2019, What is the meaning behind the structure adjustment of Xiaomi? 《小米组织架构调整, 背后有何深意?》–https://baijiahao.baidu.com/s?id=1626628597959062761&wfr=spider&for=pc

Docin.com, Lian Yu, April 2015, Xiaomi-style organizational structure case study 《小米式组织架构案例分析》– https://www.docin.com/p-1386975976.html

EqualOcean, Zekun Wang, February 2019, Xiaomi Announces Organization Restructure – https://legacy.equalocean.com/news/201902271485

Medium, April 2019, A closer look into Tencent's micro innovation strategy – https://medium.com/@wechatminiprogrammer/a-closer-look-into-tencents-micro-innovation-strategy-6dead41b4213

Research Methodoly.net, John Dudovskiy, May 2018, Xiaomi Organizational Structure: matrix and flat – https://research-methodology.net/xiaomi-organizational-structure-matrix-and-flat/

Sohu.com, from Sales And Market, February 2019, Why are more and more companies giving up flat management? 《为什么有越来越多的公司放弃了扁平化管理?》– https://www.sohu.com/a/298133487_465378

Sohu.com, Bo Ming dun, May 2018, The myth of Xiaomi's listing to create wealth, and what is more valuable is the divisional award logic behind its success 《柏明顿: 小米上市造富神话 更值钱的是其成功背后的分算奖逻辑》– https://m.sohu.com/a/231551760_188260/

Xiaomi, 2019 Annual report

On Internal competition and Amoeba style organisations

Handu Power eCommerce, Handu Yishe company introduction presentation

q.chinasspp.com, Hua Yi Nong, February 2015, Handu Yishe builds 270 "three members" teams to catch up ZARA 《韩都衣舍大建"三人团"共270小组, 追赶ZARA》– http://q.chinasspp.com/1-81469.html

QQ.com, Ma Huateng Dialogue with Qian Yingyi, October 2016, First reveal the secret! It turns out that WeChat was born like this 《马化腾对话钱颖一: 首次揭秘! 原来微信竟是这样诞生的》– https://tech.qq.com/a/20161023/010508.htm

QQ.com, Ming Brother, March 2020, In the workplace, what do you think of the phrase "victor is the king, loser is the bandit"? 《在职场上你对"胜者王侯败者寇"这种说法怎么看?》– https://page.om.qq.com/page/OWS8pSSkDmw32UovqhirQhbg0

Sohu.com, Hu Xiu Team, June 2015, Zhao Yingguang: Three transformations of Handu clothing store's "group system" under high internal competition 《赵迎光: 韩都衣舍"小组制"在内部高度竞争下的三次转型》– https://www.sohu.com/a/19463852_115207

Sohu.com, from Amoeba Management Model and Practice, January 2017, Amoeba management: small collective big business 《阿米巴经营: 小集体大事业》– https://www.sohu.com/a/123693507_570041

Sohu.com, Zhangrong Yu, Wei Shi, October 2018, What you lack is not talent, but talent "horse racing mechanism" 《你缺的不是人才, 而是人才的"赛马机制"》– https://www.sohu.com/a/259660356_100010216

Sohu.com, Chong Gong Dian Li, November 2020, Amoeba core ten words: company platformized, group enterprised 《阿米巴核心十个字: 公司平台化, 小组企业化》– https://www.sohu.com/a/434281461_100021990

Zhihu.com, Uncle Watermelon, May 2020, Is the Amoeba model suitable for Chinese companies? 《阿米巴模式适合中国企业吗?》– https://www.zhihu.com/question/382862539/answer/1257369473

On Ecosystems

360doc.com, Xin Zheng, March 2019, How were world-class giants born? Look at the construction of Alibaba ecosystem 《世界级巨头是怎样诞生的? 看阿里巴巴生态系统的构建》– http://www.360doc.com/content/19/0327/08/53746720_824425926.shtml

Cainiao, Network Overview (As of September 2016) – https://www.google.com/url?sa=t&rct=j&q=&esrc=s&source=web&cd=&ved=2ahUKEwjG_pu49t3yAhVS4aQKHZ36AecQFnoE-CAIQAQ&url=https%3A%2F%2Fwww.alizila.com%2Fwp-content%2Fuploads%2F2016%2F09%2FCainiao-Factsheet.pdf%3Fx95431&usg=AOvVaw23Q0ElARNApsDCmrS1FuK8

Daxue Consulting, Allison, April 2019, Open Innovation: Transforming your Business in China – https://daxueconsulting.com/open-innovation-in-china/

BCG Henderson Institute, François Candelon, Chenao Yu, and Jun Wang, January 2019, Get ready for the Chinese internet's Next chapter – https://www.bcg.com/en-nl/publications/2019/get-ready-for-chinese-internet-next-chapter

235

Huxiu.com, November 2014, Ali may invest in the entrepreneurship of former employees 《2000人阿里离职校友会上，彭蕾说今后阿里对离职员工创业或会进行投资》– https://www.huxiu.com/article/102700.html

OECD, Colin Mason and Ross Brown, November 2013, Entrepreneurial ecosystems and growth-oriented entrepreneurship – https://www.google.com/url?sa=t&rct=j&q=&esrc=s&source=web&cd=&ved=2ahUKEwjz273W993yAhVZ-PewKHcqoChMQFnoECAUQAQ&url=https%3A%2F%2Fwww.oecd.org%2Fcfe%2Fleed%2FEntrepreneurial-ecosystems.pdf&usg=AOvVaw2XSzFLoF--fQR1UMrNaEzp

Sohu.com, Za Ji, May 2015, Jack Ma as the head of the "Ali" entrepreneurial gang : let us check the 19 entrepreneurs who left Ali and created their own careers 《以马云为首的"阿里"创业帮：盘点19位离职创业者》– https://www.sohu.com/a/13341482_111230

Wired, David Kline, December 2017, Behind the Fall and Rise of China's Xiaomi – https://www.wired.com/story/behind-the-fall-and-rise-of-china-xiaomi/

Chapter 6, People Come and Go. Those Who Fit Stay Longer.

163.com, Lao Fang, October 2019, To let employees surpass themselves! Jack Ma: I always take "people" as the first product of Alibaba 《要让员工超越自己！马云：我一直把"人"作为阿里巴巴的第一产品》– https://www.163.com/dy/article/ESEBIR-700521BCF5.html

Central University of Finance and Economics, Chuanchuan Zhang, October 2017, Culture and the Economy: Clan, Entrepreneurship, and Development of the Private Sector in China – https://www.researchgate.net/publication/311493349_Culture_and_the_Economy_Clan_Entrepreneurship_and_Development_of_the_Private_Sector_in_China

CNN, Naomi Ng, May 2015, Chinese company treats 6,400 employees to French vacation – https://edition.cnn.com/2015/05/11/asia/china-france-company-holiday/index.html

Inkstone, Laura He, Jane Zhang and Louise Moon, January 2019, In China, the family business is out and the business family is in – https://www.inkstonenews.com/business/chinas-big-family-businesses-lack-succession-plan/article/3000444

The Irish Times, Joe Humphreys, October 2019, How to understand China: Step one, forget about God – https://www.irishtimes.com/culture/how-to-understand-china-step-one-forget-about-god-1.4037605

Quartz, Zach Wener-Fligner, May 2015, A Chinese billionaire sent 6,400 of his employees on a French vacation – https://qz.com/402326/a-chinese-billionaire-sent-6400-of-his-employees-on-a-french-vacation/

On incentive schemes and stock option programs

Baidu.com, from China Economy Network, February 2019, Optimistic about the value of the company, SF Express repurchases shares for employee incentives 《看好公司价值，顺丰回购股票，用作员工激励》– https://baijiahao.baidu.com/s?id=1624314383738009891&wfr=spider&for=pc

Baidu.com, from Sina Financial, June 2020, Interpreting 480 listed companies' cases! Implementation of employee stock ownership plan preparation, these three points need to pay attention to 《解读480家上市公司案例！实施员工持股计划准备，这三点需注意》– https://baijiahao.baidu.com/s?id=1669657747116433335&wfr=spider&for=pc

The Clute Institute, Journal of Applied Business Research, Volume 31, Number 4, Lei Luo, July/August 2015, Determinants Of Stock Option, Use By Chinese Companies – https://www.google.com/url?sa=t&rct=j&q=&esrc=s&source=web&cd=&ved=2ahUKEwiW4Ifrq-DyAhWJhvoHHSaeCP4QFnoECAIQA-Q&url=https%3A%2F%2Fclutejournals.com%2Findex.php%2FJABR%-2Farticle%2Fdownload%2F9323%2F9435%2F35679&usg=AOvVaw2Xjy8ycz3ghXbHMVCMlEHE

Fenwick & West LLP, Fred M. Greguras & Liza Morgan, Overview of Stock Option Grants in China – https://assets.fenwick.com/legacy/FenwickDocuments/Stock_Option_Grants_China.pdf

Thomson Reuters – Practical Law, Gordon (Minghao) Feng, Jasen (Ming) Li & Peter (Yi) Zhu, May 2020, Employee share plans in China: regulatory overview – https://uk.practicallaw.thomsonreuters.com/9-507-4557?transitionType=Default&contextData=(sc.Default)&firstPage=true

On Huawei ownership

Cssn.cn, Hui Zhou Xue Yuan, August 2014, Classic Case Study: Huawei Employee Stock Ownership Plan 《经典案例评析:华为员工持股计划》– http://www.cssn.cn/glx/glx_jdal/201408/t20140807_1282666.shtml

Jeffrey Towson 陶迅 Digital China and Asia Tech Strategy, Jeffrey Towson, October 2019, Huawei Is Going to Beat Trump with Human Resources, Not Technology – https://jefftowson.com/2019/10/huawei-is-going-to-beat-trump-with-human-resources-not-technology-pt-1-of-3/

Jeffrey Towson 陶迅 Digital China and Asia Tech Strategy, Jeffrey Towson, October 2019, Huawei's Employee Stock Ownership Plan (ESOP) is "Meritocracy Plus Partnership" at Scale in China Tech – https://jefftowson.com/2019/10/huaweis-employee-stock-ownership-plan-esop-is-a-great-example-of-meritocracy-plus-partnership-in-china-tech-at-scale-pt-2-of-3/

The New York Times, Raymond Zhong, April 2019, Who Owns Huawei? The Company Tried to Explain. It Got Complicated – https://www.nytimes.com/2019/04/25/technology/who-owns-huawei.html

Telecom.com, Wei Shi, April 2019, New research claims employees do not own Huawei – https://telecoms.com/496951/new-research-claims-employees-do-not-own-huawei/

The Wall Street Journal, Dan Strumpf & Yifan Wang, April 2019, Huawei Says It Is Employee-'Owned'—But Not Really – https://www.wsj.com/articles/huawei-says-it-is-employee-ownedbut-not-really-11556204552

On Yonghui

YongHui Superstores Co., Ltd., 2019 Corporate Social Responsibility Report

Fung Business Intelligence, "New Retail" in Action, Issue 10, Teresa Lam and Christy Li, November 2017, Yonghui Superstores - The Vanguard of China's Grocery Market – https://www.fbicgroup.com/

Sohu.com, Kuai Xiao Tong, March 2019, Detailed explanation of the partner system of Yonghui Supermarket 《永辉超市的合伙人制度详解》– https://www.sohu.com/a/299264466_100010274

Weixin.qq.com, Cui Heng Yu, April 2020, Let Tencent and Jingdong make a lot of money, Yong Hui supermarket is already a superior student? 《让腾讯和京东大赚的永辉超市，已经是优等生了？》– https://mp.weixin.qq.com/s/E_ZombFWfyH-fr-GlRx6nAQ

On HaiDiLao

Atlantis Press, Zeng Shiqiang, Guoqing Li, Limei Li and Huimin Deng, October 2019, On Three Characteristics of the Chinese Style Management – https://www.atlantis-press.com/proceedings/aemh-19/125919711

QQ.com, Jian Shu Tai, November 2020, It turns out that Haidilao treats its employees this way, no wonder... 《原来海底捞是这样对待员工的，怪不得......》– https://new.qq.com/rain/a/20201119A095NH00

Thepaper.cn, Xiao Bei, September 2020, Why is Haidilao's "business path" so wild? 《为什么海底捞"业务路子"这么野？》– https://www.thepaper.cn/newsDetail_forward_9059169

Sohu.com, Zhong Can Wang, September 2019, Haidilao employee incentive system 《海底捞员工激励制度》– https://www.sohu.com/a/338835730_798937

Chapter 7, It All Starts with Data.

Alibaba Group, November 2019, Alibaba Introduces Brand Databank: Data Can Appreciate and Be Deposited like Monetary Funds – https://www.alibabacloud.com/blog/alibaba-introduces-brand-databank-data-can-appreciate-and-be-deposited-like-monetary-funds_595587#:~:text=%22As%20the%20name%20implies%2C%20Brand,of%20Data%20Marketing%20Strategy%20Center%2C

Baidu.com, Shen Zhen Ju Li Chuang Xiang Scientific Technology Company, January 2020, Ali's 3 major marketing models: AIPL, FAST, GROW 《阿里3大营销模型：AIPL、FAST、GROW》– https://baijiahao.baidu.com/s?id=1655759993185953179&wfr=spider&for=pc

Baijiahao.baidu.com, Sina Financial, February 2020, Why is Huawei so important to 5G and the world? 《对于 5G 和全球来说，华为为什么如此重要？》– https://baijiahao.baidu.com/s?id=1659520726971958956&wfr=spider&for=pc

Baijiahao.baidu.com, Sina Financial, July 2020, Interview with Pinduoduo Chen Lei: AI will solve the core problems of the retail industry 《专访拼多多陈磊：AI将解决零售业的核心问题》– https://baijiahao.baidu.com/s?id=1671088526985135954&wfr=spider&for=pc

BCG Henderson Institute, François Candelon, Fangqi Yang & Daniel Wu, May 2019, Are China's Digital Companies Ready to Go Global? – https://www.bcg.com/publications/2019/china-digital-companies-ready-go-global

Bernstein, January 2018, Artificial Intelligence in China

Bilibili.com, You Chuang Yun Tian, December 2020, These 13 big data application cases will give you a thorough understanding of big data 《这13个大数据应用案例，让你彻底了解大数据》– https://www.bilibili.com/read/cv8924518/

Boston Consulting Group, Ted Chan, Nikolaus Lang, Shashank Modi, Tjun Tang and Konrad von Szczepanski, July 2020, How Chinese Digital Ecosystems Battled COVID-19 – https://www.bcg.com/publications/2020/how-chinese-digital-ecosystems-battled-covid-19

Brink, Manisha Mirchandani, February 2020, Why China Could Lead on Global Data Privacy Norms – https://www.brinknews.com/why-china-could-lead-on-global-data-privacy-norms/

Conseillers du Commerce Extérieur de la France – Chine, Rapport du Groupe de Travail Economie Numérique Chine, 2018, L'Intelligence Artificielle en Chine

Ctocio.com, Cashcow, April 2013, The great value of big data: in-depth analysis of the five successful cases of big data 《大数据的大价值：大数据五大成功案例深度解析》– https://www.ctocio.com/industry/retail/14238.html

The Economist, January 2021, The great mall of China, Why retailers everywhere should look to China – https://www.economist.com/leaders/2021/01/02/why-retailers-everywhere-should-look-to-china

The European Commission, April 2021, "Fostering a European approach to Artificial Intelligence – https://digital-strategy.ec.europa.eu/en/policies/european-approach-artificial-intelligence

European Community, April 2021, Communication from the Commission to the European Parliament, the European Council, the Council, the European Economic and Social Committee and the Committee of the Regions Fostering a European approach to Artificial Intelligence

e-Marketer, Ethan Cramer-Flood, March 2021, Unexpected surge pushes China's internet population to brink of 1 billion – https://www.emarketer.com/content/after-unexpected-surge-chinas-internet-population-on-brink-of-1-billion

Harvard Business Review, Ming Zeng, September/October 2018, Alibaba and the Future of Business – https://hbr.org/2018/09/alibaba-and-the-future-of-business

MIT Technology Review, 50 Smartest Companies in the World 2017 – https://www.technologyreview.com/lists/tr50/what-are-the-50-smartest-companies/

MIT Technology Review, 50 Smartest Companies in China 2020 – https://events.technologyreview.com/tr50-china/

Thepaper.cn, Du Wei, January 15, 2021 China's online sales increase by about 150%, luxury goods grab e-commerce dividends 《2020中国线上销售额增长约150%，奢侈品抢夺电商红利》– https://m.thepaper.cn/baijiahao_10804823

Samr.gov.cn, China Antimonopoly Bureau, November 2020, 《Guidance on Anti-monopoly in the Field of Platform Economy (Draft for Comment)》《关于平台经济领域的反垄断指南（征求意见稿）》– http://www.samr.gov.cn/hd/zjdc/202011/t20201109_323234.html

Search Engine Journal, Amy Bishop, June 2021, Google FloC Explained: A Guide for Marketers – https://www.searchenginejournal.com/google-floc-explained-a-guide-for-marketers/409379/

Sohu.com, Zhong Wu Lian, May 2020, What exactly is big data? What does it mean for our country? What impact does it have on everyone? 《大数据到底是什么？对我们的国家有什么意义？对每个人有什么影响？》– https://www.sohu.com/a/394001434_288086

Sohu.com, published by He Xun Investment Consultant, July 2020, Heavy news! Pinduoduo actually wants to use AI to grow strawberries for me to eat. Can AI enter the agricultural field? 《重磅消息！拼多多竟然要用AI种草莓给我吃 AI进军农业领域能行

吗？》 – https://www.sohu.com/a/410759207_120273974

Stock.eastmoney.com, published by Chong Qing Daily, August 2019,Gene determines Pinduoduo is an artificial intelligence company《基因决定拼多多是一家人工智能公司》 – http://stock.eastmoney.com/a/20190826217030425.html

De Volkskrant, Marije Vlaskamp, May 2021, App met gezichtsherkenning gaat restaurantvissen in Hongkong beschermen – https://www.volkskrant.nl/nieuws-achtergrond/app-met-gezichtsherkenning-gaat-restaurantvissen-in-hong-kong-beschermen-b9e394fd/?referrer=https%3A%2F%2Fwww.google.com%2F

Zgswcn.com, China Commerce Network, July 2021, What did the big guys say at 2021 World Artificial Intelligence Conference? 《2021世界人工智能大会，大佬们都说了啥？》 – https://www.zgswcn.com/article/202107/20210715140201089.html

On Shein

Business of Fashion, Chavie Lieber, June 2021, the Search for the Next Shein – https://www.businessoffashion.com/articles/retail/the-search-for-the-next-shein

Daxue Consulting, April 2021, Shein's market strategy: How the Chinese fashion brand is conquering the West – https://daxueconsulting.com/shein-market-strategy/

Forbes, Mark Faithfull, February 2022, Shein: Is China's Mysterious $15 Billion Fast Fashion Retailer Ready for Stores? – https://www.forbes.com/sites/markfaithfull/2021/02/10/shein-is-chinas-mysterious-15-billion-fast-fashion-retailer-ready-for-stores/?sh=348c936b6df5

The Wire China, Lily Meier, June 2021, Fast Fashion, Fast Profits – https://www.thewirechina.com/2021/06/06/fast-fashion-faster-profits/

On Yum

Cision (YUM press release), March 2020, Yum China Named to Fast Company's Annual List of the World's Most Innovative Companies for 2020 – https://www.prnewswire.com/news-releases/yum-china-named-to-fast-companys-annual-list-of-the-worlds-most-innovative-companies-for-2020-301021461.html

The Wire China, Matt Schiavenza, February 2021, The Yum Model – https://www.thewirechina.com/2021/02/28/the-yum-model/

PART 3 – EMPLOYING DRAGON TACTICS

163.com, from 21 Century Economy Report, November 11, 2020, Platform economy anti-monopoly sword out of the sheath 2020 Double 11 Carnival Variations, Internet giants trillion in market value evaporating《平台经济反垄断利剑出鞘，2020双11狂欢变奏, 互联网巨头万亿市值蒸发》 – https://www.163.com/money/article/FR65HO5U002580S6.html

Baijiahao.baidu.com, Zheng Yong Nian, June 2018, Zheng Yongnian, Why do Chinese entrepreneurs lack ambition?《郑永年：中国企业家为何缺少格局?》 – https://baijiahao.baidu.com/s?id=1603909119789971266&wfr=spider&for=pc

Bain, Bruno Lannes & Derek Deng, August 2020, In 2019, Foreign Brands Outgrew Chinese Brands in China – https://www.bain.com/insights/in-2019-foreign-brands-outgrew-chinese-brands-in-china-snap-chart/

Bain, Bruno Lannes, Jason Ding & François Faelli, April 2019, Consumer Products: Now's the Time to Double Down on China

– https://www.bain.com/insights/consumer-products-nows-the-time-to-double-down-on-china

Competing With China: A Strategic Framework – https://itif.org/publications/2020/08/31/competing-china-strategic-framework

CNBC, Evelyn Cheng, June 2021, China wants to build up its wine country into one that could rival France's Bordeaux – https://www.cnbc.com/2021/06/21/china-wine-ningxia-strives-to-be-france-bordeaux-amid-tariffs-on-australia.html

The Diplomat, James Carafano, Arvind Gupta and Jeff M. Smith, January 2021, The Pitfalls of the China–EU Comprehensive Agreement on Investment – https://thediplomat.com/2021/01/the-pitfalls-of-the-china-eu-comprehensive-agreement-on-investment/

The Diplomat, Xue Qing, May 2021, How China is Losing Europe – https://thediplomat.com/2021/05/how-china-is-losing-europe/

Foreign Policy, Sulmaan Wasif Khan, May 2021, Wolf Warriors Killed China's Grand Strategy And we'll all come to miss it – https://foreignpolicy.com/2021/05/28/china-grand-strategy-wolf-warrior-nationalism/

Fortune, François Candelon, Akhil Puri and Shameen Prashantham, January 2021, Your company needs a new China strategy in the 'decoupling' era – https://fortune.com/2021/01/28/china-strategy-multinationals-chinese-decoupling-market-consumers-trade-manufacturing/

Harvard Business Review, J. Stewart Black and Allen J. Morrison, May–June 2021, The Strategic Challenges of Decoupling – https://hbr.org/2021/05/the-strategic-challenges-of-decoupling

Information Technology and Innovation Foundation (ITIF), David Moschella & Robert D. Atkinson, August 2020 – https://itif.org/publications/2020/08/31/competing-china-strategic-framework

The New York Times, Li Yuan, May 2020, China's 'OK Boomer': Generations Clash Over the Nation's Future – https://www.nytimes.com/2020/05/14/technology/china-bilibili-generation-youth.html

Pew Research, Laura Silver, Kat Devlin and Christine Huang, October 2020, Unfavorable Views of China Reach Historic Highs in Many Countries – https://www.pewresearch.org/global/2020/10/06/unfavorable-views-of-china-reach-historic-highs-in-many-countries/

Sohu.com, Manager Magazine, November 2018, The "Souffrance and glory" of Chinese entrepreneurs《中国企业家们的苦难与辉煌》– https://www.sohu.com/a/278118852_479806

Sohu.com, Hui Zhi Xing Bang, December 2018, Failure, debt, and downfall are not terrible, they are all gifts from God to the successful.《失败、负债和落魄其实并不可怕，这都是上天对成功者的馈赠》– https://www.sohu.com/a/279122777_802471

The Wire China, Alec Ash, August 2021, China's New Nationalism – https://www.thewirechina.com/2021/08/08/chinas-new-nationalism/

The Wire China, Peter Martin, June 2021, China's Wolfpack – https://www.thewirechina.com/2021/06/20/chinas-wolfpack/

The Wire China, Eyck Freymann, August 2021, What If China Never Reopens? – https://www.thewirechina.com/2021/08/01/what-if-china-never-reopens/

BOOK SOURCES

The Complete I Ching (Inner Traditions, 2010) – Translation Alfred Huang

Yi Jing,Le Livre des Changements (Albin Michel, 2012) – Authors : Cyrille J.-D. Javary & Pierre Faure

The Analects, Confucius

Les Trois Sagesses Chinoises: Taoïsme, confucianisme, bouddhisme (Albin Michel, 2012) – Author : Cyrille J.-D. Javary

La Souplesse du Dragon: Les fondamentaux de la culture chinoise (Albin Michel, 2017) – Author : Cyrille J.-D. Javary

Traité de l'Efficacité (Grasset, 2001) – Author : François Jullien

Figures de l'Immanence (Grasset, 1993) – Author : François Jullien

Le Paradoxe du Poisson Rouge : Une voie chinoise pour réussir (Saint-Simon, 2015) – Author : Hesna Cailliau

Histoire de la Pensée Chinoise (Seuil, 1997) – Author : Anne Cheng

Chine, Culture et Traditions (Picquier, 2015) – Author : Jacques Pimpaneau

L'intelligence de la Chine: Le social et le mental (Gallimard, 1994) – Author : Jacques Gernet

Le Monde Chinois 1,2 & 3 (A. Colin, 1,2 & 3, 1990) – Author : Jacques Gernet

China: A New History (Harvard University Press, 2006) – Authors: John King Fairbank, Merle Goldman

Une Vie Chinoise (Kana Edition, 2009) – Authors : Philippe OTIE & KUNWU

Deng Xiaoping and the Transformation of China (Harvard University Press, 2013) – Author: Ezra F. Vogel

China Shakes the World (Mariner, 2007) – Author: James Kynge

Les trente "empereurs" qui ont fait la Chine (Perrin, 2018) – Author : Bernard BRIZAY

Les Trente Ans qui ont changé la Chine 1980-2010 (Buchet-Chastel, 2011) – Author : Caroline Puel

Paris-Pékin Express: La nouvelle Chine racontée au futur Président (François Bourin, 2017) – Author : David Baverez

The China Factor (The China Agenda, 2019) – Author: Annette Nijs,

Markets Over Mao, The Rise of Private Business in China (Peterson Institute for International Economics 2014) – Author: Nicholas R. Lardy

China's Disruptors: How Alibaba, Xiaomi, Tencent, and Other Companies are Changing the Rules of Business (Portfolio, 2015) – Author: Edward Tse

Made in China: Secret of China's Dynamic Entrepreneurs (John Wiley & Sons (Asia) – Authors: Winter Nie & Katherine Xin with Lily Zhang

Inside Chinese Business: A Guide for Managers Worldwide (Harvard Business Review Press, 2003) – Author: Ming-Jer Chen

The China Factor: Leveraging Emerging Business Strategies to Compete, Grow, and Win in the New Global Economy (Wiley, 2016) – Author: Amy Karam

Management and Organizations in the Chinese Context (Palgrave Macmillan, 2000) – Authors: Xiangming Chen, James W. Bishop and K. Dow Scott

AI Superpowers: China, Silicon Valley, and the New World Order (Houghton Mifflin Harcourt, 2018) – Author: Kai-Fu Lee

China's Next Strategic Advantage: From Imitation to Innovation (MIT Press, 2016) – Authors: George S. Yip & Bruce McKern

The End of Copycat China: The Rise of Creativity, Innovation, and Individualism in Asia (Wiley, 2014) – Author: Shaun Rein

Payback, reaping the rewards of Innovation (Harvard Business Review Press, 2007) – Authors: James P. Andrew and Harold L. Sirkin

Huawei. Leadership, Culture and Connectivity (Sage, 2017) – Authors: Tian Tao, David de Cremer and Wu Chunbo

Un succès nommé Huawei: S'inspirer du champion mondial du numérique pour réussir (Eyrolles, 2019) – Author : Vincent Ducrey

Alibaba, the House that Jack Ma Built (Harper Collins, 2018) – Author Duncan Clark

How a Remarkable Chinese Company is Changing the Face of Global Business (Pan Books, 2016) – Author: Porter Erisman

Zhang Jindong: Management Journals of Suning (China Railway Publishing House, 2011) – Author: Sun Jing

Shenzhen Superstars — How China's smartest city is challenging Silicon Valley, self-published, 2017 – author Johan Nylander